JOSEPHINE
La BELLE de NUIT

Based on a true story of music, science,
faith – and the darkest desires

Josephine deBois

authorHOUSE®

AuthorHouse™ UK
1663 Liberty Drive
Bloomington, IN 47403 USA
www.authorhouse.co.uk
Phone: 0800.197.4150

Script consultation by K.Cromme.

Published by AuthorHouse   10/24/2017

ISBN: 978-1-5462-8343-0 (sc)
ISBN: 978-1-5462-8344-7 (e)

Print information available on the last page.

Dedicated to

The Starbucks Company

for giving me a place to write - wherever I am

EXT. DESOLATED CLOISTER (ABOUT 25 YEARS AGO) - HILLSIDE - DAY

(Mozart, Requiem, Introduction). Heavy rain pours over the desolated cloister located at a hillside surrounded by gloomy mountains. Thunder and lightning. It is almost dark.

The young scientist DUILO PAIONI (23), dressed in a black cassock, is walking up the hill towards the deserted cloister. The hill near the cloister is covered by fragmented rocks and grass with only few plants in between. From the other side of the hill, GIOVANNI LANDINI (26), also in a black cassock and wearing a large broad-brimmed hat approaches the cloister. The two men meet by the huge, broken, wooden gate. Together they push the gate open.

EXT. DESOLATED CLOISTER - COURTYARD - DAY

Giovanni and Duilio walk over the cobblestones in the small courtyard. They reach the entrance of a small chapel in the corner of the courtyard. They stand together in front of the heavy wooden door waiting a short moment while facing each other before opening the door. As they push the door, it opens with a strong creaking sound.

INT. DESOLATED CLOISTER - CHAPEL - DAY

After entering the chapel, the two young men carefully close the door behind them. A large black bird flies out of a broken window with a terribly frightening screeching. MARCHETTO CACCINI (48), a large broad shouldered man, sits on a bench in front of the altar. Pictures with religious motives have fallen down from the walls of the deteriorating chapel and lie disorderly around the altar table. Duilio and Giovanni approach Marchetto at the bench. Marchetto rises. His body height matches his natural authority. The three men stand face to face. They take their hats off. Their faces become visible. Marchetto, motionless like a statue, observes the two young men mindfully. Their faces radiate energy, determination, and outstanding intelligence. Giovanni's thick black hair is combed backwards and in perfect order in spite of the rough weather. Dark eyes, Italian descent. Duilio is smaller than the others. Bright eyes, scientific appearance. The three men stand silent for a moment. Rain hammers on the roof and drips through the many defects in the building. Finally Marchetto speaks in a low voice.

                              MARCHETTO
                    (in Italian)
          My Brothers, I asked you to be here today,
          to assure me that we are now together in
          this mission.
                    (he pauses)
          Today, from my side, I can promise
          you unlimited support from our sacred
          institution - whatever it takes will be
          made available!
                    (he pauses)
          So Brothers, now is the time for you to
          give me your promise.

The three men stand in silence for a moment. The thunder,
the rain, and the wind reach peak proportions and almost
overshadow the Requiem.

                              GIOVANNI
                    (in Italian)
          I promise you Brother: I will carry this
          mission through - whatever it takes.
          I will pursue our common goal with no
          compromise.

Giovanni bows his head in obedience. Marchetto looks Duilio
in the eyes. Duilio raises his face and looks directly at
Marchetto as he speaks slightly louder than Giovanni.

                              DUILIO
                    (in Italian)
          I promise you Brother: I am fully
          committed to this endeavor. It will be
          driving all my doings. I will carry it
          through; whatever it takes. I will pursue
          our common goal with no compromise.

Duilio and Giovanni both watch Marchetto. He raises his arms
and stretches his hand towards Duilio and Giovanni. The two
men each take hold of a hand of Marchetto and, at the same
time, each other's hands, all together forming a circle.

                              MARCHETTO
                    (in Italian)
          Well so be it then. God bless you and God
          bless this mission.

The three men move close together and hold their arms around
each other's shoulders. They pull tight together looking
down on the floor in tight unity. They whisper a prayer. The
Requiem breaks softly through during the prayer and then rises
to its full, overwhelming sound.

CROSS FADE FORWARD TO PRESENT TIME - MUSIC CARRIES OVER

INT. VIENNA - CONCERT HALL - EVENING

LUDWIG MANN (23) conducts the final bars of the continuing
Requiem in front of a large symphony orchestra, a full choir
and four singers. His blond, filling hair is combed backwards,
but scattered in disorder by his energetic conducting. His
shining eyes deliver his fine sharp profile an intense,
fantastic energetic yet charming and capturing appearance, in
spite of his overall fragile posture.

Ludwig conducts smilingly and untraditionally with long
movements of his arms with which he more creates an atmosphere
than making the beats. He is extremely well connected to the
entire orchestra, the singers, the choir, and the individual
musicians. The orchestra consistently follows him flawlessly.
Behind him is a totally packed, medium sized, classic concert
hall with the audience seated on several balconies and in
small lodges.

Ludwig holds the last cords as the music totally dies out.
Nobody moves while his hands are still slightly lifted.
Finally, he lowers his hands and lets his arms fall down
along his body. He stands deeply concentrated with his head
bowed. With one hand he brushes his hair back. He turns
to the audience. An enormous applause evolves to standing
ovations. Ludwig turns and lifts his arms toward the
audience. He turns back to the orchestra and again lifts
his arms. Finally, he again faces the audience and stands
with the orchestra and the singers behind him. He smiles and
almost laughs, totally delighted as though he cannot believe
the achievement. The musicians lift their instruments as
their standing applause. Ludwig again lifts his arms and
embraces the audience. He bows deeply. He turns around and
walks between the musicians towards the door to the concert
corridor leaving the undiminished applause behind. The
singers follow him.

INT. VIENNA - CONCERT HALL - CORRIDOR - EVENING

Ludwig enters the narrow corridor behind the orchestra. The orchestra director DR. JOHAN SCHLESINGER (61) and Ludwig's manager JOSEPHINE DEBOIS (44) are waiting. Dr. Schlesinger applauds relieved as Ludwig enters the corridor. The elegant, blond, tall, well-shaped, beautiful and seductive Josephine in a tight fitting dress matching her body embraces Ludwig warmly and tightly, yet without damaging her flawless and colorful makeup.

Josephine leans back while still holding her arms around Ludwig's neck as she speaks extremely excited, with a seductive touch, tone and body language. The singers remain standing right inside the corridor and briefly organize themselves before the recall from the audience.

                    JOSEPHINE
               (in German)
          I knew. I knew it! You made it happen.
          Again, as never before! I knew you would
          do it.

Josephine leans back as she still holds Ludwig. She smiles to him sensually, then loosens her hold of him and turns around to a LADY SERVANT in black holding a tray with three big glasses of chilled beer in long Austrian-type beer glasses wet of dew. She grasps one of the glasses and hands it to Ludwig.

                    JOSEPHINE
               (in German)
          Prost!

Ludwig takes a very big sip. He gives the glass back to Josephine while turning to Dr. Schlesinger.

                    LUDWIG
               (in German)
          You see. Had we not taken the front row
          out, the sound would not have been right!

Dr. Schlesinger nods with a slight trait of exhaustion being reminded of Ludwig's endless requirements. Wiping his memories he smiles wholeheartedly and with his hand points to the entrance to the orchestra hall and starts applauding. Josephine follows suit. Ludwig gives sign to the singers to enter the concert hall and follows them back towards the entrance. Josephine and Dr. Schlesinger grasp their beers from the tray. They both take a big sip with great relief as they hear the enormous applause from inside of the concert hall.

EXT. VIENNA - CONCERT HALL - SIDE ENTRANCE - LATE EVENING

A limousine is waiting in front of the stage door. It is a dark, clear night. Ludwig, Josephine, and Dr. Schlesinger exit the concert building and walk to the car. Dr. Schlesinger shakes hands with Josephine and then with Ludwig.

> DR. SCHLESINGER
> (in German)
> Again, Dr. Mann. Thank you so much for this unforgettable event. And Josephine, thanks so much - and please, let's be in touch as soon as you can regarding the other possibilities I mentioned. It would be so great to make it happen.

The driver closes the doors of the car with Josephine and Ludwig at the backseat, then enters the car and drives slowly out of the concert hall area, through Vienna and finally through the outskirts of Vienna.

INT. VIENNA - CAR - DRIVING THROUGH VIENNA - NIGHT

Ludwig and Josephine sit quietly on the backseat. There is no other traffic in the late evening. They both look out in the darkness. Josephine moves close to Ludwig and puts her hand seductively on his lap. A silver moonlight breaks the darkness.

> CROSS FADE BACK IN TIME

EXT. NEW YORK - SUBURB - NIGHT - (23 YEARS AGO)

A light silver moonlight shines over a single, small wooden house. Only the bedroom is with light. The silence around Ludwig and Josephine in the car prevails through the flashback until suddenly a woman's frightening scream cuts through the silence.

INT. NEW YORK SUBURB - HOUSE - BEDROOM - NIGHT

GIULIA CARA (29, European) sits on her knees with her legs
spread in the middle of a large bed. Her long, dark, unordered
hair covers most of her face, shoulders and white night gown
soaked with blood. She holds her hands around her pregnant
belly and screams as blood continues to flush out of her,
totally soaking the sheets and her night gown. Her hands
are filling with blood as she tries to stop the flow and the
abortion with her hands. Screaming again she lifts the hands
and watches the blood in the hands and the flow of blood
along her arms.

A YOUNG COUPLE enters the house and runs into the bedroom. As
soon as they see the aborting woman they stop frightened by
the bloody scenery. Giulia lies on her side breathing heavily
in pain. The young woman screams and then shouts hysterically
to her husband.

                    THE YOUNG WOMAN
          Call an ambulance.

The young man picks the phone in the bedroom, but as soon as
Giulia realizes he is about to call, she gets up on her knees
and raises her bloody hands towards him in a frightening and
deadly moment.

                    GIULIA
          Please do not call. Please.

The young man and woman look puzzled at each other. The woman
moves close to Giulia to comfort her.

                    THE YOUNG WOMAN
          But you are bleeding! You are in great
          danger - you need help.

The young man dials and briefly talks over the phone. Giulia
sinks down on the bed and cries desperately.

EXT. NEW YORK - SUBURB - HOUSE - NIGHT

Two police cars with flashing lights and an ambulance are
in front of the house. The emergency staff comes out of the
house carrying Giulia on a stretcher. Her cover is soaked with
blood. A police officer stands next to his car with the young

couple and makes notes as the couple talks. The police officer looks at his watch, carefully noting the time. The young woman, still in shock, holds her hands over her eyes as she talks to the police officer and cries at the same time. The police cars and the ambulance drive away. The scenery fades away in black darkness.

CROSS FADE TO PRESENT TIME

INT. VIENNA - OUTSKIRTS - CAR, DRIVING - NIGHT

Ludwig and Josephine are continuing their drive in the darkness outside of Vienna. Ludwig is still looking out in the dark, now holding Josephine's hand. She moves even closer and leans on him. They both appear happy, relieved, and exhausted. The car stops in front of their hotel. The two just sit in silence for a moment.

EXT. VIENNA - HOTEL - NIGHT

The car doors are being opened by two servants. Ludwig and Josephine step out. Ludwig watches the dark sky over the large trees around the hotel. The moon shines a light silver light through the dark, but crystal clear scenery. Ludwig and Josephine walk up the broad staircase to the large classic hotel and, hand in hand, enter the hotel lobby.

TRANSITION TO NEXT MORNING

EXT. VIENNA - HOTEL - SUITE - TERRACE - MORNING

Ludwig sits at the large, sunny hotel suite terrace dressed in a comfortable bathrobe. The early sun is bathing the beautiful terrace, its light brown oblong floor tiles, the blooming roses along the rails, and its neatly designed, classic terrace furniture. A servant is organizing the table for breakfast from a large silver trolley and pours a big cup of coffee and hot milk for Ludwig. He enjoys the coffee and the scenery - a beautiful valley, a river, a lake and a town in the valley - while the servant continues serving the breakfast. The rays of the morning sun are reflected and broken in crystal glasses at the table. The servant exits the terrace backwards with a slight bow. At the same time Josephine enters the terrace, upbeat and full of energy, wearing an elegant, provocative nightgown and carrying a pile

of newspapers, her computer, iPhone, and note paper. She puts
it all at a side table on her side of the breakfast table and
goes over to Ludwig. She sits down across Ludwig's lap and
puts her arms around his neck while Ludwig holds his large
hot milk-coffee in his hand away from his body. Josephine
kisses Ludwig deeply, emotionally and tempting. Ludwig puts
his coffee on the table with one hand while he responds to her
kisses and seductive temptations. He touches her body under
her nightgown. Satisfied by having provoked Ludwig, Josephine
abruptly interrupts the kiss and leans slightly away from the
aroused Ludwig.

                    JOSEPHINE
               (in German)
          They all love you! I show you!

Josephine rises from Ludwig's lap, pours her coffee and
freshly squeezed orange juice, grasps one of the freshly baked
breads and sits down by the table opposite Ludwig. She takes
the pile of newspapers, puts it on her lap and reads loud for
Ludwig.

                    JOSEPHINE
          "Ludwig Mann delivered what nobody before
          thought possible...."

                    LUDWIG
               (interrupts her)
          Please - I know all this stuff people
          write.

                    JOSEPHINE
          I know, I know. OK, I will not tire you
          with that then - but it is good stuff.

Josephine puts the papers aside, hiding her disappointment.
She smiles to Ludwig. He enjoys the perfect moment of beauty
and perfection all around him. Josephine silently reads
through all the Internet messages on her smartphone. She
briefly pauses and smiles as Ludwig pours his second glass of
orange juice in the light flickering crystal glass.

                    JOSEPHINE
          Just listen to this - you will like this
          one. It's a little different.

Josephine moves to the edge of her chair and sits more upright.

                    JOSEPHINE
                (reading in English)
        "Particularly the Mozart pieces got life
        as never before - it is almost like
        Ludwig Mann knows the music better than
        the composer himself!"

Josephine, exited and happily smiling, looks over at Ludwig.

                    JOSEPHINE
        This is written in a UK paper. This
        guy always writes some pretty unusual
        comments.

                    LUDWIG
        Was he the one who claimed some music
        should simply stay on the score? That was
        a pretty profound remark - I really agree!
        With some music - whatever you do - it
        will not be what it is intended to be.

Ludwig pauses as he looks over the landscape and ponders.
After a while he looks over at Josephine as he continues the
thought.

                    LUDWIG
        I cannot deal with all of this. It
        distracts me. Why on earth does he write
        that? I don't want to be in the composer's
        shoes?

                    JOSEPHINE
        But what more can you hope for and wish
        than being compared with the creator of
        what you interpret?

                    LUDWIG
        I don't believe he really means it.
        He simply wants to make some smart
        remarks that may sound profound.

Ludwig pauses. He is distracted and irritated by the thought,
as he simply wants to enjoy the beautiful surroundings.

                         LUDWIG
                  (talks while rising)
          Let's not get bucked down in all of this.
          Let's focus on what matters in the music.
          Please!

Ludwig pushes his chair a bit away from the table. He turns
it and looks over the beautiful landscape. Josephine grasps
a little more of the delicious food. She looks concerned over
at Ludwig. Then she reads through the rest of the mails. She
waits for a moment where Ludwig is approachable.

                         JOSEPHINE
          Dr. Schlesinger asked me again about
          his idea - you remember? Now he says,
          he would support you doing the six late
          symphonies, with only one condition -
          there would also be a live performance
          here and another over there!

Ludwig holds the coffee close to his nose and enjoys the
flavor. During the following conversation a subtle, yet
controlled argument evolves. Josephine always tries to hold
back, Ludwig loses his poise.

                         LUDWIG
          I really don't think I can do it.

                         JOSEPHINE
          What? Are you kidding?

                         LUDWIG
          This guy sort of said it. I cannot bring
          some music from the score to life without
          failing.

                         JOSEPHINE
          Come on, you always say something like
          that, and you always make it in the end.

                         LUDWIG
          Well, you think so? Okay then; but how
          much do you want me to suffer? What about
          all the times I was sitting there in the
          concert corridor with the orchestra and
          the audience waiting and I just could not

go in - this feeling that whatever I did
it would be inferior to what it should be.
What about that?

> JOSEPHINE
> But this is different. You know these
> pieces, and you will perform with the
> orchestras you most love. You will be in
> New York again! You love that. It always
> lifts you. It energizes you. It inspires
> you! The sound there makes you flourish.
> And you deliver everything. You know
> that - wake up!

Ludwig symbolically kicks and hits something to get rid of his
aggression.

> LUDWIG
> Get a car. Let's make chance rule our
> life, just for a few days instead of being
> so totally organized with every minute
> lined up in schedules.

Ludwig again turns to view the landscape and then continues
to speak.

> LUDWIG
> Somehow I feel that we will lose the
> music if we just continue doing what we
> are doing - however successful we are. I
> mean, however successful all these writers
> and reviewers claim us to be - they just
> make us a story. That's what they want; a
> story. It is not really about the music!

Josephine realizes she will not get further with her wishes.

> JOSEPHINE
> OK, let me get a car - but think about
> the offer - we cannot just let it go.

Josephine rises, goes over to Ludwig and kisses him softly,
yet passionately and seductively. Ludwig reaches out for her,
but she slips away and runs back to the hotel suite. Ludwig,
slightly irritated and frustrated, pours another coffee and
walks up and down the terrace with the coffee while watching

the landscape. As the beginning of Symphony 29 fills the space around him, he smiles, raises his arms towards the music as though it comes to him through the air, picks a whole baguette and starts conducting with it. A sound from his phone in the pocket of his bathrobe signals a text message. The music stops. He picks the phone and reads. The message is from TIFFANY (23, Asian with Korean characters - "Western look" from the side "Asian" look from front - tall, slim, long black hair)

                    TIFFANY
              (text message)
         "Can I call you?"

Ludwig looks around and writes something back. Josephine appears on the terrace. She is smart and seductively dressed now and in perfect shape, upbeat and full of energy. She moves close to Ludwig and puts her arms around his neck for a soft kiss.

                    JOSEPHINE
         Just be ready to leave in an hour.
         Just bring your good mood and all your
         love and attraction to me!

Josephine moves her hands seductively along her body and then lifts her finger jokingly as she leaves the terrace.
Just as she exits the door to the suite, Josephine turns around and kisses Ludwig hot through the air. Ludwig appears slightly worried as he dials a number. He walks to a distant end of the terrace and watches the landscape as he waits for the call to go through.

INT. HONG KONG - HOTEL - SUITE - DAY

Tiffany, dressed elegantly but casual in bright colors, is standing by a panorama window and overlooking the sky-line and sea of Hong-Kong from her hotel suite. Her phone lies on a small writing desk facing the window. The phone rings. Tiffany hurries over to answer. She looks at the display and sees Ludwig's name. She immediately answers nervously. She tries to brace herself, as her eyes are wet with tears and her voice almost breaking.

                    TIFFANY
              (in German)
         Ludwig, Ludwig?

                    LUDWIG
          (in German, voice on the
          phone)
     Yes. What's going on?

                    TIFFANY
     I need your help. I am desperate. I am
     falling apart!

                    LUDWIG
     Is it the music?

                    TIFFANY
     It is everything. Yes - the music. I am
     losing it. All these concerts - over and
     over again - the music is just not there
     anymore. I know you know what I mean!
          (she pauses and continues in
          a lower voice)
     And of course my loveless life here.

Tiffany wipes her eyes. The cosmetics get messed up. She leans
her face on the glass windows towards the skyline and doesn't
care about being ugly.

                    LUDWIG
     Of course. I know exactly what you mean -
     I mean with the music.

Tiffany blows her nose close to the speaker. Black mascara
flows with the tears. It knocks on the door to the suite.

                    SERVANT
          (in Mandarin)
     They are all waiting for you downstairs
     Madame.

                    TIFFANY
          (in Mandarin)
     Tell them I got caught on a call -
     15 more minutes.

                    TIFFANY
          (in German)
     Help me. I have to play again in two
     weeks - I cannot. I just cannot.

                        LUDWIG
              What's the program?

EXT. VIENNA - HOTEL - SUITE - TERRACE - DAY

                        TIFFANY
                   (voice on the phone, as if
                   it would be the worst, she
                   weeps)
              The 4th - among others, of course.

Ludwig holds the phone a little away from his ear. He looks at
the beautiful hotel, then down at his feet, then again over
the landscape. It gets calmer on the other side of the line.

                        LUDWIG
              Calm down. Just think of when we first
              played together.
                   (he pauses, the Mozart
                   double sonata fills the
                   background)
              Is it better?
                   (he pauses again)
              Why don't you come over here? Can you
              slip away for a few days? We can go to my
              cottage - just a day or two.

                        TIFFANY
              Yes, please, please - make it happen.

                        LUDWIG
              I send you a text at latest tomorrow.
              Hang-in; don't call the next two days.

                        TIFFANY
              Of course - I know. I love you!

                        LUDWIG
              Love you!

Ludwig puts the phone back in his pocket. He watches the clock
and walks fast to the suite to get dressed, humming, while
the music fades.

EXT. VIENNA - HOTEL - IN FRONT - DAY

In front of the hotel, Josephine is signing the rental papers
for a spacious, open, sporty car. The servants are loading
the luggage in the trunk. Josephine takes the driver's seat.
Ludwig enters the car and sits next to the energetic and
upbeat Josephine. She immediately drives fast and determined
out of the hotel area. She smiles proudly to Ludwig.

> JOSEPHINE
> We go to Linz now! We will be in a
> beautiful place there tonight. I already
> organized a romantic dinner for us - and
> a menu you will never forget - not to
> mention the wines! And then we are on our
> own - all night.

She smiles seductively.

INT. LINZ - HOTEL - LOBBY - EARLY EVENING

Ludwig and Josephine enter the spacious lobby of the
old Linzer hotel. They are welcomed and recognized by a
SERVANT (35).

> SERVANT
> Welcome back, so good to have you here.

> JOSEPHINE
> Thank you. We almost missed it, like home
> (laughing)

Josephine and Ludwig are guided through the large, beautiful,
classic hotel hall.

INT. LINZ - HOTEL - SUITE - EARLY EVENING

Ludwig lies on the big bed and looks around in the beautiful
suite. Josephine is taking a shower in the background.
Ludwig's mind goes back to his first concert in the
conservatory and his first meeting with Josephine.

TRANSITIONS BACK IN TIME

INT. CONSERVATORY - CONCERT HALL - EVENING - BACK IN TIME

The young Ludwig (17) stands in front of a small orchestra conducting a Mozart symphony (29th) as part of his final examination at the conservatory. The MAESTRO (69) and a panel of teachers evaluating Ludwig are sitting on the first row. The young musicians, students of the highly prestigious school, play extremely well. Ludwig radiates his enthusiasm and enormous energy as the music shapes in his hands. He conducts very close to the musicians and elegantly, with total confidence, handling all details without any technical difficulties. The small concert room is packed. Josephine (39) is sitting in the middle of the first row. She exhibits all her womanly seductive characteristics as she watches Ludwig's conducting with the greatest attention. Everybody holds their breath as Ludwig guides the audience and the musicians through the symphony as were it his own. The music flows perfectly and fills the room magically.

Ludwig holds the last bar. The applause from the audience makes the roof fall down. The Maestro rises in the middle of the first row and with him everybody rises and applauds. Ludwig embraces the audience. He takes his seat at one of the chairs along the side of the concert hall. The next student comes up to the podium to conduct.

INT. CONSERVATORY - RECEPTION ROOM - EVENING

All students and the audience are gathered for a reception after the concert in a small, classic, elegant room which, however, needs repair. The students help serve the guests. Ludwig hands glasses of white wine to the guests. Having distributed the glasses from his tray, Ludwig is congratulated by friends and colleagues who line up in front of him. Josephine, impatient, stands waiting in the line for Ludwig. She gradually gets closer and finally stands face to face with Ludwig. He is immediately captured by Josephine's sensuality and beauty. She smiles and moves very close to Ludwig, yet initially pretending being a little shy.

                    JOSEPHINE
              (in German)
          That was very, very nice. It was so
          powerful - totally capturing. I wonder how
          you do it.

                         (she pauses while moving
                          closer and lowering her
                          voice)
          There was something magic going on!

                         LUDWIG
          I am glad you enjoyed - actually I was
          quite lucky with the orchestra this time.
          In the rehearsals they never got it. But
          then, suddenly, it just worked out.

Ludwig smiles back to Josephine. He radiates enormous energy
and joy of the moment. Josephine is impressed. It gets harder
to see who captures whom.

                         JOSEPHINE
          So what are you going to do now?

                         LUDWIG
                         (flirting with an
                          understatement of his
                          talent)
          Well, my free time - I mean the time paid
          for by the school is over, so - I assume
          I go back to my village and do the best
          I can. I miss the solitude, I guess -
          and our church has an organ - I have
          managed to make some pretty decent music
          there from time to time! I even had good
          musicians coming and perform with me - so
          maybe it will not be too bad after all.

Josephine stands quiet for a little while, still in the shy
mode, and watches Ludwig as she considers her next step.

                         JOSEPHINE
          Maybe - maybe I can offer you something
          very different -

                         LUDWIG
          And?

                         JOSEPHINE
          What about I made you a world famed
          conductor?

Ludwig is amused. He laughs slightly.

                         LUDWIG
            Well, how could I not be interested?

Josephine takes another glass of wine from the adjacent table.
She smiles capturing and charming, yet no longer appearing
shy but serious and professional, yet seductive.

                         JOSEPHINE
            OK, here is the deal - I become your
            manager; your exclusive manager. You
            conduct - and do not think of anything
            else. And I do nothing but getting
            good deals for you - and I organize
            everything.

                         LUDWIG
            Very tempting. But...

          THE PICTURE OF THE ROOM BLURS AND TRANSITIONS TO
          LUDWIG LYING ON THE BED IN THE LINZER HOTEL SUITE

INT. LINZ - HOTEL - RESTAURANT - EVENING

The waiter guides Ludwig and Josephine to their beautifully
decorated table, surrounded by plants to deliver a significant
privacy. He helps them sit down and swiftly opens a bottle of
champagne already waiting in a silver ice-bath. He opens the
bottle with only a slight puff and pours the champagne in the
pre-cooled glasses. Josephine and Ludwig touch glasses as they
taste the beautifully sparkling champagne. Josephine smiles
her most beautiful, seductive and engaging smile. They rapidly
finish their first glass. The waiter refills the glasses and
discretely retreats from the table. Ludwig and Josephine make
themselves comfortable and enjoy the moment.

                         JOSEPHINE
            You don't need to order. I took care of
            everything - everything as you like it
            the most!

Ludwig is impressed and forgets his troubled mood. He takes
the bottle of champagne and refills their glasses. Josephine
lifts her glass.

                    JOSEPHINE
     Cheers - to us.

                    LUDWIG
     How is it that somehow you always make
     exactly what I like the most - you make
     me want all that is beautiful - and
     then - well then you just give me all
     that is beautiful.
               (he pauses and ponders)
     You just read my mind - before me!
               (he continues jokingly yet
               serious)
     Sometimes I wonder if my mind is really
     mine - or if you have taken over.
               (he pauses)
     If I have a mind at all. Well - whatever
     it is, without you I wouldn't even know
     some of the pleasures in life!
               (feeling dizzy he pauses)
     I think we had quite a bit of wine.

                    JOSEPHINE
               (overhearing Ludwig's last
               comment)
     Well, you give beauty to the world like
     nobody else, so you deserve the beauty
     of the world. It's very simple - don't
     complicate thing.

Their flirty adulation to each other gets interrupted by the
waiter, who serves a very small portion of the finest sea
food and pours a golden Riesling in their glasses. The dew
condenses on the glasses as he pours the gently chilled wine.
The waiter leaves them. Josephine gets back to her seductive
mode and looks Ludwig deep in the eyes.

                    JOSEPHINE
     And now - tell me about the recordings
     and the concerts.

Ludwig tries to go on playing the game, but concern comes back
in his mind. He protracts his answer by lifting his glass,
moving his chair, eating a bite of the seafood with his free
hand, and drinking a sip of wine.

                              LUDWIG
          I cannot do all six symphonies. I don't
          really understand them.
                    (he pauses)
          I can do the four of them. And for the
          live performance I will need something
          else in between - Beethoven's 4th - I mean
          the piano concert. Something like that.
                    (he pauses)
          And then we should disc the Requiem - now
          I just got it right.

Josephine looks thoughtful and slightly suspicious at Ludwig
for a short moment. The waiter refills her Riesling. She
drinks while Ludwig finishes the food. They both take big sips
of the wine. The servant again refills their glasses.

                            JOSEPHINE
          I know how you feel about this kinds of
          collections of masterpieces. I know - I
          know.

She takes another big sip.

                            JOSEPHINE
          Maybe Mozart himself did not really feel
          good about all the symphonies either or
          at least parts of them.

                              LUDWIG
          What I feel is all I have - wherever
          that feeling comes from. And I have to
          live with it. And please, let's not ignore
          that - it bubbles up from somewhere, deep
          down, unexplainable, like the music itself.

Ludwig realizes how the wine carries them away. The servant
pours two big glasses of red wine. He gently swirls the wine
in the glasses to saturate the bouquet over the wine. He
carefully checks the bouquet and the cork. Josephine tastes
the red wine. With a nod she shows her acceptance.

                            JOSEPHINE
          OK. What about a pianist then. There is
          not time for that. You cannot just get a
          pianist from one day to the other to play

both here and over there and up to your
standards, right?

Ludwig, pretty enchanted by Josephine and the wine, is
something in between boyish and calculating.

> LUDWIG
> Well. I will come up with something - and
> then you just make it happen; as usual!

> JOSEPHINE
> (slightly suspicious, yet
> business oriented)
> I wonder what you really are up to.
> But OK, then that's it: four recordings
> and two live concerts both with a
> Beethoven piano concert in between.
> (she pauses)
> And you make your recording of the
> Requiem.

Both are relieved. The main course is served. They eat in
silence, making the quiet sounds of fork and knife and their
glasses sound loud in Ludwig's head as if it would be music.
Josephine looks at Ludwig with all her charm. She prepares for
the moment to talk. She leans forward to the table and puts
both elbows on the table as the servant removes her plate. She
holds her wine glass in both hands and looks at Ludwig over
the glass and through the strong bouquet of the red wine.

> JOSEPHINE
> Tell me something. Did I give you
> everything we agreed when we made our
> deal - you remember?

> LUDWIG
> Of course I remember. Oh yes - of
> course - everything ...

Ludwig feels desires from deep down bubbling up in his
mind. Fearful of himself and of losing the ties to the depth
Josephine provides, he continues in a low voice.

> LUDWIG
> - and even more. It is almost unreal -
> deep - satisfying ...

                    (he pauses)
          ... necessary.

Ludwig abruptly takes Josephine's hand and holds it firmly
and pulls her a bit closer. Josephine holds Ludwig's hand with
both her hands.

                    JOSEPHINE
          Maybe you could offer me something?

Ludwig for a moment is confused. Then he realizes what
Josephine is talking about. He get slightly conflicted and
worried but smiles to her. Josephine seductively moves the
very closest, almost lying over the table.

                    JOSEPHINE
               (whispering)
          Strictly speaking we are just in a
          business relationship! Right?

She smiles and so does Ludwig.

                    LUDWIG
               (whispering back)
          So - what's the proposal.

                    JOSEPHINE
          The proposal is very simple - we marry.
          Yes we marry!.

The waiter pours a well-chilled desert wine and serves a very
small portion of fruits. He rapidly clears the table and steps
away.

                    LUDWIG
          But, in reality we are already. We have no
          limits!

Josephine shakes her head - unconvinced. She pulls her hands
back and moves a bit away from the table. She looks at Ludwig
and then down on her hands. She makes her eyes slightly wet,
faking tears.

                    JOSEPHINE
          Well, then you never know what the future
          may bring.

> (she pauses and continues in
> a broken voice)
> I want to know and to see my future - our
> future. Yes - our future.

Ludwig immediately gets worried. He wipes his conflicting thoughts and moves close to the table and reaches out for Josephine's hands. He gathers them in his hands and pulls them close to his face and kisses them softly and emotionally as is he afraid of losing her. He keeps holding her hands and then looks over at her. He puts her hands at the table. He takes her glass with wine and hands it to her. He takes his own glass. They both move close together until their faces meet at the middle of the table. Ludwig kisses her softly.

                    LUDWIG
          (whispering)
     Will you?

                    JOSEPHINE
     You know how you need me, deep, and I
     need you.

They both again move close together. Josephine kisses Ludwig sensually while he totally gives in to her.

INT. EUROPE - AIRPORT - ARRIVAL AREA - DAY

Ludwig walks swiftly into the arrival area of the airport. He looks a little nervously at the screen announcing flight arrivals. As he realizes Tiffany's plane has already arrived he looks impatiently around in the arrival area. Suddenly he sees Tiffany way down the broad arrival hall. Tiffany has seen Ludwig and is running with small "Asian" steps towards him like she is floating over the floor. She carries a small carry-on. Her long, dark hair is set up above her head. She wears elegant, but convenient clothes for a long flight and travel. Her Asian type make-up is flawless in spite of the long travel. As she gets close to Ludwig, she lifts her hands. Ludwig sees her move like in slow-motion. He sees her beautiful face and happiness as she gets closer and closer. Ludwig lifts his arms and runs towards her. They reach each other in the middle of the large arrival hall and embrace as they turn around and around. As they stop, motions become real time. The music stops. They are endlessly happy and loving being together.

                              LUDWIG
                        (in German)
                 You made it. Let's get out of here.

Ludwig puts his arm around her. They start walking.

                              LUDWIG
                 I have a car outside.
                        (he pauses)
                 Was it tough?

                              TIFFANY
                 Not too bad.

She doesn't know what to say. Ludwig grasps a baggage trolley
standing idle.

                              LUDWIG
                 Come on, let's move fast.

Tiffany jumps on the trolley. They have fun while Ludwig
rapidly rolls through the arrival area to significant
amusement of other passengers.

                              TIFFANY
                        (excited with her hands
                        raised)
                 Wohooooo!

They exit the arrival hall.

EXT. EUROPE - MOUNTAIN ROADS - CAR - DAY

Ludwig and Tiffany drive away from the airport and into the
countryside. A heavy rhythm rock music love song again fills
the space and overshadows their talking. The music rocks
the car and energizes them as they are seen to have fun
talking about everything and nothing - the travel, the music,
the past, their love, their longings, their fun and their
respective situations. After a while, jet-lag hits. Tiffany
falls in a deep sleep as they drive. The music stops. It is
quiet as Ludwig continues driving. He reaches the foot of
the mountains and continues the steep drive up through the
mountains. The landscape becomes totally deserted with no
cars and houses around. Ludwig, relaxed and happy, enjoys the
difficult ride and the silence in his mind. They reach the

height where trees are very scarce. The drive continues along steep hillsides. Finally, the road ends at the edge of the mountain of Ludwig's cottage, only reachable by foot about a hundred meters further up the mountain. Ludwig stops the car. He opens the door and sits a moment enjoying the crisp cool air and the silence with only the faint, soft sound of the wind between the surrounding mountain peaks. He enjoys the gorgeous sight over the mountains. He looks at the sleeping Tiffany. He exits the car.

EXT. COTTAGE - PARKING - EARLY EVENING

The cottage with two parts, a main cottage and a smaller annex, is situated on a small plateau with an unhindered view of the surrounding mountains. The cottages are built in massive wood and have grass covered roofs. The main cottage is situated right next to a very steep hillside. The smaller cottage is behind the main cottage. Close to the small cottage there is another steep hillside. Between the cottages is a small courtyard with a manual water pump. Tiffany is still in deep sleep. Ludwig exits the car. He walks up to the cottages and unlocks the doors. He enters the small cottage.

INT. COTTAGE - SMALL COTTAGE - EVENING

Inside the small cottage there is a narrow bed. The outside walls of the cottages are of the same raw, massive wood as the inner walls. Totally familiar with the place and everything being in order exactly as he last left it, Ludwig takes a big blanket from a shelf and puts it on the small bed. He exits the small cottage leaving the door open.

EXT. COTTAGE - COURTYARD - EVENING

Ludwig goes to the manual water pump in the middle of the small courtyard between the cottages. He pumps full of energy and lets all the first water pass. When clean and clear water flushes from the pump he puts his head under the stream while still pumping with one hand. Refreshed and relieved with water dripping from his face he watches the beautiful scenery around the cottage. Full of energy he runs and jumps down the hill back to the car. He lifts Tiffany out of the car and carries her in his arms as he walks back to the cottages. Ludwig carries Tiffany as though he just saved her from drowning. The music (beginning of 5th/2rd movement) breaks into the picture and totally fills the space as Ludwig carries Tiffany gently up the steep path to the cottages.

INT. COTTAGE - SMALL COTTAGE - EARLY EVENING

Ludwig puts Tiffany on the small bed. He covers her with the blanket on the bed. He pushes it firmly around her to protect against the crisp temperature at the high location. He sits briefly at the edge of the bed and watches her deeply relaxed face. He kisses her gently on the forehead. Energized he rises, stands and watches her quietly for a few moments and then silently exits the cottage closing the door behind him.

EXT. COTTAGE - MAIN COTTAGE - EARLY EVENING

Ludwig walks over to the main cottage. Like the small cottage, it is built in heavy, massive wood trunks which form both the inside and the outside of the cottage walls. He enters the main cottage.

INT. COTTAGE - MAIN COTTAGE - EVENING

Ludwig enters the main cottage. There is a very large wooden table in the room and a fireplace. Two old pianos are standing side by side along the wall facing the steep mountain side. From two windows one sees the impressive mountainous scenery. In a corner of the room there is a small kitchen and a fireplace. He goes over to the two pianos and strikes a few keys. The pianos are quite out of tune.

                              LUDWIG
            Wow my friends - you haven't been used for
            quite a while. Don't worry - I take care
            of you.

Ludwig walks over to a small cabinet by the kitchen and finds a piano tuning rod. He takes the front covers of the pianos away to get access to all the knots and strings. He starts tuning the pianos.

                                        CROSS FADE AHEAD IN TIME

After tuning Ludwig strikes a few final cords on both pianos. He nods satisfied with the tuning.

LUDWIG
Great. Well done old friend.
(in low voice)
I should just stay here with you folks -
much nicer.

Ludwig puts the piano tuning rod back in the cabinet. He looks satisfied around and exits the cottage in great mood.

EXT. COTTAGE - COURTYARD - EVENING

Ludwig stands for a moment between the two cottages and again watches the scenery. He breathes the clear and crisp air like it feeds him energy. He enters the small cottage.

INT. COTTAGE - SMALL COTTAGE - EVENING

The jet-lagged Tiffany still sleeps exactly as Ludwig left her. He sits down at the edge of her bed. He softly puts his hand on hers. He sits for a while. Tiffany opens her eyes. She looks slightly confused around, and then at Ludwig. He leans forward and kisses her softly on the chin. He makes a little sound to wake her up.

INT. BERLIN - AIRPORT - ARRIVAL AREA - DAY

Josephine enters the arrival hall in the airport. She is in an elegant business dress. She exits the arrival hall.

EXT. BERLIN - AIRPORT - PARKING - DAY

Josephine walks swiftly and determined to the parking spot for limos right outside the arrival terminal. The driver BRUNO (35, formally dressed as driver, tall, slim) is waiting for her.

BRUNO
(in German)
Good morning Josephine.

JOSEPHINE
(in German)
Bruno. Good to see you.

Bruno puts her carry-on in the trunk. He opens the car door for Josephine, waits for Josephine to take seat, then goes to the driver's seat and starts driving.

INT. BERLIN - LIMO - DAY

                    JOSEPHINE
          So how are things Bruno? How are the
          kids?

                    BRUNO
          Viola starts to get teeth. Pretty noisy
          nights. - How was your trip?

                    JOSEPHINE
          Short, on time, and easy; just as it
          should always be.
                    (pauses)
          And Bruno - as I mentioned, I have to
          get the flight to Zurich right after this
          meeting. Is the traffic easy today?

                    BRUNO
          Oh Yes. Many people have a day off today.
          I will get you there on time. If we are
          late we just do some shortcuts!

They drive through the streets of Berlin towards the city center and the concert hall area. Josephine watches the streets passing. She is tense, focused and serious.

EXT. BERLIN - OFFICE BUILDING - PARKING - DAY

Bruno stops the car in front of a large, modern building. He exits the car and opens the door for Josephine.

                    BRUNO
          I will be right here - any time!

INT. BERLIN - OFFICE BUILDING - FOYER

The RECEPTIONIST (23, blond, well-shaped and fit German woman) rises as she sees Josephine entering and stands ready as Josephine reaches the reception.

THE RECEPTIONIST
(in German)
Dr. Schlesinger is expecting you. He is on
his way down.

The elevator door opens. Dr. Schlesinger steps out and walks
smiling with his hand stretched forward to greet Josephine.
She greets him. They shake hands. Dr. Schlesinger guides
Josephine to the elevator.

INT. BERLIN - OFFICE BUILDING - SCHLESINGER OFFICE - DAY

Josephine and Dr. Schlesinger enter the spacious office at the
top-floor. The glass walls at two sides of the corner office
provide a stunning view. All other walls are covered with
photographs and painting of leading conductors, musicians,
original classic paintings, golden records from key classic
recordings, and a few violins. Dr. Schlesinger picks a
folder with a few sheets of papers from his desk. He invites
Josephine to sit in a comfortable armchair by a small table
in the corner of the office. He opens the folder as they both
sit down.

DR. SCHLESINGER
(in German)
I amended the agreement. It is now
four recordings with all the copyrights
to the Vienna Orchestra Foundation.
There are two live performances. One
in Vienna, the other in New York. There
are four rehearsals for each recording.
One piece in each live performance
is the 4th piano concert or the 5th at
your discretion - these with only two
rehearsals - everything to be done within
three months from now. In addition, we do
the recording of the Requiem.
(he pauses and looks over at
Josephine)
And the money: 100.000 EUR cash at
signature and 400.000 EUR at completion
of the last concert and, as usual,
we pay all your direct expenses for
travel, accommodation etc. Same, same as
previously.
(he pauses and smiles)

So, I believe this should be it then -
and I tell you: everybody here is so
excited to see this moving.

Dr. Schlesinger pushes a copy of the agreement over the table
to Josephine. She pulls the agreement closer with two fingers,
but leaves it on the table. She talks slightly subdue.

                    JOSEPHINE
It's fine Joseph - just one thing.
We need to make it 250.000 now and
750.000 when we are done.

                    DR. SCHLESINGER
                (surprised)
But Josephine, this is a major change.
And you know, our recordings do not bring
that much revenue anymore; even though
these of course will be classics and sell
forever.
                (he pauses)
You know, in the moment we release the
recordings you have copies everywhere -
you can even download them almost at the
same time as we publish! - you wouldn't
believe how this landscape is changing.

                    JOSEPHINE
Joseph, you know how it is working
with Ludwig. He sets higher and higher
allowances to go on. And, this is top
secret, Joseph - just between you and me,
right. But he entrusted me that this will
be his last recordings. He wants to stop
conducting after this. Joseph, we both
know that he has said something like this
before - but I know, it is different this
time.
                (she pauses for a little
                while and pretends slightly
                embarrassed)
I can assure you Joseph that this is his
last. But - should it even happen that he
records ever again, I promise it will be
with your company.

Josephine opens her hands at the table. She looks at Dr.
Schlesinger. They know each other well. Dr. Schlesinger takes
a deep breath.

> DR. SCHLESINGER
> OK. So - OK. But no more changes then.

Dr. Schlesinger takes the draft contracts. He corrects
the numbers in hand writing. He signs both contracts and
initializes by the changes. He pushes the agreements over the
table to Josephine. She signs and initializes. Dr. Schlesinger
goes to his writing desk and takes a checkbook from the
drawer. He fills a check out, signs it and hands it to
Josephine. They shake hands.

> DR. SCHLESINGER
> Thank you for your confidence. One more
> thing - we need the name of the pianist;
> sooner rather than later - we have to
> start advertising, you know.

> JOSEPHINE
> Ludwig is on it. He will tell me in three
> days. I will let you know immediately.

> DR. SCHLESINGER
> Where is he now?

> JOSEPHINE
> Hiding again in his cottage to get
> inspired and energized, as he says. As
> usual, he will call me as soon as he
> reaches a village nearby and gets radio
> contact.

EXT. BERLIN - OFFICE BUILDING - PARKING - DAY

Bruno opens the door of the limo for Josephine and greets Dr.
Schlesinger. As Josephine is about to enter the car she turns
around to Dr. Schlesinger.

> JOSEPHINE
> Joseph, can I ask you a favor? - it is
> something entirely different.
> Something private.

                    DR. SCHLESINGER
Of course - just tell me what it is.

                    JOSEPHINE
I am going to marry soon - very soon
actually - and I wonder - would you join
the wedding ceremony - as a witness? It
will be a very small event in the first
place. Just for the formalities - later on
there will be a big party, and you will
of course be invited there too.

                    DR. SCHLESINGER
How wonderful news. And what an honor
for me!

                    JOSEPHINE
Thanks Joseph. It will be somewhere here
in Europe, probably near Vienna, so it
will be easy for you. I will follow up.
Maybe at the same time as we have the
concert there, so it will be easy for you.

Josephine smiles gratefully and happy to Dr. Schlesinger. She
enters the car. The car drives away.

INT. BERLIN - CAR - DAY

Bruno drives Josephine back through the streets of Berlin.
Josephine watches the town passing by.

                    BRUNO
We are a little short of time - do you
mind I take a shortcut?

                    JOSEPHINE
Not at all Bruno.

Bruno turns into a narrow road. They reach a small square
which they rapidly drive through. On the opposite side they
enter a very narrow passage. Here and there some prostitutes
are hanging around leaning to the house walls. Josephine
watches the girls, initially with discrete interest. As they
pass one of the girls dressed in a tempting black leather
suit, Josephine turns around and watches the girl through the
rear window of the car. She turns back and sits for a short

moment and watches her hands. She moves the hands softly along her legs and exhales softly. Suddenly, irritated, she hits her formal business dress hard with her hand.

> JOSEPHINE
> (whispering to herself)
> I hate this dress!

Josephine looks distressed at the streets passing.

> JOSEPHINE
> Good it soon is over.

Bruno turns onto a major road. As they have passed the dense traffic, Bruno speeds up. They rapidly reach the airport.

INT. ZURICH - HOTEL COURTYARD - DAY

The prestigious hotel limousine stops in front of the entry to Hotel Baur au Lac. The chauffeur swiftly exits the car and opens the passenger door for Josephine. She rapidly enters the hotel. The chauffeur hands her luggage to a servant, THOMAS (21, dressed in official hotel suit). He immediately follows Josephine.

INT. ZURICH - HOTEL - BAUR AU LAC - SUITE - DAY

Josephine and Thomas enter a suite overlooking the lake. Josephine looks around in the familiar surroundings.

> JOSEPHINE
> Thanks Thomas - just put it over there.

Thomas exits. Josephine, familiar with the suite, rapidly unpacks. She sets her hair, make-up and dress and rapidly exits the suite.

INT. ZURICH - BANK - FOYER - DAY

Josephine enters the lobby of a major Swiss bank. She immediately goes to the receptionist.

> JOSEPHINE
> (German)
> I am Josephine deBois. I have an
> appointment with Mr. Ziegler.

The receptionist looks through a list with an overview of the appointments of the day.

> THE RECEPTIONIST
> (in Swiss German)
> Welcome Mrs. deBois. Mr. Ziegler is
> expecting you - he will be with you in a
> moment.

Josephine walks to the elevators and waits. After a few moments GIUSEPPE ZIEGLER (50, flawlessly dressed in a neutral suit as appropriate for a Swiss banker) steps out of the elevator. He greets Josephine. They both enter the lift.

INT. ZURICH - BANK - ZIEGLER OFFICE - DAY

Josephine and Mr. Ziegler enter the office. It is very spacious, but lightly furnished with simple, elegant furniture. Josephine, obviously familiar with the place, immediately goes to one of two chairs in front of the large and very wide desk of Mr. Ziegler.

> MR. ZIEGLER
> (in German)
> Great to see you again Josephine. I see
> the business is running well - actually
> very well indeed!

> JOSEPHINE
> (in German)
> Giuseppe, I cannot tell you how happy I
> am with the achievements. It is totally
> beyond everything we projected. Well -
> of course we did not really know what to
> expect.
> (she pauses)
> Giuseppe, this is actually the reason why
> I am here today. I don't need the credit
> lines any more. So, I wonder if we could
> close those and just keep my personal
> accounts?

> MR. ZIEGLER
> Well, as you know, the credits don't
> cost you anything. Your guarantors have
> provided you unlimited credit, fully

guaranteed - and you have the strongest
guarantors one can possibly get, sacred.
So you can just leave it as is.

                    JOSEPHINE
I know Giuseppe. Still - I like to cancel.
You know - simplicity makes peace of mind.
Please just put everything on my personal
accounts. It should be a pretty decent
amount by now.

                    MR. ZIEGLER
Let me check for you.

Mr. Ziegler opens his computer and gets the summary of the
accounts on his screen. Josephine, unnoticed, looks a little
nervously around in the office while Mr. Ziegler looks for the
data. He writes a few numbers on a small piece of paper and
hands it to Josephine.

                    MR. ZIEGLER
It will be about 200 million Swiss if we
add it all up.

                    JOSEPHINE
OK. Please move ahead then. Can we do
it now?

                    MR. ZIEGLER
Sure. So everything to your personal
account?

                    JOSEPHINE
Yes, please.

Mr. Ziegler enters the requests in the systems. He prints a
few documents out and reads carefully through them. He turns
to Josephine and puts the papers in front of her.

                    MR. ZIEGLER
So, this is the closure of all current
arrangements. And here is the deposit
notice to your personal account. The
exact amount is 201,117,399.29 Swiss.

Mr. Ziegler signs the documents - all in duplicate. All pages
are initialized. Josephine signs. Mr. Ziegler carefully gathers
the signed documents. He hands one set of copies to Josephine
in a small folder.

                    MR. ZIEGLER
          So here is the receipt for your personal
          account. The total deposit is now
          249,499,377.01 Swiss. I have canceled all
          your credit cards except the one linked
          to your personal account.
                    (he watches the screen)
          Well, wait a minute. There is still an
          active credit card for Ludwig Mann. Do you
          want this to remain active?

                    JOSEPHINE
          Yes, please keep it active for now - but
          limit the e-banking access to me only.

                    MR. ZIEGLER
          OK - and where do we send mailings
          regarding the account?

                    JOSEPHINE
          Please keep everything here - I will pick
          it up from time to time - as usual.

Mr. Ziegler finished the details on the computer.

                    JOSEPHINE
          Oh, one more thing. Could you please
          credit this check to the account, but
          please let me have 100,000 in cash now.

Josephine hands Mr. Ziegler the check. He turns it around for
her to sign on the back. He talks briefly on the phone. Then
he enters the new numbers in the system and hands Josephine a
receipt.

                    MR. ZIEGLER
          The cash will be here in a sec. So, that's
          it then?

                    JOSEPHINE
          Yes, thanks a lot Giuseppe.

They rise. A woman enters the office and hands an envelope to Mr. Ziegler. He hands it to Josephine.

> MR. ZIEGLER
> Your cash!

Josephine puts the envelope in her handbag without counting the money. They walk to the exit.

> MR. ZIEGLER
> I will notify the guarantors of the change.

> JOSEPHINE
> Of course Giuseppe - but - well - could you do me a favor. Wait until the end of the month please.

Josephine sends a begging glance to Mr. Ziegler.

> MR. ZIEGLER
> Sure Josephine - I can do that - had you been asking for more credit it would be different, of course. But since you are essentially freeing the guarantors from any obligation, there is no urgency.

> JOSEPHINE
> Thanks - you have always been perfect.

INT. ZURICH - BANK - FOYER - DAY

Josephine exits the elevator to the foyer. She walks fast through the large hallway and exits to the street.

INT. ZURICH - HOTEL - BAUR AU LAC - SUITE - DAY

Josephine relaxes in the comfortable sofa in the middle of the suite. Thomas enters with a bottle of chilled, white wine. He puts it at the table by the sofa.

> JOSEPHINE
> Thanks Thomas - please let me have a glass - right away.

Thomas pours a glass and exits backwards with a gentle bow.
He closes the door to the suite silently. Josephine, relieved,
watches the beautiful scenery as she enjoys her drink.

                         JOSEPHINE
                  (whispering to herself)
              So far so good.

INT. COTTAGE - SMALL COTTAGE - MORNING

Ludwig sits at Tiffany's bed side. Tiffany is awake. Ludwig
kisses her softly on the forehead. The light in the small
cottage is soft. The impressive landscape is visible through a
small window.

                         LUDWIG
              You look like a Hopper painting.

Tiffany rises in the bed resting on her elbows. She laughs.

                         LUDWIG
              I make you some breakfast.

                         TIFFANY
              All right "SIR" - I will be there in
              a sec.

Ludwig rises and exits.

INT. COTTAGE - MAIN COTTAGE - MORNING

Ludwig puts the kettle on the fire. As the water is boiling,
he puts grounded coffee in two big cups and pours the boiling
water on the coffee, stirs briefly and places the cups on the
table. The coffee grains sediment. He unpacks a large bread
and puts it on the table together with a pack of butter.
He finds a big knife in the kitchen and starts cutting the
bread in thick slices. Tiffany enters, still wearing the same
clothes. She carries a few note papers which she puts on the
table. She sits down opposite Ludwig.

He hands her a coffee cup, a huge slice of bread, and the big
knife.

                    LUDWIG
          Just let the coffee sediment.

Tiffany holds the warm mug between her hands and inhales the
soothing coffee aroma. The vapors spread from the coffee in
the still chilly room. The only sound in the room is from the
fireplace.

                    LUDWIG
          So, tell me about the music.

Ludwig drinks his coffee and eats the rough bread. Tiffany
butters the bread while talking.

                    TIFFANY
          I canceled my concerts.
                  (she puts a piece of sugar
                  on a spoon, and watches it
                  melting, as she slowly puts
                  the spoon inside the coffee)
          I simply lost the music. The essence. Or
          the reason. Or the - I don't know - the
          meaning? It's just an empty cover. Like a
          butterfly, who left it's cocoon. But I am
          just the skin, not the butterfly.
                  (she pauses)
          I stand embedded in success, and yet:
          I am doing a lousy job.
                  (she pauses)
          You know what I mean - the music is gone.

Tiffany pauses for a while. She watches the fire, she watches
Ludwig, and she briefly looks at the scores placed at the end
of the table. Her eyes get blank from tears.

                    TIFFANY
          The manager - and Father, they are
          furious. They will force me to play - I
          just cannot.

Tiffany loses a tear, but immediately sweeps it away. She
tries not to cry but to be assertive..

                    TIFFANY
                  (a bit childish)
          I won't do it; whatever they say.

LUDWIG
Anything else going on?

TIFFANY
(talking in a very low voice)
Well, yes a lot actually. You know what it
is about.
(she looks directly at
Ludwig)
Do we really have to live this kind of
life - isn't it time to break out?

Ludwig for a moment hides his face in the hands. He is
troubled for a moment but tries to pretend being on top of the
situation.

LUDWIG
You should have said "no" - we could have
made it. Think of the music we made - and
we were not even trained.

TIFFANY
You know I couldn't. It was Father, it
was the tradition - the culture, the
ambitions. Nobody cared about our love.
The music - well, for him it was just
an instrument to power. You know, I was
imprisoned.

Ludwig hesitates before he continues, a bit shy to admit his
dark side. He initially looks down as he speaks.

LUDWIG
I know what happened; I know - and it
put me in prison too. This dark prison.
This deep desire I don't want, but cannot
escape - except with you.
(he pauses and looks at
Tiffany)
I just cannot say "NO" - the dark forces
drive me. They pub up, they erupt, and I
cannot resist. Even the most extreme - I
just cannot. Only if I were with you -
then it would be easy - I know that.

They sit for a while in silence.

                    LUDWIG
              (assertive)
          Let's forget this misery!

Ludwig, determined brushes all the troubles away. He becomes
happy, smiling and relaxed in the tranquility of the place, and
with peace of mind as he is with his deep and only real love.

                    LUDWIG
          Let's check music.

Ludwig walks over to the pianos and takes seat by one of them.

                    LUDWIG
              (very gentle, but assertive)
          Come on - I tuned them while you slept.
          Let me hear. Come over here - let's work
          on it a bit!

Ludwig points at the other piano chair. Tiffany sniffs back
her tears and takes the scores. She takes seat by the other
piano. She is shaky and uncertain.

                    LUDWIG
          Do the second movement first. Do it
          without the introduction. Go right to it!

Tiffany plays the first bars of the first solo piano part of
the second movement. The tempo is high. She looks at the keys
as she plays. Ludwig interrupts her.

                    LUDWIG
              (very directive)
          Now, again, but look somewhere else - out
          of the window or something - just not the
          keys. Whatever - and then softer. Put the
          tempo down a bit.

Tiffany plays again. The tempo is a bit slower. The cords
more separated. Ludwig stops her again. He gets energized and
forgets everything else as he is in his favorite element of
diving deep into music.

        TRANSITIONS TO ONLY THE PICTURE AND THE SOUND OF THE MUSIC
                            WITH THE TALKING NOT HEARD

Ludwig raises his hands and explains. Tiffany repeats again. Her mind appears away from her troubles. Ludwig plays the orchestra part of the 2rd movement. They reach the next piano solo bars. Tiffany plays through. As she reaches the following orchestra part, the full orchestra music fills the room. The walls of the cottage vanish and the music merges with the landscape around them.

                                        MUSIC CARRIES OVER

EXT. AUSTRIA - CHURCH - SQUARE - SUNDOWN

Josephine opens the huge and heavy wooden doors to the church using the whole weight of her body. The doors open slowly. Josephine slips in as soon as the space between the doors is sufficient. She enters the church. The doors close with an echoing sound in the church room.

INT. AUSTRIA - CHURCH - SUNDOWN

High gloomy columns reach to the high ceiling in the huge church room. Josephine's slow steps on the granite floor echo in the room. The church is almost dark with only a slight flickering light from groups of candles around small altars in chapels along the sides of the main, large church room. Josephine looks around and finds the confessional by the remote side. She holds her handbag close to her body and walks to the confessional. She kneels down by the confessional. She hears a voice from inside.

                    THE VOICE
                (in Italian)
        You have something to tell me?

                    JOSEPHINE
                (in Italian)
        Yes!

                    THE VOICE
        Please -.

                    JOSEPHINE
        I like to marry - I mean, I am going to
        marry.

Pause.

                    THE VOICE
               (unusually loud)
This is not what we expect from you at
this time. It will distract!

                    JOSEPHINE
I know. But I can still fulfill my
obligations.

                    THE VOICE

And with whom?

                    JOSEPHINE

Him. Himself!

Josephine looks down at her hands on her lap. Then she looks up
and out in the huge dark space of the church's gloomy darkness.

                    THE VOICE
               (whispering)
This is impossible. You know that - it's
insane - try to think it through. It will
totally destroy the project.

Silence. Josephine looks at her hands.

                    THE VOICE
               (in a frightening tone,
               increasing volume)
If you continue down this path I cannot
promise you anything anymore - except
one thing - you will be doomed: a traitor
towards humanity, our faith and our
sacred institution.

                    JOSEPHINE
               (pretending being a bit
               stupid)
But, I can still deliver what I promised
you. And I cannot deny the love I .....

                    THE VOICE
               (interrupting)
Stop please. You make it worse and worse.
Love! Are you out of your mind? I cannot
believe this. Love to Ludwig Mann. You

must be out of your mind. Listen, this
love simply cannot exist! Stop it - or it
will be stopped!

The chapel echoes from the shouting of the last words. The
curtain in the confessional is pulled abruptly.
Josephine rises. She smiles satisfied. The doors to the church
are slowly opened. Giulia (56) appears in the door. She walks
slowly forward to one of the small chapels and kneels by
the altar. Her back is totally bent forward. She is poorly
dressed. Josephine, having expected to see Giulia, walks
determined, but discretely over to the same altar. She kneels
next to the Giulia and moves close to her. The light from the
candles flicker in their faces. Giulia looks at the beautiful
face of Josephine. She whispers in a horse, low voice as she
looks towards the altar.

                    GIULIA
              (whispering in Italian)
          What is such a beauty praying for in this
          place?

                    JOSEPHINE
              (in Italian)
          I pray for being married.

                    GIULIA
          Why should you not be married - unless,
          of course, you do not meet love?

Giulia turns her face to Josephine. Her aged face shines
friendly in the flickering light. She sees Josephine has tears
in her eyes. Josephine fakes sorrow.

                    JOSEPHINE
              (faking her situation)
          I do meet love - at least I believe so.
          Well, I do. And I do love. But I am asked
          not to follow my love.

The both sit in prayer. Giulia turns her face.

                    GIULIA
              (whispering)
          Let's leave this place. I come here every
          single day.

(she tries to rise)
Can you help me a bit, please?

                    JOSEPHINE
     Of course!

Josephine looks cautiously around. She supports Giulia and
helps her to get up. They walk to the huge wooden doors of
the church. Josephine pulls a door open. They exit with Giulia
holding Josephine's arm for comfort and support.

EXT. AUSTRIA - CHURCH - SUNDOWN

It is dark. A dense fog has gathered around the hill.
Josephine and Giulia walk onto the square in front of the
church. The wooden doors close heavily behind them with an
echoing sound. They walk into the fog. The church disappears
from their sight. They stand in the middle of the square
embedded in the dense fog with none of the buildings around
them being visible. Giulia turns to Josephine. Drops of water
from condensed fog gather on their faces. They see each other,
but nothing else in the dense fog.

                    GIULIA
     Thank you dear.

                    JOSEPHINE
     Shall I help you all the way home?

                    GIULIA
     That would be very kind!
          (she points into the
          dense fog)
     I live in a house right over there
     somewhere. It should be that way.

They start walking on the slippery cobblestones over the
square through the fog in the direction Giulia pointed. They
become invisible as they disappear in the fog.

EXT. AUSTRIA - GIULIA APARTMENT - SUNDOWN

Josephine and Giulia stop by the door to the downstairs in
one of the very old houses around the square in front of the
church.

GIULIA

Thanks again dear. Here we are.

Josephine again discretely turns around as to ensure they are
alone and not being watched. She turns to Giulia.

JOSEPHINE

Let me follow you all the way down - I
like to see you safe home.

GIULIA

Oh, thank you dear. I wish I could offer
you something for your help.

JOSEPHINE

I have a small kirsch - maybe we could
share.

Giulia looks at Josephine with a subtle smile.

INT. AUSTRIA - GIULIA APARTMENT - SUNDOWN

Josephine and Giulia are in Giulia's apartment. Giulia turns
an old electric switch by the door of the simple, very small
room. A weak light from a single bulb hanging from the low
roof barely illuminates the room. The walls in the room are
slightly moist. Giulia points to a chair by a wobbly table as
she walks over to a small cabinet on the wall. While Josephine
sits down by the table, Giulia takes a bottle of kirsch and
two small schnapps glasses from the cabinet. She holds the
bottle against the light and checks, with difficulty squeezing
her eyes, if any contents is left. She hobbles over to the
table while she looks at the glasses, again with difficulty.
She grasps a towel hanging over one of the two chairs by the
table, cleans the glasses, again squeezes her eyes to see
if the glasses are clean and finally pours the kirsch with
shaking hands. Josephine holds her handbag close to her body
while she watches a few small old oil paintings on the wall.
Giulia takes seat opposite Josephine. She pushes a glass over
to Josephine and lifts her own to greet. Josephine lifts her
glass. They touch glasses and both enjoy the first, warming
and soothing sip. Giulia notices Josephine is looking around
in the room.

GIULIA

Yes my lady, this is all we get.

Josephine pretends innocence and ignorance of the activities in the church.

                    JOSEPHINE
          Who is "we"? You mean the church over
          there?

                    GIULIA
          Well, it is not really a church, you know.
          Yes, - the building is a church ...
                    (she pauses)
          ... it is used for something else now.

                    JOSEPHINE
          So what is it then?

Giulia looks down for a moment, then takes her glass. They drink the last kirsch left in the glasses. Giulia refills both glasses. The small drops of kirsch floating down the side of the bottle reach the rough wooden surface of the table and make rings on the table.

                    GIULIA
                    (with slightly hoarse)
          Nobody really knows. The little I know
          is that they helped me long ago. But not
          for free, not for free. No, I had to help
          them. I had to do something for them
          which I should never talk about, they
          said.
                    (she pauses, looks up to
                    Josephine while gathering
                    her thoughts and strength)
          I was ready to do whatever. It was life
          or death for me; that's how they get us -
          they have many like me which will do
          exactly as they say - we have no choice.
                    (she pauses)
          When it became my turn, I did everything
          they asked me - but things went wrong.
          They were furious. They wanted to get
          rid of me - but somehow the police got
          involved. That saved me.

Giulia pauses. She wants to speak more but holds. She looks over at Josephine.

                    GIULIA
          So why were you there?

                  JOSEPHINE
          I was there to confess and pray.

Giulia smiles to Josephine. She smiles back. They both take
another sip of the kirsch. Josephine discretely put her hand
in her handbag, takes a small bottle and pours a fresh glass
to Giulia and herself. She adds the contents of her hand
discretely to Giulia's glass. They again empty the glasses.
Giulia pours the last kirsch from the bottle in the glasses.
Giulia looks Josephine directly in the eyes. She shivers
briefly.

                    GIULIA
                (whispering)
          Nobody comes in that church if they are
          free.
                (she shivers)
          I need some rest dear.

Giulia rises and walks with uncertain steps over to the bed.
Josephine rises and helps Giulia.

                    GIULIA
          Thanks my Lady. Just leave me alone now.

                  JOSEPHINE
          Thanks for letting me come. Let me just
          clean up.

Josephine cleans the glasses and the bottle carefully with
paper towels from her bag. She cleans the table. She looks
over at Giulia in the bed. Giulia's eyes are closed. She lies
on her back. Her face is peaceful and relaxed. Josephine
silently exits the room.

INT. VIENNA - HOTEL - SUITE - EVENING

Josephine enters the luxurious room. In the small lobby of the
suite she briefly looks through letters and messages waiting.
She enters the main, very spacious room. She calls a waiter
and lies down on the sofa. She looks around in the room. She
gets up and goes to the windows and pulls the curtains tight.
A young waiter enters.

JOSEPHINE
(in German)
Please bring me a bottle of white wine -
totally dry.

Josephine undresses and puts all her clothes in the hotel bag
for cleaning. She goes to the bathroom and showers briefly.
Dressed in a comfortable bathrobe she takes seat in front
of the mirror for make-up. She makes her hair and applies
make-up to her face, slightly overdone and vulgar. She goes
to the sofa again and makes herself comfortable. She smiles.
The waiter enters with the wine and a splendid crystal glass
on a silver tray. He discretely looks at Josephine, pours a
big glass of the chilled wine and hands it to her. She takes
the glass and smiles provocatively to the waiter as he leaves
the room with the bag for dry cleaning. Josephine takes a
big sip of the wine, leans back and relaxes. She looks at
the impression of her dark red lipstick on the glass, smiles
slightly and almost laughs.

JOSEPHINE
So far so good! One less who knows
anything.

She empties the glass, takes the bottle and slightly carelessly
refills her glass. She leans back and continues drinking.

INT. COTTAGE - MAIN COTTAGE - EVENING

It is dark outside. The only light in the cottage is from a
few candle lights and the fireplace. Tiffany sits by the table
and studies the score. Ludwig is roasting a steak and potatoes
at the fireplace. He has poured a big glass of red wine for
Tiffany; she enjoys while reading through the scores. The wind
becomes violent and loud. The covers over the windows shake
in the strong wind and occasionally hammer against the walls.
The candles in the room flicker. Tiffany enjoys the wine and
the scores undisturbed. Ludwig talks with his eyes focused on
the cooking.

LUDWIG
I have two concerts coming up where I
like you to be in with either the 4th,
the 5th, or both. Before and after there
will be a Mozart symphony - also to be
recorded.

                    (he pauses)
          Could you do that for me?

Tiffany looks up from the scores.

                         TIFFANY
          Why do you even ask? You know I would
          love to.
                    (She pauses)
          There may be some contractual issues with
          my manager and all that stuff.

                         LUDWIG
          I would not worry about that. My manager
          can deal with that - we can probably pay
          our way. She is good at that - very good.

Tiffany takes her glass and holds it with both hands smiling
unsentimental to Ludwig over the glass. The reflexes from the
candles and the fireplace are flickering in her glass. The
sound of the wind outside has become very strong. Distant
thunder is heard. Glimpses of lightening reach into the room.
The windows are shaking - all unnoticed by them.

                         TIFFANY
          Yes, I am in!

                         LUDWIG
          Great.
                    (he pauses)
          We should have done it long ago.

                         TIFFANY
          We were like the clouds. How can they
          resist the wind. How can they avoid
          moving? How can they avoid moving towards
          the horizon and dissolve.
                    (she pauses)
          Well, some say "a cloud never dies".

Ludwig brings the dishes and the well prepared food to the
table. They eat without talking and follow their minds.

      THE PICTURE FOCUSES ON TIFFANY AND FOLLOWS HER MIND BACK IN
                                                             TIME

EXT. KOREA - MANSION - EARLY EVENING - BACK IN TIME

The sun is setting in a mountainous Korean landscape in a spectacular scenery. The mansion, built over dark wood with traditional Asian styled roofs, is located right to a steep, deep, vertical slope. A few screams from birds settling for the night sound. The huge mansion surrounds a small courtyard covered by gravel with small groups of meticulously maintained and pruned trees. Around the mansion, by the edge to the surrounding forest, are several small guesthouses. A large wooden frame holding a huge bell is located close to the entrance to the courtyard. A wide wooden terrace around the main building is directly facing the steep, deep slope and provides a place for watching the scenery. Rooms facing away from the mansion are located directly to the connecting terrace.

The young, teenage Tiffany walks onto the terrace from her room in the main building. The gentle, chilly evening wind pulls and spreads her white, long dress and her long, dark hair. She goes to the edge of the terrace and watches the scenery. Her eyes are wet and distant. With one hand she touches the wooden rails and lets her fingers slide gently over the dark, moist wood. A distant, light sound of cars approaching the mansion breaks the silence. Tiffany watches two black cars stop in front of the house. Three servants, ready for the expected arrival, immediately go to the cars and open the doors. Tiffany watches five Asian, formally business dressed men stepping out of the cars. The drivers, dressed in black suits and wearing black, slightly oversized caps, stay in the cars. The guests are guided to the main building. Four of the men carry light business folders. They rapidly enter the house. The silence prevails. It becomes dark. There is light in a few of the many windows in the mansion. The light is switched on in the room behind Tiffany. The door between the terrace and her room is open. Only a curtain covers the door opening. Tiffany turns around and walks over the broad terrace to the door while taking care not to fall on the slightly moist and slippery wooden floor. As she reaches the doorway, she holds the curtain to the side with her left hand and enters the room holding her dress close to her body.

INT. KOREA - MANSION - TIFFANY ROOM - EVENING

The personal servant of Tiffany for years, YOUNG-HOO (42), in traditional Korean dress is making Tiffany's Korean type bed in the not too spacious, but beautifully and lightly decorated traditional room. As Tiffany enters, Young-hoo steps back from the bed and bows deeply. His hands slide over his knees as he bows deeply. As he rises, he notices with worry Tiffany's sad appearance.

                    YOUNG-HOO
              (in Korean)
        Your bed is ready. Anything else?

Tiffany shakes her head slightly, almost invisibly while her lips suggest she whispers. Young-hoo again bows deeply and with his head bent down walks backwards to the door opening to the inside of the mansion. As he reaches the curtain, he again bows deeply and leaves the room. Tiffany switches the feeble light by the bed off. She lies on the traditional bed flat on her back and watches the room in the dim silver light from the moon rising over the mountains. The curtain to the terrace continues to flicker slightly in the light breeze. Tiffany places her arms on the bed along her body. Her long black hair spreads on the bed along her neck and shoulders. She breathes through her gently open mouth. She closes her eyes.

Loud voices break through the silence for a moment. Tiffany opens her eyes. She rises and walks silently to the door opening facing the inside of the mansion. She holds the curtain slightly to the side. On the other side of the building she recognizes her father talking exited in his meeting room. The door to the room is partially open. Worried, Tiffany quietly exits to the dark connecting terrace.

EXT. KOREA - MANSION - GALLERY - EVENING

Tiffany walks softly on her bare feet on the broad wooden floor of the terrace. The floor creaks slightly as she walks. By the sound she holds her steps and breath. She slowly gets closer to the partially open door to the meeting room. Inside she sees the business men gathering their papers while talking friendly and exited. She sees her father HOON-KWAN (45) approach the senior guest, clearly the leader of the visiting delegation. He reaches the slightly overweight but agile and aristocratic man, KI-SION CHUNG (48). They embrace each other wholeheartedly and firmly for a short moment. A servant enters the room carrying a tray with small glasses and a bottle of liquor. She fills the glasses and gives the tray to Hoon-kwan. He goes from person to person and hands each a glass. He gives sign to the servant to leave the room. All men gather in the

middle of the room. Tiffany silently moves closer to the door.
She sees the individuals clearly through the slightly open
door. Hoon-kwan raises his glass.

                    HOON-KWAN
               (in Korean)
          Finally we are united. We will control
          this whole industry throughout the
          World! -

He raises his glass towards Ki-sion Chung.

                    HOON-KWAN
          - and become a true family!

The men empty their glasses and cheer. Hoon-kwan takes the
bottle and refills all the glasses. Again, the men touch
glasses. They put the empty glasses on the table. The servant
enters the room to guide the guests back to the cars. The men
gather their folders and they all exit the meeting room.

Tiffany walks quietly back to her room.

INT. KOREA - MANSION - TIFFANY ROOM - EVENING

Tiffany enters her room. She carefully watches the space
behind her. She rapidly goes to her bed and lies down, almost
as before. She lies with open eyes as she follows the sound of
the men entering the cars in front of the mansion. She hears
the cheerful bidding goodbye by Hoon-kwan. The doors of the
cars close and the engines start. She hears the cars driving
over the crunching stones down the narrow, steep and twisted
road. The sound of the cars fades. She hears the steps of
Hoon-kwan as he walks back to his studio in the main building.
She lies with open, anxious eyes. The breeze stops. The
curtain over the door to the terrace hangs still. It becomes
totally quiet. Only a few screams of wild animals break the
silence in the dark night. Tiffany closes her eyes.

EXT. KOREA - MANSION - NIGHT

The moon shines over the mansion, the steep slope, and the
dark soft mountain hills.

INT. KOREA - MANSION - TIFFANY ROOM - NIGHT

Tiffany is sleeping. It is pouring rain outside. The water
from the rain flushes down on the terrace from the roofs.
A loud scream from a woman breaks through the noise of the
pouring water. Tiffany wakes up instantly. She immediately
rises and sits half upright on the bed supported by her
elbows. She is slightly confused and orients herself. Again
she hears the loud woman voice. She recognizes the voice as
her mother's. She runs to the door.

EXT. KOREA - MANSION - GALLERY - NIGHT

Across the open space in the mansion Tiffany sees light from
Hoon-kwan's studio. She hears violent arguing of the father
and her mother MYUNG-HEE (40, Asian, slim). Frightened, Tiffany
walks onto the connecting terrace and swiftly towards the
studio. Outside the studio she stops. She watches the violent
argument through the doorway.

                    MYUNG-HEE
               (in Korean)
          This was done to me. And I did my duty.
          You got your life just as you wanted it.
          I tell you. I will not let you do this to
          my daughter.

Myung-hee falls on her knees in the middle of the room,
distant from Hoon-kwan. She hides her face in her hands
as she cries from her heart. Hoon-kwan violently hammers
his hand on a small table in the room and sweeps precious
porcelain items from the table. The porcelain figures and
vases splinter on the floor. Myung-hee screams as the pieces
of porcelain hit her and the floor around her. Hoon-kwan does
not approach Myung-hee but talks angrily from the distance
across the room.

                    HOON-KWAN
          You do as I say. You do your duties which
          extend to your daughter, our family and
          our enterprise. I don't want to hear your
          ridiculous moaning and praying. You know
          what you have to do.

Myung-hee rises and walks as fast as possible without running
to the back of the room while she unsuccessfully tries to

control her crying. Tiffany holds her hands over her mouth
while she frightened watches her mother leave the room. She
swiftly turns around and runs back to her room.

INT. KOREA - MANSION - TIFFANY ROOM - NIGHT

Tiffany enters her room still holding her hands over her mouth.
She runs to the terrace door and watches the water pouring from
the roof and splashing on the terrace floor. She cries.

                                        FORWARD IN TIME

INT. KOREA - MANSION - DINNER ROOM - DAY

Tiffany is sitting on the floor by the middle of one side of
a long, precious and nicely decorated, traditional low, long
Korean dining table. She wears a long, soft and light, totally
white dress covering her entirely and spreading over the floor
around her. Tiffany's long hair is meticulously and tightly
set up. Hoon-kwan, in casual, yet elegant and modern dress,
is sitting by the end of the table to Tiffany's right. Myung-
hee is sitting by the end of the table to Tiffany's left,
also in a modern dress. The table is tastefully loaded with
delicious dishes in traditional, precious Korean handcrafted
tableware. In the corner of the spacious room GYUNG-HEE
(40, Asian, strong resemblance to Tiffany) is calmly playing
soothing, discrete music on a kayagum. The walls are wooden
with precious pieces of traditional arts. The light is soft
from windows covered by small rectangular transparent paper.
Young-hoo, in traditional dress, is sitting on his knees next
to Tiffany. One woman servant is sitting next to Myung-hee and
another is sitting next to Hoon-kwan. Myung-hee is nervously
eating very slowly. Hoon-kwan is eating with healthy appetite,
but visibly concerned.

                        HOON-KWAN
            My daughter; in the last days your mother
            and I have discussed your future.
                  (he pauses)
            We have decided it is time for you to
            marry and we are very happy today to tell
            you -

He is interrupted by Tiffany. She lifts her head from the
tea cup and looks straight forward as she knowingly, totally

inappropriately, interrupts her father and speaks while she
continues to look straight through the room.

                         TIFFANY
             ---- Dear father, please let me continue
             to focus on my music. I am doing
             everything as you and mother asked me to
             do - and I am becoming one of the most
             outstanding musicians in the world - as
             you asked me. Marriage for me is..

Tiffany is interrupted by Hoon-kwan. He speaks extremely
angrily and loud. With a violent move with his hand he orders
Gyung-hee to stop playing. The servants fearfully retract a
few steps from the table with their heads bowed.

                         HOON-KWAN
             I did not ask for your comments.
             Yes, you have become a world famous
             musician. But your duties go beyond that.
             Your mother and I have made our best
             efforts to find a way to ensure your
             happiness while at the same time ensuring
             the family, our enterprise, your position
             in the arts, and the future of -

                         TRANSITION TO TIFFANY'S MIND

The voice of Hoon-kwan fades and in the space of Tiffany's mind
sounds with an echo of the words "marriage" - "enterprise" -
"happiness". Tiffany sees the small bowl with soy sauce turn
into a bowl of blood. The bowl transforms to the bloody hands
of Tiffany and Ludwig mixing blood in a flowering European
garden under a rain of tulip leaves. The leaves of a flower
decoration on the table transform to tulip leaves. Tiffany's
inner sight turns totally blood red as she faints.

                         TRANSITION BACK TO DINING ROOM

Tiffany falls forward and hits the table in the middle of the
numerous dishes.

                         PICTURE SLOWS IN THE FALL

The black soy sauce from one bowl hit in the fall splashes
over Tiffany's white gown. Young-hoo and a servant move to

her rescue. Sitting on each side of Tiffany they lift her to a sitting, upright position. They hold the upper arms of the still unconscious Tiffany firmly to support her and avoid she falls forward while they nervously look at Hoon-kwan.

PICTURE BACK TO REGULAR MOTION

Myung-hee rises to get to Tiffany, but Hoon-kwan angrily orders her to sit.

> HOON-KWAN
> (shouting)
> You stay where you are!

As Tiffany slowly becomes conscious, she looks straight and unfocused forward as in a trance. Half of her white gown is soaked in the black liquid from the table and merges with her black hair which has loosened in the fall and now falls over her shoulders and body and almost entirely covers her face. She sits as a sculpture soaked in black blood. Hoon-kwan rises and angrily walks to the side of the table opposite Tiffany. As he stands in front of the barely conscious Tiffany he speaks and shouts angrily.

> HOON-KWAN
> This is the last time we talk about this.
> There is no further discussion of your
> duties.

Hoon-kwan turns towards Myung-hee as his anger peaks. He shouts while barely able to control himself.

> HOON-KWAN
> And you - you know what your duties are!

Hoon-kwan leaves the room. The servants bow deeply towards him as he exits. Young-hoo and the servant next to Tiffany continue to support her. Myung-hee sits quietly with her head bowed while tears drop on her hands and on her lap.

EXT. KOREAN - MANSION - COURTYARD - DAY

Tiffany, beautifully dressed as a traditional Korean bride, is standing in the courtyard of the mansion close to the main entrance of the house flanked by Hoon-kwan, Myung-hee, Ki-sion, and the groom's mother MI-SOOK CHUNG (45, traditional Korean woman). Tiffany is devastated, as close to tears as can be. Young-hoo is standing behind Tiffany. The courtyard is packed with colorfully dressed guests - half transitionally, half modernly dressed. The huge group forms an open space in front of Tiffany and to the entrance to the courtyard and the narrow road leading up to the mansion. Behind the many guests and all around the courtyard are tables made ready with delicious foods and drinks. A Buddhist priest is standing in the open circle to Tiffany's left. The many guests are situated to leave an empty space as a narrow path between them to the large bell in the courtyard. In the distance, down on the small road the groom, CHU-HIN (about 10 years older than Tiffany, slightly overweight, not particularly attractive), traditionally dressed, appears while slowly approaching the mansion on horseback. It becomes quiet in the courtyard. The guests move slightly backwards to enlarge the open circle as Chu-hin enters the courtyard. He descends from the horse and walks slowly up to Tiffany. As he reaches Tiffany they reach out to each other with both hands and hold each other hands while turning their sides to the open space and the guests. The Buddhist priest walks up to the couple and, with his back to the open circle, raise his arms to Tiffany and Chu-hin. He speaks distantly and softly. His soft voice to the couple is barely heard in the otherwise totally quiet courtyard. As his talk ends, the guest erupt in cheer while Chu-hin moves close to Tiffany for a kiss. As Chu-hin slightly forcefully kisses her, she moves backwards as much as possible to minimize contact during the kiss. Behind Tiffany, Young-hoo bows his head in order not to witness the kiss. Friends of Tiffany among the guests watch the kissing with worry. The wedding party moves forward with the cheerful guests enjoying the wonderful servings while mingling together. Tiffany and Chu-hin remain standing while couples among the guests pass by to convey their congratulations. Tiffany drinks whatever is offered and gradually becomes visibly drunk.

EXT. KOREA - MANSION - COURTYARD - NIGHT

The guest gather in the courtyard in the flickering light from torches placed all alone the sides of the courtyard. Tiffany and Chu-hin enter a large, old, black, prestigious car. Tiffany, sitting to the right on the backseat, moves into the corner of the car, avoiding Chu-hin. She is doing her best to sit right up. She looks straight forward and does not pay attention to her surroundings. Chu-hin, in great mood, waves to the excited guests as the car slowly drives out of the courtyard. Young-hoo watches the departure with worry. Chu-hin carefully puts his hand softly on Tiffany's and smiles to her. Tiffany, uncomfortable with the touch, pulls her hand back. Chu-hin, disappointed, puts his hands on his lap and is quiet as the car drives out of the mansion.

EXT. KOREA - MANSION CHU-HIN - COURTYARD - NIGHT

The car with Tiffany and Chu-hin arrives in front of the large mansion. Two servants immediately come to the car, open the doors and assist Tiffany, barely able to walk straight. They all walk to the entry of the mansion and enter the building

INT. KOREA - MANSION CHU-HIN - WEDDING SUITE - NIGHT

Tiffany, dressed in a light, white nightgown, is sitting sad and distant at the edge of the wedding bed in the beautiful, traditional, dimly illuminated room. In her drunken state she is supporting herself with her arms to the back. Chu-hin is standing drunk from the party in the middle of the room in his night gown watching Tiffany with great desire and sympathy. He goes to the bed and sits next to Tiffany. With a finger under Tiffany's chin he turns her face towards his. He sees her wet, drunken and indifferent eyes. He smiles gently to her and approaches her for a kiss. Tiffany turns her face away, uncomfortable by his touch and falls drunken back on the bed. Chu-hin again tries to kiss Tiffany. Again she turns away. In spite of Tiffany's total lack of response Chu-hin makes love with her. His mood changes to disappointed violence. Tiffany gets in total disorder under the encounter where she is torn around in the bed by Chu-hin in the hope she would mobilize a response. While finally Chu-hin is heavily breathing and groaning, the passive and drunk Tiffany is looking at the ceiling while she endures the final moment. Finished under a deep exhale Chu-hin slides to the side. He watches Tiffany. His eyes becomes wet as he falls asleep. Tiffany, lies indifferent and drunk on her back with her legs flat and spread on the bed.

FORWARD IN TIME

INT. KOREA - MANSION CHU-HIN - LIVING ROOM - EARLY EVENING

Chu-hin is pouring a glass of whiskey while standing in his
comfortable, preciously, and modernly furnished living room.
He is visibly drunk and obviously upset as he walks around in
the room and violently pushes furniture and decorations. He
takes a newspaper from a small table, reads briefly through
the headlines, and throws the newspaper in disorder on a sofa.
Tiffany enters the room, neatly dressed and ready to go out.

                    TIFFANY
          I am going out now.

                    CHU-HIN
          Please do not go tonight - please stay
          with me.

                    TIFFANY
          But we agreed already.

                    CHU-HIN
          I know, but please stay with me.

                    TIFFANY
          I cannot!

                    CHU-HIN
              (devastated, changes mood)
          I don't want you to leave tonight.
          Stay home.

                    TIFFANY
              (upset)
          But we agreed I could leave tonight. My
          friends are waiting. The car is already
          here.

                    CHU-HIN
          I just told you - I don't want you to go
          out tonight.

                    TIFFANY
              (angrily)
          But I must. We agreed already. I cannot
          be here every evening - like in a prison.

Chu-hin violently smashes his glass towards the table. The whiskey spills all over. He angrily moves forward towards Tiffany shouting.

                    CHU-HIN
          Did you say prison?

Tiffany, frightened moves backwards. She turns to rapidly exit the room. Chu-hin grasps her arm and violently pulls her back. As he holds her, closely face to face, he sees her eyes flashing with rage and hatred. He shouts, pulls and damages her clothes totally, grasps her hair violently and pulls her head backwards. Tiffany screams and resists with all her power trying to get loose. She slaps him in the head. Chocked by the hit, Chu-hin loosens the grip of Tiffany. She turns and runs out of the room. Devastated Chu-hin stands back, he raises a fallen chair, takes seat on the chair and hides his head in his hands, crying desperately.

                              BACK TO PRESENT

INT. COTTAGE - MAIN COTTAGE - EVENING - PRESENT TIME

Tiffany and Ludwig have finished the meal. Ludwig refills Tiffany's glass with the rich red wine. They are both carried away by the wine. The violent weather has reached disastrous proportions. The cottage vibrates in the storm, the rain and the lightening. Ludwig and Tiffany look out of window, then go to the bed, and fall heavily on the bed next to each other in their pretty drunk state. They instantly fall asleep.

Ludwig wakes up abruptly and sits up screaming.

                    LUDWIG
          No ...!

Tiffany rises, sits next to Ludwig and holds her arms around him.

                    TIFFANY
          You are here with me - don't scream!

Ludwig wakes up and calms down.

                    TIFFANY
          What happened?

                         LUDWIG
           I just remembered when you had to
           leave me.

He watches his scar and takes Tiffany's arm to see her scar.
He touches it softly.

                         TIFFANY
           See. I never really left you.

Ludwig gets calm. Tiffany kisses him softly, smiling and
unsentimental. Her long, black hair covers them as she takes
her arms around Ludwig and lies on him. They embrace in
love and total satisfaction and unity. They fall asleep while
the weather outside deteriorates and continues to shake the
cottage.

                                        TRANSITION TO MORNING

INT. COTTAGE - MAIN COTTAGE - MORNING

A very dim light shines into the cottage. The storm and the
rain have stopped. The morning is quiet. Ludwig gets up,
carefully puts the blanket around Tiffany, takes two hoodies
out of a cupboard, and puts one of them on.

                         LUDWIG
           Come, we can just make it.

Ludwig exits the cottage swiftly and full of energy.

EXT. COTTAGE - COURTYARD - DAY

Ludwig quickly goes to the edge of the cottage area by the
steep precipice. A small bench is placed right at the edge.
He sits down and watches the snow-covered mountain peaks. The
sun breaks through over the peaks in a spectacular scenery
of light. Music blends into the scenery (5th, 2rd movement).
Tiffany comes, running, also wearing a hoodie. Ludwig points
exited at the terrific scenery. The music continues as they
speak (mid 5th). He points to the scenery around them.

                         LUDWIG
              Great - right?

Ludwig notices Tiffany is still worried.

                    LUDWIG
          We got it right yesterday - you will do
          great! Just play as you did.

Ludwig laughs to cheer Tiffany up. Tiffany, while enjoying the
moment, still appears worried by her memories of the past. She
overcomes the worry and smiles, but is still a bit subdue as
she speaks.

                    TIFFANY
          Will do. But then? It is not just the
          music, you know.
                    (she pauses)
          For you too - ?

INT. NEW YORK - AIRPORT - ARRIVAL AREA - NIGHT

Josephine walks through the arrival area of a NY airport.
She swiftly goes to the area for rented cars. The staff
immediately follows her to a car right outside the arrival
area and gives her the car key. Josephine signs on an
electronic portable terminal, throws her carry-on on the back
seat, enters the car and swiftly drives out of the airport.

EXT. NEW YORK - PRIVATE CLINIC - EVENING

Josephine stops the car behind a small, one floor high clinic
building. She leaves the car right by the entry and walks to
a back door. The door is opened from the inside as Josephine
gets close. Josephine enters.

INT. NEW YORK - PRIVATE CLINIC - EVENING

Duilio closes the back door immediately as Josephine has
entered.

                    DUILIO
          This way.

Josephine follows Duilio down a short corridor. From a door at
the end they enter a small operation room.

NEW YORK - PRIVATE CLINIC - OPERATION ROOM - EVENING

One female doctor and one assistant, both dressed up for sterile work, stand ready in the small operation room. Nobody talks. A young female assistant in the back of the room is filling a syringe with a sample from a small test tube. Behind her working space are a number of liquid air containers.

INT. NEW YORK - AIRPORT - DEPARTURE AREA - EVENING

Josephine drives up in front of the departure area. She steps out of the car and leaves it on the spot. She takes the boarding card from her handbag and immediately proceeds through Security to the gates.

INT. COTTAGE - MAIN COTTAGE - DAY

Ludwig quickly cleans up in the main cottage.

INT. COTTAGE - SMALL COTTAGE - DAY

Tiffany tidies the small cottage up.

EXT. COTTAGE - COURTYARD - DAY

Tiffany and Ludwig stand together in the small courtyard. Ludwig locks the doors. He carries their luggage as they walk down the hill to the car. He puts the luggage in the trunk. They stand together by the car for a moment and watch the landscape as goodbye. They enter the car. Ludwig starts driving.

EXT. VIENNA - HOTEL - SUITE - TERRACE - DAY

Josephine, dressed practical, yet smart for work, is on an outdoor terrace overlooking a magnificent mountainous scenery. Her small table is crowded with her papers, computers, and cellphones amidst several served pots of coffee and soft drinks. Her phone rings.

                         LUDWIG
              (voice on Josephine's phone)
          It's me. I am on my way.

                    JOSEPHINE
       Finally!
              (pause)
       You better be on your way! You have the
       first rehearsal in a few days.
       Have you forgotten? - I have promoted this
       concert a lot. Expectations are through
       the roof!
              (pause)
       And then you just disappear and I am
       sitting here alone managing all this
       stuff and not sure what is next.

Ludwig ignores Josephine's complaints and temper.

                    LUDWIG
              (voice)
       I thought about the pianist...

                    JOSEPHINE
              (interrupting)
       So did I; and I have some very strong
       proposals....

                    LUDWIG
              (interrupting)
       The name of my choice is Tiffany Yun.

Josephine abruptly rises irritated and goes to the edge of the
terrace not to disturb other guests at the terrace restaurant
as she shouts on the phone.

                    JOSEPHINE
       What?

                    LUDWIG
              (voice)
       I am sure she can do something quite
       unique.

Josephine is very upset.

                    JOSEPHINE
       What on earth are you thinking?

This makes absolutely no sense. She is not
a great name! She will draw the profile of
the concerts in a totally wrong direction,
meaning down, down. Do you hear me? DOWN!

Josephine tries to control herself.

                    JOSEPHINE
- it - makes - no - sense. No sense
whatsoever.

                    LUDWIG
Trust me. I have been thinking about it
a lot. I know what she can do. It will
be a landmark concert. The music will be
deeper than with the usual "big" names -
you know, they barely have the time. We
disk with them Sunday morning and off
they go and we sit there with a pretty
boring recording. I just don't want that
kind of stuff anymore.

                    JOSEPHINE
               (suspicious)
Is she the one that mailed to you recently
and asked you for help with concerts?

                    LUDWIG
... and that reminded me of how she
played. You know how I remember
everything I hear.

                    JOSEPHINE
I do not want your name to be compromised
by your generosity. This is about building
you. Not about doing a favor to a sad
girl. It is about profiling you with the
strongest names you can get. And, we
are asking top ticket prices for these
concerts!

                    LUDWIG
               (voice on phone upset)
Just listen to me - I know what I am
doing here. This will be the best of
music you can get - and that's what's it's

about, right? She will move these concerts
to the edge of music!

Josephine realizes Ludwig's determination.

                    JOSEPHINE
          No chance to change your mind?

                    LUDWIG
          No chance. You better get hold of her
          manager.

                    JOSEPHINE
          OK, I will contact her manager - if she
          has one - and get this in place. And I
          see you this evening here at the hotel.
          I have something very important to
          tell you. Maybe even two very important
          things - you will be happy.

Ludwig hangs up.

                    JOSEPHINE
              (to the dead end)
          Love you.

EXT. VIENNA - HOTEL - EARLY EVENING

It is early evening. Ludwig steps out of the car right in
front of the hotel. He hands the car key to a waiting servant.
The servant takes Ludwig's carry-on from the trunk and follows
him into the hotel.

INT. VIENNA - HOTEL - FOYER - EARLY EVENING

The last light of the days fades inside the lobby and is taken
over by artificial warm lights inside the hotel.

                    THE SERVANT
              (in Austrian German)
          Mrs. deBois is already here. Let me follow
          you up.

INT. VIENNA - HOTEL - SUITE - EARLY EVENING

Ludwig enters the suite. He has hardly closed the door behind
him before Josephine appears very lightly and challenging
dressed. She immediately embraces Ludwig. She kisses Ludwig
violently and passionately and pulls him into the suite. The
room is very dimly illuminates by a few candles.

                    JOSEPHINE
          They are expecting us for dinner in
          a bit.

She pushes Ludwig to the large bed covered and surrounded
by silk curtains. She challenges Ludwig seductively and
totally captures him. Ludwig goes with the flow and forgets
everything else than the seductive Josephine. They have
passionate love.

INT. VIENNA - HOTEL - RESTAURANT - EVENING

Ludwig and Josephine are in the restaurant by their usual
table.

                    JOSEPHINE
          I talked to this manager of your "Tiffany
          Yun" this morning. Can you believe it - he
          wanted me to buy her out of his contract
          with her - and he didn't even know where
          she is these days! Can you believe it?

Ludwig watches Josephine while he ponders about her.

                    LUDWIG
          You must have a secret source of energy.
          You just do everything, so fast -
          sometimes your energy frightens me!

                    JOSEPHINE
               (faking)
          I missed you - that's why!

Ludwig smiles and laughs softly. Josephine stretches her hand
over the table to Ludwig and holds his hand on the table.

                    LUDWIG
          What happened then?

                         JOSEPHINE
          Well, since you so absolutely want that
          woman, I bought her for you!
                    (she raises her finger as a
                    reminder)
          And I tell you, she was not cheap!

Josephine continues holding Ludwig's hands and fake her
loneliness.

                         JOSEPHINE
          Well - that's what I did for you!

Josephine pulls her hands back, leans back and continues in
an upset tone.

                         JOSEPHINE
          And now this manager would try to figure
          out where in the world his client is and
          try to convince her to agree to these
          concerts. He better finds her right away.

They sit in silence for a while.

                         JOSEPHINE
          So, that's where I am. We do not have her
          acceptance at this moment. But she would
          be pretty dammed stupid if she does not
          accept. Every pianist will pay anything
          to perform with you. This guy will call
          as soon as he finds her.
                    (she pauses)
          I just wonder. How on earth can a manager
          not know where his is client?
                    (she pauses)
          Don't you think that a bit strange.

Josephine takes her glass, watches the contents absent minded
while swirling it. Ludwig pretends ignorance.

                         LUDWIG
          Well, maybe he is just not as effective a
          manager as you are - and as attractive!

The servant comes to the table and serves them delicate
pieces of steak, very thinly sliced.

                    THE WAITER
          Mrs. deBois - would you like a red wine ?

                    JOSEPHINE
          Just sparkling, please.

                    LUDWIG
          (a bit uninterested in wines
          and dinners)
          Well then - a glass of the Brunello please.

They both enjoy the meal. Josephine leans forward and takes
Ludwig's hand.

                    JOSEPHINE
          Lu, I am pregnant! We are going to have a
          child!

It is very quiet around them. There is no visible response
from Ludwig. Josephine, slightly irritated, continues.

                    JOSEPHINE
          Did you hear what I said?

                    LUDWIG
          (taking a big sip of the
          Brunello)
          Of course .... It's just such a surprise.

                    JOSEPHINE
          Now, come on - it cannot be a total
          surprise Mr.
                    (she pauses before
                    continuing businesslike)
          We must marry now. We cannot have all
          kind of rumors around - it will derail
          our course. We must marry - right away.

Ludwig reaches out for the Brunello and pours another glass.
The servant rapidly comes to his assistance. Ludwig holds
the glass with both hands. He puts his elbows at the table
and holds the glass right under his nose to enjoy the strong
flavor. He reaches out for Josephine

                              LUDWIG
             Of course ...

Josephine lifts her sparkling water in a glass identical to
Ludwig's. She holds it with both hands with her elbows at
the table. She enjoys the sparkling sprinkles on her lips
as she looks seductively over the glass towards Ludwig and
captures him. They both move their glasses towards each other.
The glasses meet and sound at the middle of the table. They
both bottom their glasses. They eat in total silence. They
rise and leave the restaurant holding each other totally and
passionately tight, yet appropriate for the place.

EXT. DESOLATED CLOISTER - ROAD TO - EVENING

In the early evening, in the last daylight a car passes
through the narrow, empty streets of the small deserted
village on the mountain side. Cats are sitting on the granite
walls that span between the houses. Giovanni watches the
depressing scenery from the backseat of the car. The car exits
the small village and drives towards the small, old deserted
cloister further up the mountainside until the street ends
half a kilometer from the cloister. Giovanni exits the car and
watches the village below him. The driver stands waiting right
next to the car. The Mozart Requiem breaks through.

                            GIOVANNI
                        (in Italian)
             Turn the lights off please - and wait.

Giovanni starts walking up towards the cloister. The sound of
the small stones grinding under his feet breaks through the
music.

EXT. DESOLATED CLOISTER - COURTYARD - EVENING

Giovanni reaches the dark cloister and walks into the
courtyard between the low buildings. A few birds, frightened
by Giovanni, fly away screaming. Giovanni continues towards
the door to the chapel. He opens the door and slowly enters.

INT. DESOLATED CLOISTER - CHAPEL - EVENING

The choir from the requiem fills the space together with the
echo of the closing door. Marchetto sits on the bench in front
of the remains of the old altar. Giovanni walks slowly up to
Marchetto and takes seat next to him. They sit side by side in
silence for a while.

                    MARCHETTO
               (in Italian)
          I did not expect that we would need to
          meet here ever again!

                    GIOVANNI
               (in Italian)
          I know. But - there is something I want
          you to know. And I want to tell you in
          person.

                    MARCHETTO
          Well - so tell me.

                    GIOVANNI
          Josephine has fallen in love and wishes
          to marry.

                    MARCHETTO
          Well, and - ?

                    GIOVANNI
          She wants to marry Ludwig Mann.

Marchetto pulls the bonnet from his head and turns towards
Giovanni. 25 years older than at their first meeting in the
cloister, he is even more frightening. His dress is extremely
precious and reflects his current high rank. Precious jewelry
occasionally becomes visible as he moves.

                    MARCHETTO
          What? - what are you saying Brother?
               (he pauses)
          Just stop it!

                    GIOVANNI
          She is extremely persistent, we..

Marchetto, having gathered his thoughts, interrupts Giovanni
abruptly and extremely irritated.

MARCHETTO
If she marries Ludwig it will be your
total failure. And -

Marchetto rises. He speaks louder. The requiem continues.

MARCHETTO
- and, if this marriage should bear fruit
and they start talking about emotions as
love and what have you - then, Brother, it
will be the total catastrophe. You know
that, right? So what are you going to do?

GIOVANNI
I am so sorry. Perhaps you could give me
advice. Please Brother - help me. One more
time.

Giovanni rises. The two men stand face to face. Screams from
wild animals are heard from the outside. The last light of the
day is almost gone. Marchetto tries to calm down to properly
map his options.

MARCHETTO
What about Duilio? Where does he see this
whole thing going?

GIOVANNI
As far as I can tell he wants to move on.
He believes that, so far, he has done an
excellent job: Ludwig is doing extremely
well; he acts as any human being - even
as a pretty successful human being. So he
sees it totally on track - "it cannot be
better," he says!

MARCHETTO
Is that what you consider successful? For
me, it is the exact opposite....

GIOVANNI
... no, no no. The point is that
Duilio still expects to show there are

shortcomings in the mind of Ludwig that
will prove our point - lack of devotion,
faithfulness, fidelity, and truthfulness -
his mind will be defect, something will be
missing. He will be without a soul - Duilio
will prove that. He firmly believes we are
on track. We will prove the divinity of
the pure creation of humans and humanity.
"Continue" - that's what he says.

                    MARCHETTO
Listen Brother. I am not so sure anymore.
To me, this is very simple! Ludwig is way
too close to being human. The whole thing
must stop - NOW.

Marchetto walks fuming around in the chapel.

                    MARCHETTO
And this marriage. It must never ever
bear fruit - imagine the consequences -
and this "love" - ha, love! It must be
eliminated. This whole story is not in
our favor anymore - get rid of the whole
thing. It is out of control.
          (he pauses)
Get - rid - of - it. EVERYTHING.
That is what you need to do; that's my
advice to you, as you asked for - and
Brother, if you cannot get rid of it,
well - then I will do whatever needs to
be done.
          (he pauses. The music
          intensifies through the
          conversation)
I sense a catastrophe Brother.

Marchetto steps away from Giovanni and rises in his full
figure.

                    MARCHETTO
Go Brother. Go and have it done. You have
my blessing to use any measures. I say any
measures. I will ensure you forgiveness
for all you do in the name of the Holy
Spirit. Do not disappoint me!

Giovanni bows and walks to the chapel door. He exits the chapel. Marchetto sits alone on the bench as the door closes with an echo. The music fades. It gets totally quiet.

INT. VIENNA - CAR - DRIVING THROUGH VIENNA - DAY

Ludwig sits on the backseat in the car with a cafe latte and a croissant. The driver swiftly gets to the streets of Vienna. The Mozart Symphony in A sounds in Ludwig's mind.

EXT. VIENNA - CONCERT HALL - SIDE ENTRANCE - NIGHT

The car stops in front of the side entrance to the concert hall. The driver opens the door. Ludwig exits. The music director, Dr. FRANZ HASSE (45), having waited by the side entrance, walks swiftly to the car, embraces Ludwig and greets him wholeheartedly.

> DR. FRANZ
> (in German)
> I cannot tell how happy I am to see you here Dr. Mann. How is Josephine?

> LUDWIG
> Thanks Franz. She is well - still sleeping!

They enter the concert building.

INT. VIENNA - CONCERT HALL - CORRIDOR - DAY

Ludwig and Dr. Franz walk through the narrow corridors to the door of the conductor's room. Dr. Franz opens the door. Ludwig enters the room.

INT. VIENNA - CONCERT HALL - CONDUCTOR ROOM - MORNING

Ludwig puts his coffee cup on a small table, he goes to a small sink with a mirror above, he looks at himself in the mirror, he makes faces, and finally briefly refreshes himself. He dries his face in a large towel, talks to himself into the towel, and exits the conductor's room to the corridor where Dr. Franz is waiting.

INT. VIENNA - CONCERT HALL - CORRIDOR - DAY

Dr. Franz guides Ludwig through the corridors to the entrance
of the concert hall. They stand briefly by the entrance. Dr.
Franz looks at Ludwig to ensure he is ready. Ludwig nods. They
enter the concert hall.

INT. VIENNA - CONCERT HALL - ORCHESTRA - DAY

The musicians are already prepared. Some are walking around
talking, others are exercising their parts or tuning their
instruments. The sound in the room resonates crystal clear;
the light at the orchestra is strong. Outside of the podium,
the medium sized concert hall is dark and empty. Ludwig steps
up on the conductor podium. Dr. Franz stands next to the
podium. The musicians find their places. It becomes quiet.

                    DR. FRANZ
          Dr. Mann, it is a while ago you were here
          and I speak for the whole orchestra that
          we have been looking forward to having
          you here again - a lot. Welcome to this
          rehearsal and concert. We are looking
          forward.

Dr. Franz shakes hand with Ludwig. Ludwig looks over the
orchestra. He smiles and is full of charm and energy, yet
extremely focused, tense and very nervous.

                    LUDWIG
          Well my friends, I am happy to be back -
          yes, it has been a while - but now let's
          see how we have developed.
               (he pauses briefly)
          So, Mozart, Symphony in A - number 29!

Ludwig straightens his back as he looks over the orchestra
and orients himself on the exact location of the various
musicians. He talks loud.

                    LUDWIG
          Well, let's try it out!

Ludwig raises his hands as to start conducting. The musicians
are ready and look up at Ludwig. He lowers his hands. He
is interrupting his own sentences as he speaks abruptly
and breathes between the words. He smiles and captures the
orchestra in a charming and inclusive way.

                    LUDWIG
          This small symphony is such a nice
          piece - simple and beautiful - quite
          a contrast to the other parts of the
          program. So, friends, keep it simple.

Ludwig holds his hands motionless while waiting for the total
silence. He makes the first beat. The orchestra follows - a
little stiff and a little rigid. Ludwig lets the orchestra play
up to and into the forte (bar 15). He strikes the forte full
of energy and smile. He interrupts.

                    LUDWIG
          It's good. But my friends, make it much
          softer at the beginning - much, much
          softer. Almost mystic somehow. Yes
          mystic - and lighter, just for a start.
          Let's try again - just the first bars.

Ludwig waits again for total silence. He makes the first
beat - almost invisibly. The orchestra follows beautifully and
soft. Ludwig listens thoughtfully. He does not conduct stroke
by stroke but fluently shapes the tune with his hands and is
followed flawlessly and fully understood by the orchestra. He
interrupts at the 6th bar.

                    LUDWIG
          Better - but friends - please, please more
          fluent up to the forte - like this.

Ludwig conducts while he gently hums the tune for the
orchestra.

                    LUDWIG
          Now, again please.

Ludwig again waits for the silence and makes the first beat.
The orchestra follows.

                              THE MUSIC CARRIES THROUGH

EXT. VIENNA - SUBURB - TOWN SQUARE - DAY   120

A taxi stops at a small square in the old village. The
houses around the square are old, but very well maintained.
The small church at the square is very well kept. There are
small, busy cafes around the romantic place and various kinds
of colorful flowers in flower boxes by all windows of the
houses. Josephine, neutrally and elegantly dressed, exits a
taxi. She pays the driver. While waiting for the receipt, she
watches the scenery. She holds her handbag close to her body
as she walks to a small building next to the church. She
rings the bell by a robust wooden door. While she waits she
looks back over the square. The door opens. An elderly, very
slim woman dressed totally in black opens the door slightly
and looks questioning at Josephine.

                      JOSEPHINE
               (softly, in German)
          I have an appointment with Pastor Graupner.
          My name is deBois - Josephine deBois.

                      THE WOMAN
               (in Austrian German)
          A moment please.

The door closes. Josephine waits for a while. She looks
impatiently on her watch. The door opens. The woman lets
Josephine in.

                      THE WOMAN
          Pastor Graupner is ready to meet you.

INT. VIENNA - HOUSE GRAUPNER - DAY

Josephine enters the building. The woman swiftly closes the
door. Josephine follows the woman through a small entry
hall to a narrow corridor. The floors in the hall and in
the corridor are of old cobblestones. The walls are painted
white, directly on uneven large granite stones. Josephine, on
high heels, walks with difficulty on the uneven surface. They
enter a short, narrow side corridor, also with white granite
stone walls. A large black crucifix at the end of the corridor
is the only decoration. They stop by a solid wooden door to
Pastor Graupner's office. The woman knocks softly on the door

and waits for a sound from the room. As a voice is heard, she opens the door slightly and speaks into the office.

                    THE WOMAN
          Mrs. deBois is here.

                    PASTOR GRAUPNER
                 (in Austrian German)
          Please let her come in.

INT. VIENNA - HOUSE GRAUPNER - OFFICE - DAY

Josephine enters the office. PASTOR GRAUPNER (67), a small, overweight and kind man, stands behind his desk made of old, solid wood. A crucifix is on the wall behind him. The room is spacious and high ceilinged. Pastor Graupner greets Josephine with a handshake over the desk. He points to a chair located opposite the desk. Josephine, tense, sits down. Pastor Graupner appears overly modest and restrained.

                    PASTOR GRAUPNER
                 (in Austrian German)
          I am very happy to see you Mrs.
          deBois - and I am delighted that you are
          considering a donation to our church.

                    JOSEPHINE
          It is a pleasure. I have always been
          impressed by this church - it means a lot
          to me.
                 (she pauses and continues
                  with fake modesty)
          I know, of course, that times are tough,
          so I really would like to help.

                    PASTOR GRAUPNER
          And could you perhaps tell me how you
          consider to help us?

                    JOSEPHINE
          I would like to give my support regularly.
          Say every year.
                 (she pauses)
          My proposal is fifty thousand today.

Pastor Graupner leans forward over his desk clearly
astonished, yet pleased by Josephine's generosity. Josephine
takes an envelope from her handbag, holds it for a short
moment while watching Pastor Graupner. As he continues
to appear content Josephine puts the envelope quietly on
the desk close to her side. Pastor Graupner watches the
envelope.

> PASTOR GRAUPNER
> That's indeed generous Mrs. I cannot thank
> you enough. I am sure you will find it
> worthwhile - and, needless to say, I shall
> do my utmost to help you all I can in
> return.

> JOSEPHINE
> I do not expect anything in return
> Pastor.

Pastor Graupner reaches out for the envelope. Over the broad
desk he has to stretch out quite a bit to reach it. He places
the envelope on his side on the desk. Josephine smiles to him
and then looks a bit shy down as she speaks.

> JOSEPHINE
> Well, perhaps Pastor, I wonder if you
> could help me with a small thing?

Josephine looks up and smiles in her most pleasant and
charming way as she continues pretending being a bit shy.

> PASTOR GRAUPNER
> Just let me know Mrs. deBois - I shall do
> my best.

> JOSEPHINE
> I am going to marry. I would like to
> marry in your church - it means a lot
> to me.

Pastor Graupner, delighted by the manageable proposal smiles
wholeheartedly as he speaks with all the charm he is able to
mobilize.

> PASTOR GRAUPNER

With the highest pleasure. I shall be glad
to conduct the ceremony myself.

JOSEPHINE
Wonderful, could you do it this Saturday?

PASTOR GRAUPNER
But, Mrs. deBois, our procedures require
a month.

JOSEPHINE
(plays the naive)
But Pastor, we travel so much and we will
be away for so long - we cannot wait for
all the happiness of marriage.

Pastor Graupner looks at the desk. He folds his hands.
Josephine takes another, slightly larger envelope from her
handbag. She keeps it in her hand.

JOSEPHINE
Pastor Graupner, I know of course that
there are expenses for the church by a
wedding and for yourself - but I can help
with that.

Josephine puts the envelope on the desk and pushes it well
over the desk to Pastor Graupner. The envelope obviously
contains a huge amount of money. Pastor Graupner folds his
hands on the desk, looks at the envelope, half ashamed, half
exited. He takes a sheet of paper from a drawer in the desk
and rapidly reads through it.

PASTOR GRAUPNER
Well Mrs. deBois, I can see we have a
service this Saturday - so I may be able
to do it right after - but it will be in
the small chapel then.
(he pauses while trying to
focus his mind)
But what I need from you right away
then is the name of your future husband
and his data; and then, of course, the
names of witnesses - we need two. And
also the necessary papers - mainly birth
certificates.

Josephine takes a slim folder from her handbag.

                    JOSEPHINE
          It should all be here Pastor. All the data
          and papers you just mentioned.

Pastor Graupner takes the folder and rapidly browses through
the papers. He opens a small drawer in his desk and opens a
computer. He enters the names and searches. For a moment he
looks surprised and focused on the small screen. Josephine
fiercely looks at him. The pastor's eyes goes to the two
envelopes on the table. He tries to read the contents of the
second envelope from its size.

                    PASTOR GRAUPNER
               (takes the envelope)
          Well Mrs. deBois - so please be in the
          small chapel at 4 o'clock on Saturday -
          all of you.

                    JOSEPHINE
               (again smiling shy)
          Thank you so much.

Pastor Graupner lowers his voice.

                    PASTOR GRAUPNER
          How wonderful. You and Ludwig Mann will
          have the most beautiful future. Nothing
          can be more complete, more beautiful and
          more honest than a marriage of two minds
          like yours. I am honored to seal this
          unique marriage for our Lord and Savior.

Pastor Graupner nods modestly as he speaks. He and Josephine
rise. Pastor Graupner follows Josephine to the door. He opens
and holds the door for Josephine. The woman in black rapidly
appears. Pastor Graupner and Josephine shake hands by the
door. Josephine exits the office.

EXT. VIENNA - HOTEL - SUITE - TERRACE - NIGHT

Ludwig sits worried by the table on the terrace with a cup of
coffee. He again hears the music in his mind. He shakes his
head as he disagrees. The only light is from the lamps in the

suite. He hides his head in his hands and lets the music start
all over. Still unhappy he leans back and tries to relax and
again starts the symphony in his mind. He appears a bit more
content. Josephine enters the suite. She calls from inside the
suite while she kicks her shoes off in the small lobby.

                    JOSEPHINE
        I am here. Are you here?

Josephine enters the terrace. Ludwig again sits by the table
resting his head in his hands. Josephine goes behind him and
puts her hands on his shoulders. She lets her hands slide
sensually down on his chest.

                    JOSEPHINE
        How was it? Was it OK?

Josephine takes a chair to sit face to face with Ludwig on the
same side of the table and smiles to cheer him up.

                    JOSEPHINE
        Did they play well?

                    LUDWIG
        I just could not get it right. It was
        never there. There is a disconnect. I
        imagine the piece one way and somehow
        deep inside I feel differently. I don't
        understand. I don't know what to do.
            (he pauses)
        I know it must sound strange to you -
        even to me actually.

Ludwig again hides his face in his hands. Josephine goes
behind him and holds his head between her hands to calm him
down. She talks very directive.

                    JOSEPHINE
        Now stop this. Don't do this again.
        I know you have these deep feelings about
        the music. But whatever you feel, your
        audience loves what you do - they feel
        differently - they love what you do.
            (she pauses)

I know that you don't care. But, you mean
a lot to them. They all agree you are the
greatest. They adore you.

Josephine sits down, still touching Ludwig.

                    JOSEPHINE
          Keep going. You know how it is.
          Suddenly you get it right. "Out of the
          blue". It's somewhere waiting.
          Be patient, please.

Josephine pauses a moment, considering how to move on. She
decides to diffuse the issue by talking about something
else. She gets up and sits down on the edge of the table,
seductively with her breast at the level of Ludwig's eyes.
                    JOSEPHINE
          I have a surprise for you. I arranged our
          marriage - right before the concert. Just
          you and me - and the witnesses.

                    LUDWIG
               (surprised)
          What - just before the concert?

                    JOSEPHINE
          Yes exactly. And then you make the best
          performance ever, right after.
          Isn't that romantic?

                    LUDWIG
          But what about a party, guests and
          whatever goes with a wedding?

                    JOSEPHINE
          We do that later, after the recordings.
          Maybe over there!

Josephine rises, and sits down on Ludwig's lap. She kisses
Ludwig passionately and loosens his shirt and trousers.

                    JOSEPHINE
          I have it all under control. Even the
          beautiful ring you are going to give me!
               (she rises)
          I am waiting for you in there!

She gives Ludwig a tender kiss, walks inside and switches
the lights off. Ludwig sits in the darkness. He lets the
music sound again and lets it stop, turns his chair, leans
back over the table and looks up in the air to the stars.
The second movement sounds and fills the space. He puts his
hand on his forehead. The second movement starts again. He
listens attentively. The music seems to make sense to him. He
falls asleep.

                              MUSIC FADES TO NEXT SCENE

INT. VIENNA - CHURCH GRAUPNER - DAY

Ludwig and Josephine stand in front of the altar in the small
chapel of Pastor Graupner's church. Josephine is in a completely
white, yet not classical wedding dress. Ludwig is dressed for
the upcoming evening's performance. Dr. Schlesinger stands next
to Josephine. Dr. Franz stands next to Ludwig. Pastor Graupner
stands facing the couple in his official cassock for weddings.
The second movement of the Mozart 29th symphony sounds in
the background. Josephine holds Ludwig's arm tight as Pastor
Graupner declares them husband and wife. Ludwig puts a slightly
red diamond ring on Josephine's finger. She looks passionately
and satisfied at Ludwig as they kiss softly and appropriately.
Pastor Graupner lifts his arms and delivers his blessing.
He walks in front as they all walk through the beautifully
decorated church. A few church guests watch the small ceremony
from the seats close to the church entrance.

EXT. VIENNA - CHURCH GRAUPNER - DAY

They all gather in front of the church. A photographer lines
them all up in front of the church door.

                         LUDWIG
                (whispering to Josephine)
            Who organized this chap to come?

                         JOSEPHINE
                     (whispering)
            I did - we need this moment forever.
                     (she pauses)
            He is very well connected. The
            picture will be published everywhere

> instantly - so the whole world will know
> about us - isn't it wonderful?

Josephine holds Ludwig's arm even tighter. The photographer
positions them all for the perfect wedding picture. He goes
back to the camera, looks and changes his mind. He goes back
and positions them slightly differently. Finally he shoots the
pictures with the charmingly smiling Josephine, the worried
Ludwig, the businesslike witnesses and the appropriately
neutral Pastor Graupner. Ludwig and Josephine shake hands
with Pastor Graupner who smiles warmly, yet slightly worried.
Josephine and Ludwig thank Dr. Schlesinger and Dr. Franz.
They all walk to two waiting limousines. The drivers open
the doors. Josephine and Ludwig enter one of the cars. Dr.
Schlesinger and Dr. Franz enter the other. Both cars drive
out from the small square and directly to the concert hall in
Vienna. The music intensifies (29th) as they drive and fades out
as the limos stop by the stage entrance to the concert hall.

EXT. VIENNA - CONCERT HALL - SIDE ENTRANCE - EVENING

The limos stop by the stage entrance to the concert building.
Some concert guests have already gathered in front of the
building. By the stage entrance, several enthusiastic fans of
Ludwig ask for autographs and take photographs. Ludwig, very
absent minded, signs for a few of the fans. Josephine smiles
overwhelmingly and charmingly to counterweight Ludwig's gloomy
mood. They all enter the concert building.

INT. VIENNA - CONCERT HALL - CORRIDOR - EVENING

Dr. Schlesinger, Franz, Josephine and Ludwig enter the
corridor. Dr. Franz is tense. Dr. Schlesinger is uplifted and
in a splendid mood. Ludwig is extremely tense. Josephine is
worried as she watches and feels Ludwig's mood.

> DR. FRANZ
> The conductor's room is ready for you Dr.
> Mann. - And Mrs. deBois; the suitcase you
> sent earlier is in the adjacent room, as
> you wished.
> (he turns to Schlesinger)
> I have a seat reserved for you - and you
> can be with me in the director's suite
> until the performance - just follow me.

                    DR. SCHLESINGER
          Oh thank you. It's a pleasure, it's a joy!
          Dr. Mann, I cannot tell you how I look
          forward.

Josephine and Ludwig continue through the corridor. Ludwig
enters the conductor's room.

INT. VIENNA - CONCERT HALL - CONDUCTOR ROOM - EVENING

Ludwig enters the conductor's room. He tries to refresh
himself by pouring plenty of water from a sink on his face.
It's not enough, and he puts his entire head below the tap, as
he did in the mountains.

INT. VIENNA - CONCERT HALL - FOYER - EVENING

The audience is gathering in the concert hall.

INT. VIENNA - CONCERT HALL - CORRIDOR - EVENING

The musicians start walking through the corridors and gather
in the concert hall. Dr. Franz and Dr. Schlesinger exit the
director's suite.

INT. VIENNA - CONCERT HALL - DRESSING ROOM - EVENING

Josephine, in an evening dress, is finishing her make-up. Her
face is serious and tense - almost rude, irritated and angry.
Her movements reflect her true gloomy mood.

INT. VIENNA - CONCERT HALL - CORRIDOR - EVENING

Josephine exits her room and walks through the corridor to
Ludwig's room. She knocks softly on the door. There is no
answer. She knocks again. As there is no answer, she softly
calls Ludwig's name. As there still is no answer she carefully
opens the door. Ludwig is still sitting at the piano chair,
his head bent forward, water dropping from his face. Josephine
swiftly enters.

INT. VIENNA - CONCERT HALL - CONDUCTOR ROOM - EVENING

Josephine closes the door behind her. She quickly grabs a
towel, puts it on Ludwig's head and dries it.

                    JOSEPHINE
          Look at me.

Ludwig looks Josephine in the eyes with undiminished worry.
She holds her hands behind his head and holds it close to
herself and looks straight in Ludwig's eyes. With some efforts
she mobilizes a smile.

                    JOSEPHINE
          Don't do this. Come back. Come back.

                    LUDWIG
          I cannot do this. I have known it all the
          way. There is a disconnect. I have not got
          it right!

                    JOSEPHINE
          Now, come on, remember all those totally
          complex and terribly difficult pieces you
          have done. And you have always got it
          right. You always got it right. And these
          things tonight, they are so simple. It
          is easy stuff. Look at me. You will do it
          again. Go in there and it comes out of
          the blue to you - and to all of us.

                    LUDWIG
          It is different this time.

It knocks on the door. Dr. Franz is outside.

                    DR. FRANZ
          Dr. Mann, we are all ready. Maybe you
          should come now; then we dim the light in
          the hall and we get rolling.

Josephine goes to the door. She opens it slightly. She smiles.

                    JOSEPHINE
          Please give us a few more minutes.

Dr. Franz realizes the situation.

                         DR. FRANZ
          OK, I will keep it going for five more
          minutes.

Josephine locks the door and walks back to Ludwig. He
continues his worries.

                         LUDWIG
          I cannot do it - let's get out of here.

Josephine walks behind Ludwig as she considers her next steps.
Her face is unkind and scheming. She talks to Ludwig from
behind his back, pretending giving up.

                         JOSEPHINE
          OK - let's get out then.
                (she pauses)
          Well, I better get started with damage
          control. I don't know what to do really -
          it will certainly be difficult to rescue
          the concerts coming up - New York is out
          of the window. You realize that, right?

She walks around in the room and watches Ludwig discretely. As
she realizes her comments affects Ludwig, she suddenly falls
on her knees in front of him and seductively puts her elbows
on his lap while moving her head close to his.

                         JOSEPHINE
          Do this one for me - do it for me as a
          wedding present. Just go in there. You
          will get it right. The musicians know you
          so well, so even if you make changes now
          they will follow.
                (pauses and fakes sadness)
          Don't let us fall apart - imagine how
          that would be?

She puts her head on his knees. Ludwig seems to compose
himself a bit. Captured by Josephine and his desires for her,
and considering his plans, he gives in to the forces within
him. He puts his hands around Josephine's head. She looks up
at him. Their faces are very close.

                    LUDWIG
               (whispering)
          OK - I try.

Ludwig gets up. He looks himself briefly in the mirror and
exits to the corridor.

INT. VIENNA - CONCERT HALL - CORRIDOR - EVENING

Ludwig walks swiftly through the corridor, never stopping or
hesitating. He reaches the entrance to the concert hall. Dr.
Franz is waiting. He looks enormously relieved and tries to
stop Ludwig by the entrance in order to dim the light before
Ludwig's entry. Ludwig greets him briefly and walks straight
into the concert room. Dr. Franz, hectic, gives sign for the
light in the hall to be totally dimmed.

INT. VIENNA - CONCERT HALL - ORCHESTRA - EVENING

An instant applause lifts the roof as Ludwig enters the
concert hall. He keeps going without looking left or right
until he reaches the podium. He steps up on the conductor's
stand. He bows only once and briefly to the audience. He turns
around. He stands for a while facing the orchestra looking
down. He looks up and makes small signs to the individual
musicians to signal his need for their total attention. He
leans down towards the concert master.

                    LUDWIG
               (whispering)
          I change it a bit - just follow me!

The concert master nods. He signals the need for attention to
the musicians. Ludwig stands straight up at the stand. He is
pale. He holds the moment. He looks up. He lifts his hands.
The musicians lift their instruments. He lowers his hands in
the first deep beat. The Symphony sounds perfectly. As the
music follows, Ludwig's face changes to his inspiring and
totally joyful face as he realizes he got it.

                         THE SOUND DIMINISHES AND CARRIES OVER

INT. DESOLATED CHAPEL - DAY

Marchetto and Giovanni are standing in the chapel. They are
in the middle of a conversation. Marchetto is extremely upset
and agitating. They are standing face to face.

                    MARCHETTO
          .. and Brother, I cannot believe this.
          The - marriage - just - happened.
                    (Marchetto walks up to the
                    altar as he continues)
          I first wanted to meet you here since
          I heard that the marriage was moving
          forward, in spite of what we had agreed.
                    (he turns around and again
                    faces Giovanni)
          - and then, what did I just learn?
          It happened Brother. It happened!
                    (he pauses)
          How on earth, Brother, could you not stop
          it? How? Don't you follow them? Are you
          not totally aware of every step they take?
          How on earth can you run a project like
          this without being on top of every dammed
          detail?
                    (scorn and ironic tone)
          How can you be so careless in the midst
          of all your scientific scrutiny and deep
          thinking about everything we do? You
          are in charge of a mission to answer
          fundamental questions about who we are as
          human beings, what creation and faith is,
          what makes humans humans -
                    (shouting)
          - and you don't even know what I can
          easily find out myself!

Marchetto shakes his head and again walks agitated around in
the chapel. Giovanni sees Marchetto in a halo of light on the
background of the altar and its damaged picture of a religious
motive.

                    MARCHETTO
          At least tell me you know what to do
          now. Tell me you know that this mission
          must stop now before it is totally out
          of your control and endangers the entire

existence of our sacred institution. We
discussed this already, we agreed already,
but what have you done?
>   (he pauses while angrily
>   watching the apparently
>   ashamed Giovanni)
Tell me you know. Tell me you know that
whatever is left on this earth of this
program must simply be eliminated. As I
said before. Get - rid - of - everything!
Every one that knows and everything they
know and everything that remains of this
disaster. Understood?

Giovanni nods and looks at Marchetto as he speaks softly but
convincingly.

>   GIOVANNI
>   (tumbles over his words)
> But Brother, don't blame everything on
> me. Don't forget that we were facing -
> and we still are - the biggest threat
> against our faith. We all saw this project
> as an ideal defense. We could prove our
> case - yes - we could prove that humanity
> and all that goes with it is beyond the
> explainable. You know what I mean. We
> went into this together and we ...

Marchetto, totally unconvinced by Giovanni's defense,
interrupts and talks furiously with his face inches from
Giovanni's face. He first whispers and slowly lets his voice
increase in strength.

>   MARCHETTO
> The idea may have been good Brother - but
> your execution is simply lousy. So don't
> exonerate yourself and don't blame any
> other than yourself. You asked for and you
> got the full responsibility for the entire
> mission! We pumped resources unlimited
> and endlessly into it on your requests.
> You asked for it, you got it, you did it -
> and now you get us out of it!

Outraged Marchetto leaves the chapel. The door closes heavily and loud. The music from the last bars of the Vienna concert again fills the space.

THE CHAPEL FADES AWAY AND MERGES TO THE VIENNA CONCERT.

INT. VIENNA - CONCERT HALL - NIGHT

Ludwig happily makes the last beats. The audience instantly stands up and applauds. The applaud lifts the roof. Ludwig is pale, but composed. He shines, smiles and almost laughs to the orchestra. He lifts his arms. They all rise. Ludwig turns around and faces the audience with lifted arms as a greeting. The musicians join the ocean of applause with small beats on their instruments. Ludwig turns and walks between the musicians to the concert corridor entrance.

INT. VIENNA - CONCERT HALL - CORRIDOR - NIGHT

Josephine and Dr. Franz are waiting for Ludwig. Dr. Franz applauds enthusiastically, while Josephine runs to Ludwig and kisses him softly on the chin. The applause from the concert hall increases. Before Dr. Franz leads Ludwig back to the entrance, Josephine briefly brings his dress and hair in order. Ludwig again walks between the musicians as the applause intensifies. He stands in front of the musicians. They rise. He faces the audience and bows deeply and then holds his hand at his chest as a thank you.

INT. VIENNA - HOTEL - FOYER - EVENING

As Ludwig and Josephine walk through the large lobby a servant comes to Ludwig.

                    THE SERVANT
               (in Austrian German)
          Dr. Mann, there have been a number of
          calls for you - I believe something urgent.

                    LUDWIG
          Oh thanks. My cell phone has been off -
          let me check.
               (he adds jokingly)
          You know, for good reasons I switch it off
          during the performances.

Ludwig finds his cell phone and switches it on. A large number
of unanswered calls show up on the display He moves a bit to
the side and dials for the voice messages. His face becomes
serious and worried. The Requiem sounds. He turns towards
Josephine while listening to the last part of the message.

                    LUDWIG
          It's Leopold. Mother is ill.
          Seriously he says. Something has happened
          to her. I have to go there.

Josephine looks slightly irritated by the potential
interference with the moment and her tight plans ahead.

                    JOSEPHINE
          I will organize a flight tomorrow
          morning, and a car when you land. And, -
          I organize a flight directly to the US
          thereafter. Don't worry. We will get it
          right.

                    LUDWIG
          Tomorrow may be too late. I can't wait
          until tomorrow. Please check if there is a
          late flight - or simply organize a flight.

Ludwig thanks the servant and starts walking fast towards the
broad staircase. Josephine, breath-taken, follows him. They
enter their suite.

INT. EUROPE - CAR - MOUNTAINOUS ROAD - EARLY MORNING

The Limo drives up the steep mountain roads. The traffic gets
scarce. After a while they meet no cars. Ludwig watches the
landscape as they climb up through the large deserted area
and head towards the village high up in the mountains. The
village and the church situated above become visible in the
distance. They reach the village and drive through the narrow
streets. In the very early hours of the day no people are in
the streets. Finally they stop in front of Ludwig's house.

INT. EUROPE - HOUSE LUDWIG - CORRIDOR - EARLY MORNING

Ludwig enters the very narrow corridor in the house. The interior walls of the house are all of massive wood trunks from the large logs forming the outside as well as the inside of the house walls. The light in the hall is very dim. On the walls are photographs, small mirrors, paper clips of silhouettes, small water colors, and a few oil paintings. LEOPOLD (AGE 75) enters the corridor from the adjacent room. He is very slim with thin gray hair. He walks uncertain and is bent slightly forward. He embraces Ludwig, and is looking extremely worried and sad.

                    LEOPOLD
               (in Italian; with a breaking
               voice)
          She stopped breathing several times.
          I thought she was dead - I called the
          pastor. He is in there. But when I
          mentioned you would be on your way, she
          got strength.

                    LUDWIG
               (in Italian)
          Thanks Leopold. You have always been so
          good to us.

They walk into the living room and continue towards the door to the mother's room. They open the door silently and enter.

INT. EUROPE - LUDWIG HOUSE - MOTHER ROOM - EARLY MORNING

Soft light. Ludwig's mother CHIARA (AGE 52) is in a narrow bed by the wall of the room, sitting half up supported by many large pillows behind her back. With her grayish hair and pale face she looks old and fragile, but gentle and still with fine traits. The PASTOR (AGE 65) is standing by the bed end carefully watching Chiara. Ludwig goes to the side of the bed, takes Chiara's hand and holds it firmly. Chiara opens her eyes, recognizes Ludwig, and smiles.

                    CHIARA
               (low voice in Italian)
          I saw you coming.

Chiara closes her eyes while she smiles and keeps holding
Ludwig's hand firmly.

> LUDWIG
> (in Italian)
> Mother, look at me please. What happened?

Leopold brings a chair. Ludwig sits down next to the bed and
watches Chiara. They are both smiling. There is a brief moment
of silence and relief. Ludwig leans forward to hear her feeble
voice.

> LUDWIG
> (whispering)
> You are beautiful as always, mother.

> CHIARA
> (whispering)
> Well my son. I know what is going
> to happen. I feel it. It happened so
> suddenly - I just got so weak.
> (she pauses to get her
> breath)
> I am not old - I was feeling so good
> always - why suddenly this?

Chiara gives a sign to the pastor and Leopold to leave the
room. The two men quietly exit backwards. Chiara opens her
eyes and composes herself in spite of her weakness.

> CHIARA
> Go to the small chest of drawers over
> there. Open the upper drawer.

Ludwig, a bit surprised, walks over to the chest of drawers
and opens. He looks at Chiara.

> CHIARA
> Now, find the small box in the very back
> of the drawer and put it in your pocket!

Ludwig finds a small dark red and green wooden box at the
size of a business card. He looks at it.

> CHIARA
> Put it in your pocket.

                        LUDWIG
            But what is?

                        CHIARA
            Just keep it. And don't lose it.
            Follow up on what is in there. Promise!

                        LUDWIG
            But please, tell me about...

Ludwig puts the small box in his pocket. He sits down again in
the chair next to the bed, holding Chiara's hand.

                        CHIARA
            You know, your father died before you were
            born. But there is something else to it.
            Maybe that's what takes me away too. I am
            sure. You need to know.

Chiara gets tears in her eyes. She closes her eyes firmly in
great pain.

                        LUDWIG
            Tell me now. How did he die mother?

                        CHIARA
            He went into the mountains one morning.
            He never came back. We did not even find
            any trace of him.

After a while Chiara turns towards Ludwig.

                        CHIARA
            I know dear, it must be impossible for
            you to understand. But we had nothing
            when he was gone — and then we were
            offered this way out.

Chiara closes her eyes. She turns her face away from Ludwig.

                        CHIARA
            But what you did made it all worthwhile.

Sitting in silence, Ludwig gets tears in his eyes.

                          CHIARA
          Do you remember when you had the piano
          tuned. You did it by yourself and then
          you got your friends here and learned
          them to sing. And the notes they used -
          you remember - all these unbelievable
          things you did?
                    (she pauses)
          It was magic - yes magic!

For a moment, Chiara is more awake.

  LUDWIG LOOKS OVER AT THE PIANO IN THE CORNER OF THE ROOM. HE
                                              THINKS BACK

INT. EUROPE - HOUSE LUDWIG - DAY - BACK IN TIME

Ludwig, as a small boy enters the room and takes the grown
up Ludwig by the hand leading him to the piano room. There
he sits in front of the piano, on top of a pile of books on
a chair to reach the keyboard. He writes notes on a piece of
rough paper. The lines for the notes he has made by an almost
straight piece of wood. He writes with the last little pieces
of a pencil. Two small girls and two small boys (poor farmer
children) sit exited and smiling around Ludwig. Old Ludwig
sits down next to him. The small Ludwig hands a sheet to each
of the children (Mozart's Ave Verum).

                          LUDWIG
                    (in Italian)
          This is for you, this is for you, here is
          yours and here is yours.

Small Ludwig looks old Ludwig straight in the eyes. Old Ludwig
smiles but does not get a sheet. The four children look at the
notes without any clue of what it is. They look at Ludwig. He
takes the sheet from the smallest of the girls. He puts it on
the piano, points at each of the notes while he plays them one
by one at the piano. He looks at the girl.

                          LUDWIG
          Now it's you!

He points at the notes, she sings uncertain. He supports her
with the piano. She misses most notes, but gets some. Ludwig
smiles to her.

LUDWIG
Again!

The small girl gets it much better. They have fun and laugh.
Ludwig adds a few notes from other voices at the piano. He
turns to the second girl. He shows her the notes one by one.
He asks her to sing. After a few tries she gets it. Ludwig
repeats with the two boys. They all move closer to him.
Finally they sing the piece quite beautifully with Ludwig
supporting them with the piano. They laugh. The girls start
dancing lightly and slowly around in the room while they sing
the text. Ludwig rises from the piano. The children play with
the music.

LUDWIG
Now again - without the piano.

He conducts lightly as they sing through the piece well in
tune. Old Ludwig sits behind him, watching and smiling.

TRANSITION TO PRESENT TIME

INT. EUROPE - HOUSE LUDWIG - MOTHER ROOM - DAY

Giulia briefly opens her eyes slightly. Ludwig realizes she
still listens and continues speaking to keep her with him.

LUDWIG
You had almost nothing, mother - still
you gave me everything. I tell you, the
music we made here and in our church was
the best. I so often wish me back here.

Suddenly the strength of Giulia's hand diminishes.

LUDWIG
Mother, looks at me - look at me please.

Ludwig rises. He calls the pastor and Leopold. The pastor
touches Giulia's neck. She is dead. The pastor, peculiarly
stone faced, blesses Giulia from the bed end and puts a small
wooden cross on her chest. The three men stand side by side
for a few moments by the bed. Ludwig kneels down next to
the bed. He kisses Giulia's hand, and briefly holds her hand
against his forehead. The Pastor folds Giulia's hands around

the small wooden cross. The three men walk out to the small
corridor and stand together for a moment before leaving the
house. The pastor is clearly struggling, deeply concerned for
Ludwig.

                         PASTOR
          God bless you Ludwig. It meant everything
          for her that you came.

                         LUDWIG
          Of course I would come - had I just known
          earlier I could have been here more.
                    (he looks at Leopold)

                         LEOPOLD
          She did not want to bother you. I think
          she thought she would recover - and why
          should she die - so suddenly - it made no
          sense. But then, as she realized ...
                    (he tries to control
                     himself)
          .. then, of course, she urgently wanted to
          see you. We never really understood what
          was wrong with her.

                         LUDWIG
          Well Leopold - you have done the best you
          could. And it is what it is now.
                    (he turns to the pastor)
          I assume we can do the funeral right
          away?

                         PASTOR
          Of course Ludwig. Actually before you
          arrived she expressed some strong wishes
          for the funeral. She was very firm on
          that. She must have been thinking about
          it for quite a while. Somehow it had been
          planned already, very detailed - I was a
          bit surprised.
                    (he pauses)
          I can follow up with you. The expenses
          will be quite a bit more than usual.

                         LUDWIG
          Just tell me how much.

The three men shake hands and exit the house.

INT. EUROPE - CHURCH LUDWIG - DAY

The walls in the church are white. Light shines into the
small room through a few, small circular windows in the
side walls. A black crucifix is hanging on the East wall
under a window for the Eastern sun. About six rows of
benches flank the corridor leading through the middle of
the room up to the crucifix. In the back of the room there
is a small organ. Up around the organ there are places
for singers. Four men carry the coffin up in front of the
crucifix and place it on a small elevation on the floor.
Ludwig and Leopold stand in the doorway to the church and
watch solemnly. The men turn around and walk to the exit.
Ludwig steps aside as the four men pass him. He walks up to
the coffin. He stands in front of the coffin and looks up
towards the crucifix. He bows his head and stands quiet for
a moment. Leopold stays by the entry inside the church and
watches. Ludwig turns around, walks to the door and exits
the church together with Leopold.

EXT. EUROPE - CHURCH LUDWIG - OUTSIDE - DAY

Ludwig and Leopold close the doors to the church. The
doors close with a strong sound that echoes in the quiet
surrounding. They all enter the cars and drive back down
the mountainous roads. As they reach the village Ludwig's
mind fades back in time. He looks down the street and
sees himself as a small boy around 5 years old running
towards him.

                                        BACK IN TIME

EXT. EUROPE - VILLAGE LUDWIG - DAY

Ludwig, as a small boy, runs into Leopold's shop. Leopold
stands behind the counter. The shop trades books and
utilities. In the back of the shop there is a small section
for musical instruments. There are a few pianos and, in a few
cabinets with glass doors along the walls, there are a few
violins and wind instruments exhibited.

INT. EUROPE - SHOP LEOPOLD - DAY - BACK IN TIME

Ludwig runs up to the counter. The small boy is barely able
to look over it. He stands with his hands lifted to reach the
edge of the counter. Leopold walks from the back of the shop
to the counter.

                    LEOPOLD
            (in Italian)
        What is it Ludwig?

                    LUDWIG
            (in Italian)
        How does one tune a piano? I want the old
        piano in the house to play!

Ludwig jumps with excitement and impatience on the spot in
front of the counter. Leopold smiles to him.

                    LEOPOLD
        Well Ludwig. This is a very difficult
        thing to do; only trained piano tuners
        can do it.

                    LUDWIG
        Please, show me how you do it.
        Please - please. Show me, show me.

                    LEOPOLD
        OK, OK - let me show you a little bit
        then.

Leopold takes a tuning fork from the glass cabinet, a piano
tuner rod, and a small piece of triangular wood to put
between the strings. He walks over to one of the pianos, pulls
a chair over to Ludwig and then sits down on the piano bench.
He removes the front cover of the piano. He beats on the
tuning fork and puts its foot on the side of the piano. The
"A" sounds clearly. He listens carefully. Ludwig's eyes shine
in delight as he listens to the sound. Leopold hits the "A" on
the piano. It is pretty much out of tune.

                    LEOPOLD
        So, this is the "A". First you make
        this match the tuning fork. That's the
        beginning.

Leopold tightens the knots. He puts the wooden piece between the strings for one string to be tuned. Then he tightens the knots for the other A-strings. After a little while the "A" is perfect. He looks at Ludwig.

> LEOPOLD
> Can you hear it. Now this is right.
> Then let's go to the "A" below - that's
> called an octave.

Leopold hits the lower "A" and repeats the process. He looks at Ludwig who smiles extremely happily and jumps up and down in the chair with excitement. Leopold then hits the quint and wants to start bringing it into tune.

> LUDWIG
> Please let me do it.

Ludwig looks begging at the pretty surprised Leopold. He hands Ludwig the tools. Ludwig hits the quint. He fits the piano tuner rod on the knot and tightens it using all his strength. Then he squeezes the wooden piece between the strings and tunes the remaining strings one by one.

In the end, by their mutual efforts, the whole piano is in perfect tune.

> LEOPOLD
> Wow Ludwig. How can you do that?

> LUDWIG
> You just showed me.

Ludwig jumps down from the chair. He looks up at Leopold full of excitement.

> LUDWIG
> Please, can I borrow the rod - just until
> tomorrow, and the wood.

> LEOPOLD
> Well, but only - I say only - only until
> tomorrow. But you also need the tuner
> fork.

> LUDWIG

No, I don't need that - I remember.

                    LEOPOLD
          OK; I pass by tomorrow and say "hello"
          to your mother and then you show me the
          piano in perfect tune!

Leopold smiles to Ludwig. He lifts his hand and raises his
finger. Ludwig runs out of the shop.

EXT. EUROPE - VILLAGE - DAY - BACK IN TIME

Ludwig watches the small boy running to the mother's house.
The picture from the past diffuses.

                              CROSS TO PRESENT TIME

EXT. EUROPE - VILLAGE - DAY - PRESENT TIME

The car with Ludwig and Leopold reach Leopold's house.
Leopold exits the car, he greats Ludwig goodbye and enters
his house.

                    LUDWIG
          (addressing the driver)
          Please drive me down to the village
          further down the valley. I have a few
          messages to send. It will just be a few
          minutes - afterward we go back to the
          house. You can just stay in the inn.
          We should be all done the day after
          tomorrow.

The car starts driving.

INT. EUROPE - HOUSE LUDWIG - DAY

Ludwig enters the house. From the small hallway he goes into
the living room. He looks over at the door to his mother's
room; then he steps over to the room he had as a child.
He recognizes all the things on the tables and the walls;
everything seems very much to be as he left it years ago. He
goes over to the bed, located under a small wooden window. He
lies down on the bed with all his clothes on. He puts a large
pillow under his head and looks at a photo on the wall. There

are 10 children, about seven year's old, sitting on a row in an otherwise empty concert hall. They are very attentive, sitting on the front of the too large chairs for children and supporting themselves with their hands on the front edges of the chairs. Ludwig's mind goes into the picture.

TRANSITION BACK IN TIME TO ADMISSION TEST

INT. CONSERVATORY - CONCERT HALL - DAY - BACK IN TIME

The children stop talking. They are nervous and keep their mouths tightly shut while they look totally focused to the side entrance. A large WOMAN (45) steps onto the stage. She is a formal, straight, typical German, and slightly unpleasantly commanding. The children watch her with great attention. It is clearly a nerve-racking event, climaxing endless, exhausting tests before this final round.

                    WOMAN
               (in German)
          You can all be proud of being here. You
          are the few among the many that have
          applied. But only two of you will be
          selected today and admitted to lessons for
          a full year with the Maestro.
               (she pauses briefly and
               looks at the children)
          Today, you will all play for the Maestro -
          no more than ten minutes.
          The Maestro himself will then make his
          choices.

The MAESTRO (55) walks, slightly forward bent, down to the middle of the hall, finds a seat and sits down. He leans forward, puts his arms on the row in front of him, and pays the utmost attention to the events in the room. There are two grand pianos on the stage, facing each other. The commanding woman stands next to the grand pianos at the stage with the list of the student names.

                    WOMAN
          Before we start I have to tell you
          that, very unfortunate for those of
          you that have selected pieces with an
          accompaniment from a second piano either
          as an orchestra transcript or as a pure

second voice, we have a problem: our
pianist has become acutely ill this
morning and we have not been able to find
a replacement with the short notice. We
have also been unable to reach him for
the scores.
          (she pauses)
Those of you that cannot meaningfully play
today because of this will be admitted
directly to next year's final test - you
will not have to pass all the preliminary
tests.

The woman gives sign to the first child in the row.

                    WOMAN
          Your name and pieces?

                              TRANSITION BACK TO PRESENT

INT. EUROPE - HOUSE LUDWIG - EVENING

Ludwig sits in the bed. He takes the framed photo down
from wall and watches it from very short distance. On the
picture, Tiffany is seen sitting next to him at the end of
the row of children. As Ludwig watches the picture, the
voice of the woman penetrates his mind.

                    WOMAN
          Next - Tiffany - where are you?

Ludwig moves the picture a little away struck by the woman's
unpleasant voice.

                         TRANSITION TO CONSERVATORY BACK IN TIME

INT. CONSERVATORY - CONCERT HALL - DAY - BACK IN TIME

The woman looks through the list of names on the paper in her
hand and then looks down the row of the children. Tiffany, at
the end of the row, raises her hand and jumps down from her
chair supported by her hands on the edge of the chair. She
stands with her hands folded while waiting for the woman to
give her direction.

                    THE WOMAN

So, what are your pieces?

                    TIFFANY
          (very quiet, in German with
          an Asian accent)
     Mozart double sonata, K448.

                    WOMAN
     That's impossible without the other voice.
     It will be meaningless for you to play
     alone.

The woman looks down at the Maestro. He nods. Tears pour out
of Tiffany's eyes as she stands totally still. The woman is
unaffected by Tiffany's woes.

                    WOMAN
     And the second piece?

Tiffany looks up at the woman through her tear-wet eyes.
She tries to say the name of the next piece. But she
cannot. Ludwig is sitting right behind Tiffany watching her
attentively. He is impressed by Tiffany and totally devastated
by what happens. He raises his hand. The woman ignores him
and continues in her commanding voice.

                    WOMAN
     You want to play your second piece now, or
     what?

Tiffany still cannot get her word out.

                    WOMAN
     Tiffany you can sit down!

Ludwig jumps down from his chair and stands next to Tiffany.
He raises his hand as he speaks loud.

                    LUDWIG
     I can play the second voice for Tiffany.

                    WOMAN
          (irritated)
     How on earth would you do that without
     rehearsing - and we don't even have the
     score here. I told you!

LUDWIG
But, I heard it once.

WOMAN
You heard it?

The woman increasingly irritated looks down at the Maestro. He
opens his hands as a question mark.

MAESTRO
Start with the second movement then.

Ludwig jumps up at the stage and takes seat by the piano to
the right as seen from the Maestro. Tiffany follows and takes
seat by the piano bench to the left. They see each other
across the two grand pianos and look intensely in each other's
eyes for the first time. Tiffany lowers her hands towards
the piano keys. Ludwig, totally unaffected and fully on top
of the challenge, smiles back to her. While looking directly
towards Ludwig, Tiffany starts playing. Ludwig joins totally
flawlessly. Tiffany feels totally supported and magically led
through the music. They play without body language. Short into
the piece they are interrupted. As they stop they look at each
other. Ludwig smiles unimpressed as if he had played this
piece with Tiffany a million times and puts his hands on his
lap supporting himself as he looks down at the other students.

WOMAN
Good, and what is your second piece?

Tiffany remains sitting by the piano with her hands again
folded.

TIFFANY
Beethoven, - the 4th.

WOMAN
(slightly kinder to Tiffany)
Well, then we will have to leave it here.
But at least you have played something
today!

LUDWIG
I like it a lot. I can do the orchestra
part!

While Tiffany and Ludwig played Mozart, the Maestro has moved
up on the stage. He stands behind Ludwig as he addresses
Tiffany.

                    THE MAESTRO
          Please, for the first movement - just the
          beginning solo and the very first part of
          the orchestra.

Tiffany looks over at Ludwig. Her eyes then move up in the
empty air as she starts playing the first bars. Again, she
plays softly, with total control, and without body language.
Ludwig takes over at the orchestra part. The Maestro stops him
after a few bars and puts his hands on his shoulder.

                    THE MAESTRO
          Excellent, please - let's go to the second
          movement; just briefly.

Ludwig plays the first heavy orchestra bars with high
determination and strength. He looks at Tiffany. There is
total silence before the piano part. Then Tiffany plays
through the solo piano, slowly yet continuous while her eyes
are unfocused and directed to the space above the piano
as though she binds the cords together as they stand and
fade in the air. Ludwig plays the following few bars of the
orchestra score. Tiffany follows with the short piano solo.
Ludwig continues fully enjoying and absorbed in the music. The
Maestro stops them. He looks at Ludwig.

                    THE MAESTRO
          So we have heard you both. Thank you.

                    LUDWIG
          But I didn't play my own pieces.

                    THE MAESTRO
          Well - I heard enough for now.

Ludwig and Tiffany look pretty worried and disappointed. They
start moving back to their seats among the other students.
The Maestro smiles friendly but professionally to Ludwig and
Tiffany. He turns to the lady and whispers something to her.
She speaks to the children.

                    THE WOMAN
          The Maestro has made his decision.
          Tiffany and Ludwig have been selected.

Ludwig, standing next to Tiffany, smiles proud and happy while
Tiffany is stunned by surprise. The woman looks directly at
Ludwig and Tiffany.

                    THE WOMAN
          You both qualify for a full, free year
          at the school and you both will have
          two lessons with the Maestro weekly. The
          enrollment office will take care of you
          immediately.

The woman turns to the rest of the children and addresses
them in a formal tone.

                    THE WOMAN
          Thanks you for your participation!
          For those of you that were not selected
          today, you may apply again next year; at
          equal terms with other applicants.

                                        BACK TO PRESENT

INT. EUROPE - HOUSE LUDWIG - EVENING - PRESENT TIME

Ludwig smiles as he puts the photo on the shelf besides him.
He closes his eyes and falls asleep.

                              DREAM TRANSITIONS BACK IN TIME

INT. EUROPE - MANSION - DINING ROOM - DAY - BACK IN TIME

The teenage Ludwig and Tiffany sit side by side by the dining
table with Tiffany's parents. The parents sit opposite Ludwig
and Tiffany. The father, Hoon-kwan, is, already at his young
age, a serious, stout, dictatorial, highly influential, and
slightly overweight Asian businessman. The mother, Myung-hee,
in her young age, is a gentle, beautiful Asian woman with a
soft spoken, extremely kind appearance; and behaviors a little
beyond what is appropriate for an extraordinary wealthy Asian
couple, but acceptable in the European setting. Two Asian
servants formally dressed in black and white stand behind the

parents and serve the meal. Hoon-kwan is slightly reserved and moody and talks only little while he takes food from the tray held by the servants, extremely respectful to the point of fear. Myung-hee looks happily at Ludwig and Tiffany while she clearly makes every effort to create a positive atmosphere. She smiles to Ludwig and Tiffany from a truly loving and caring heart. Mozart's double sonata gently fills the space. As the meal is over, tiffany and Ludwig leave the room. From the windows one sees Tiffany and Ludwig walking through the blooming garden of the mansion. Myung-hee follows them smiling with her eyes. Hoon-kwan briefly looks after them with dismay and leaves the room.

     MUSIC CARRIES OVER AND THE SCENE FADES TO THE CONSERVATORY
                                         GARDEN

EXT. CONSERVATORY - GARDEN - DAY

Ludwig (17) is sitting on the lawn in the conservatory garden on a sunny and clear, early summer day. He reads a message from Tiffany on his phone. The music instantly changes to a Requiem Choir which breaks strongly and totally overwhelmingly into the scenery. Ludwig rises.

                             LUDWIG
            (shouts)
     No!

                                   MUSIC CARRIES OVER

EXT. EUROPE - STREETS OF THE CITY - DAY

Ludwig runs frightened down the beautiful streets and alleys of the town, running and running, the whole way, to total exhaustion, and almost collapsing as he arrives in front of Tiffany's house.

                         MUSIC CONTINUES TO CARRY OVER

EXT. EUROPE - MANSION - GARDEN - DAY

Ludwig reaches the tall, black metal gate to Tiffany's mansion. He rings the bell. The gate opens. He runs up to the large, extremely well kept, prestigious and rich mansion. He runs up the broad staircase to the main entrance. He rings

the bell. Gyung-hee (39), the servant of Tiffany's mother,
opens the door. She recognizes Ludwig. As she apparently have
expected Ludwig, she instantly points to the garden while she
speaks with compassion.

                    MYUNG-HEE
          She is in garden.

Ludwig runs down the large garden. Tiffany sits in a corner of
the wonderful, blooming garden in a light, white, long summer
dress. The long dress reaches to the ground. Her long black
hair lies over her shoulders and covers her face. She turns
around as Ludwig approaches and holds her hair away from her
face. Her eyes meets Ludwig's. He runs to her and falls on his
knees in front of her and holds his arms around her legs. He
looks up at her. The music continues in the background.

                    LUDWIG
          Don't leave. Please. Please don't leave.

                    TIFFANY
          It's father - there is nothing I can do.

Tiffany pauses while she gathers courage to continue. She
holds her hands around Ludwig's head and leans forward placing
her head just above his. Her long black hair covers them both.
She speaks softly without eye contact.

                    TIFFANY
          We can belong together anyway - and one
          day it will happen. Please - I promise.

Tiffany leans her head back and moves her hair back with both
hands as she straightens her back. Ludwig looks up at her. He
takes her hands briefly and firmly, then holds his arms around
her legs and finally puts his head on her lap as the obvious
answer. Tiffany again bends her body over his. She sees a
grafting knife by one of the fruit trees. She rises and walks
over to pick it up. She walks back and again sits face to face
with Ludwig. Courageous she shows Ludwig the knife.

                    TIFFANY
          Let us mix blood - then we will always
          belong to each other - always.

The music intensifies and totally fills the space. Tiffany cuts a blood vessel pretty deep at her left arm open with no sign of pain. Blood is pouring out. She cuts Ludwig, also deep. He shows pain. They watch the blood pouring out of their arms. Ludwig holds his hands as a bowl for the blood. He holds the blood while Tiffany gathers his blood in her hands. They mix the blood in the hands and over the cuts. Tiffany covers Ludwig face with the mixed blood from her hands. Ludwig covers Tiffany's face with the blood from his hands. They smile happy and devoted in tranquility.

Ludwig's view of Tiffany becomes blurred. The blood runs down Tiffany's neck and colors her white dress deep red. The blood continues to flow. She rises and stands right up. Her black hair covers her face completely. The blood flowing gradually colors Tiffany's dress totally red. The blood continues and flows along her neck. She spreads her arms and opens her palms against Ludwig. She takes her bloody hands to her face and moves her hair. As her face becomes visible, she opens her mouth as she tries to speak. Blood starts flowing from the sides of her open mouth. She stands as a bleeding black, red and white sculpture. She spreads and lifts her arms and lifts her head to view the sky above her.

BACK TO PRESENT TIME

INT. EUROPE - HOUSE LUDWIG - EVENING - PRESENT TIME

Ludwig wakes with a scream and sits bewildered in the bed. Realizing he had been dreaming he again lies down. He watches the small scar on his wrist and puts his hand gently over it, as to protect the memory. He wipes his face to take the cold sweat away. He falls asleep again.

EXT. EUROPE - CHURCH LUDWIG - OUTSIDE - DAY

Ludwig stands in front of the entrance to the church and greets the guests for the funeral one by one as they enter. He recognizes all the local people. Many embrace him. A black limousine stops a little away from the church. Duilio steps out. He goes to the entrance wearing a big bucket of violet flowers. Ludwig greats him and shakes hand without knowing who he is.

DUILIO

>   (in Italian)
>   I condole. I am one of the many friends
>   of your mother.

>   LUDWIG
>   (in Italian)
>   You are most welcome.

Duilio enters the church. Ludwig continues to greet the
guests as they arrive. When most guests have arrived Ludwig
enters the church and takes seat at the front row. Leopold
is sitting next to him. A few more guests are still arriving
and take their seats back in the church. Finally, the pastor
arrives. He is wearing a black cassock; he greats Ludwig and
walks up to the coffin. He turns around and stands facing
the coffin and the communion with the crucifix behind him.
He bows his head. The organ starts playing a soft traditional
Bach hymn.

EXT. EUROPE - CHURCH LUDWIG - OUTSIDE - DAY

Ludwig stands next to the coffin as it is loaded into the
hearse. He watches the beautiful flowers on the coffin and
notices the large bucket of unusual violet flowers. All other
guests stand behind the car and watch as it starts driving
slowly down the mountainous road. As the car disappears Ludwig
turns around towards the guests.

>   LUDWIG
>   (in Italian)
>   The urn will be put to rest here at the
>   churchyard tomorrow. For now please join
>   me for a small serving.

Ludwig points to a small picturesque house about a hundred
meters from the church. They all walk to the house and enter.

INT. EUROPE - CHURCH LUDWIG - HOUSE - DAY

Inside the house, Ludwig and the pastor greet each guest
as they enter. A few women of the church offer the guests a
glass of wine from trays they carry around among the guests.
The local guests embrace Ludwig as they enter the house. The
guests gather in small group and chat friendly and quietly.

Leopold comes over to Ludwig. He drags his feet a bit. He shakes hands with Ludwig and smiles warmly. With his bent back Leopold has a little trouble looking Ludwig directly in the eyes. Ludwig reciprocates his warm smile.

                    LEOPOLD
               (in German)
          I have something for you.

Leopold takes small box from his pocket and gives it to Ludwig. Ludwig opens it and finds a small metal object wrapped in fine paper. He takes the paper of. It is the tuning fork.

                    LEOPOLD
          Do you remember it?

                    LUDWIG
          Sure - you let me listen to that the
          first time in your workshop and the
          sound just stayed with me forever. I
          always played in exactly that tune - any
          orchestra - always!

                    LEOPOLD
               (in a jokingly tone)
          Of course, I noticed that. Well, just in
          case. I like you to have it now. The tone
          of this will always keep you connected to
          the absolute.

They both laugh. Leopold embraces Ludwig. Ludwig, clearly very moved and really without words, looks at the tuning fork. He wraps it carefully in the paper, puts it in the box and puts the box in the pocket of his jacket. He looks around in the room. He watches Duilio in the background of the room. Duilio is in conversation with a local woman, GIULIA CESTI (AGE 55). She looks exited at Duilio who talks quietly. Duilio shakes hands with her, they embrace each other and Duilio quietly leaves the party. Ludwig watches through the window as Duilio enters his waiting car. Ludwig walks over to Giulia. She smiles to him and wholeheartedly embraces him.

                    GIULIA
               (in Italian)

My lovely Ludwig - so long I did not see
you. But somehow you were always here.

                    LUDWIG
          (in Italian)
I know Guli. I wish I was here much more.

                    GIULIA
I know. Your mother always told me.

                    LUDWIG
Who is this man you talked to. I never
saw him before.

                    GIULIA
He was here many, many years ago; before
your time. They were close somehow - just
as friends, well maybe a bit more, I am
not sure. I saw him a few times when he
was around. It was such a surprise to see
him again.
          (she pauses)
It was about the time when you were born.
But he sort of faded away and did not
show up here again - until today. Somehow
he helped your mother. I really do not
know more about him. Your mother didn't
want to talk about him. I asked her a few
times and .....

                    LUDWIG
          (interrupting)
And - when was that?

                    GUILIA
... It was before you were born, right
after your father disappeared.
          (she pauses)
It was a very difficult time for her -
being alone. But I think he helped her.
          (pause)
She actually traveled away for some time
and somebody must have helped her with
that. Anyway - nothing of this matters
any more now.

                          LUDWIG
        Don't worry Guli - I was just curious.
        Mother wanted it like that - so let it be
        like that. Still I wonder who told this
        man about the funeral today. Everybody
        living here knows, of course, but him?

                          GIULIA
        I don't know ...

                          LUDWIG
        Let's not worry. It is what it is - and
        it's all over now.

EXT. EUROPE - CHURCH LUDWIG - OUTSIDE - DAY

The guests from the funeral leave. Ludwig greets each of them
goodbye. As he is alone by the church and relieved by the
funeral being over he decides to walk down to the town.

        THE DOUBLE SONATA 2RD MOVEMENT SOFTLY FILLS SPACE AS LUDWIG IS
                SEEN WALKING DOWN THE STREET AND DIMINISHING

EXT. EUROPE - HOUSE LUDWIG - OUTSIDE - DAY

In the morning sun Ludwig locks the house and hides the large
key below a stone close by the entrance.

EXT. EUROPE - CHURCH LUDWIG - OUTSIDE - DAY

Ludwig goes to the graveyard and stands for a moment by the
grave where the urn had been placed. The driver stands waiting
with the car by the entry to the churchyard. Ludwig whispers
inaudibly a few words as a last goodbye, he looks up and
watches the landscape and the crisp clear air as to hold it
all in his mind. He turns and walks to the car.

INT. EUROPE - TOWN LUDWIG - CAR - DAY

Ludwig switches his phone on while driving. The car stops in
the town further down the valley in front of a small grocery
store. Ludwig steps out.

EXT. EUROPE - TOWN LUDWIG - DAY

Ludwig stands next to the car and dials Josephine. The call
goes through.

> LUDWIG
>
> It's me.

> JOSEPHINE
>
> (agitated voice on the
> phone)
> What on earth happened? I was worried
> to death! Have you forgotten about
> everything?

> LUDWIG
>
> Of course not, but.....

Josephine abruptly interrupts. Ludwig gets upset by Josephine's
lack of interest in even hearing what had happened.

> JOSEPHINE
>
> Look, you cannot just be out of contact
> or switch your phone off, or whatever you
> are doing. I need to know! Not just me as
> your - "your wife", also me as your manager.
> (she shouts)
> Don't you know what we have coming up?

While Josephine explodes in the phone Ludwig holds the phone
a good distance from his ear.

> LUDWIG
>
> Listen, I am on my way.

> JOSEPHINE
>
> (continues agitated)
> For Christ sake; the New York rehearsals
> are coming up. So much is at stake. You
> have to get there. Everything is in
> place, except you!

> LUDWIG
>
> I know. I will be there. I have not
> forgotten, of course. Just get me a flight
> today. I go directly to the airport - I

will even be a bit early over there then,
I believe - good for the jet-lag.

While talking Ludwig finds the small box. He puts it on the
roof of the car and takes the small handwritten note with
telephone numbers.

                    LUDWIG
          Just remind me. The telephone numbers in
          New York start with what digits?

                    JOSEPHINE
          They usually begin with 212.
          Anyhow. I will do the phone calls.
          Don't worry about that.

INT. NEW YORK - PENTHOUSE DUILIO - DAY - PRESENT TIME

The apartment is a huge penthouse, modernly designed and with
an unhindered view over Manhattan. All over there are piles
of books, papers, musical scores, and manuscripts. It is a bit
of an organized mess. A grand piano stands in the middle of
the biggest room. From the piano, there is a total, free view
over the skyline. The piano is covered with scores. Duilio
puts a CD with Mozart's symphony 29 in the CD player. The
sound fills the room softly. While listening he is dressing
up in a black, formal suit. He listens very attentively to the
music. He makes his tie while looking across the town. ALESSIA
(48) enters the room. She is a full blown "Italian Beauty"; her
large black hair is falling over and covering her shoulders.
She is mature, at her peak just an inch from starting to
decline as she becomes older. She is dressed in an Italian,
colorful nightgown. Alessia goes to the table in the kitchen
area. She puts a cartridge in the espresso machine, adds milk
to the milk foamer, toasts a croissant and sits down on a tall
chair by a high, narrow, modernly designed table. She leans
forward, puts her elbows on the tall table and watches Duilio.

                    ALESSIA
               (in Italian)
          So what's up today? You did not sleep much.

                    DUILIO
               (in Italian)

It is "board meeting day". We have to
decide on the Honorary Lecture for the
Annual Meeting. I hope to be elected -

                    ALESSIA
And?

                    DUILIO
- and I have a good story to tell - a
story that actually must be told.

Alessia plays with her croissant in her ambivalent feelings of
jealousy, love, and slight anger, as she feels less important
than Duilio's science.

                    ALESSIA
You better have a very good story to tell.

Duilio briefly pauses working on his tie.

                    DUILIO
My mind may often be elsewhere, but my
heart never is.

Alessia decides to stop complaining, smiles, walks over to
Duilio and helps him with his tie.

                    ALESSIA
When you change the world, please take
care that there is also espresso in the
New World and our bakery. And music,
please.

Alessia corrects Duilio's tie and adjust imperfections of his
dress. She lovingly puts her arms around his neck, leans back
to watch Duilio while still holding her arms around him and
finally moves forward for a not too warm goodbye kiss. Duilio
walks over to the small elevator that opens directly to the
apartment and exits. Alessia walks to the window and watches
the skyline. Her face is sad and slightly indifferent.

EXT. NEW YORK - SOCIETY OF SCIENCES - STREET - DAY

Duilio stands for a short moment in front of the high and
robust stone building of the Society of Sciences. He looks up
to the top, composes himself and enters the building.

INT. NEW YORK - SOCIETY OF SCIENCES - LOBBY

Duilio enters the large hallway. He goes to THE RECEPTIONIST
and hands her his coat. She smiles.

                    THE RECEPTIONIST
          Good morning Dr. They are all here
          already!

INT. NEW YORK - SOCIETY OF SCIENCES - MEETING ROOM - DAY

The Chairman of the Board and 10 board members of the
Society, all formally dressed in black suits, stand chatting
in small groups in the classic board room. Most board members
are more than 50 years old. The room is big for the small
number of people. There is a huge, polished table surrounded
by tall leather chairs, a large fireplace and portraits of
previous chairmen of the society and famous scientists on
the walls. The chairman, Dr. ALBERT RYESLING (AGE 60), an
impressive, large man with gray hair and a well cut beard,
immediately recognizes Duilio as he enters.

                    ALBERT RYESLING
          So Gentlemen, we are all here - please
          take your seats.

The board members go to their designated seats. Albert
Ryesling sits by the end of the table. Duilio sits on his
right side. As it gets quiet, the chairman opens a very slim
folder on the table in front of him. He raises his voice and
speaks quite officially, yet with a warm and pleasantly deep
tone.

                    ALBERT RYESLING
          Gentlemen - I cannot say how proud I am
          being here with you today. Our society has
          reached its hundred years anniversary and
          we are today one of the most respected
          societies of science in the world. All
          thanks to what our predecessors and you
          have done. Our voice is heard all over
          the world and our opinions in fundamental
          matters of science and related topics
          are highly respected. Our impact has

increased ever since the foundation
of our society and it has never been
stronger.

The Chairman pauses and smiles as he looks over the board
members. They all looks back at him.

> ALBERT RYESLING
> (in a more relaxed mode)
> Today we have a very simple agenda.
> "All" we have to do is to agree on
> the keynote lecture for our annual
> meeting - also our hundred years
> anniversary. Therefore this lecture will
> obviously have particular significance.
> So gentlemen can we please discuss the
> proposals.
> > (he pauses and looks down
> > the table to Mario)
> Mario, you have been leading our selection
> process. So, please...

The Chairman looks at MARIO (AGE 46) who is sitting by the
very opposite end of the table. He has a huge pile of papers
in front of him. He takes a small folder from the pile and
opens it while looking at the Chairman.

> MARIO
> Mr. Chairman, we reviewed more than a
> hundred proposals and, as discussed, our
> focus for selection for this particular
> meeting was on proposals with profound
> impact not only on the sciences, but also
> on society in general.

Mario talks with high intensity, commitment and dedication
while slightly suppressing his eagerness to avoid appearing
biased by enthusiasm.

> MARIO
> Many of the proposals we therefore spent
> quite some time on were related one way
> or the other to the interphase between
> the human mind and technological devices;
> and the resulting impact on the society.

Many proposals were about the expansion
of the human mind by directly interfacing
the brain with computers or other devises.
In this group of applications there
were examples such as implanting chips
in the brain matter in order to widen
the scope or capacity of the human mind
and, as another aspect, to treat in a
revolutionary new way diseases currently
outside the scope of treatments. So:
Influencing the human mind and curing
diseases were major topics of many
applications.
      (pauses)
Gentlemen, we found these proposals to
match our objectives; but as we dived
deeper into the applications we felt
that a talk on this type of subjects
due to the early stages of the evolution
of the involved sciences was at risk to
become too much like science fiction -
not realistic at this point in time. We
therefore put these proposals to the side
for now. I am sure you will agree Mr.
Chairman.

              ALBERT RYESLING
      (with friendly irony)
Please tell me what you decided to do
rather than what you decided not to do.

              MARIO
      (smiling and then
      continuing)
There was a proposal, Mr. Chairman, which
the team saw as having a huge impact not
only on the sciences but far beyond -
exactly as we decided should be the focus
for this lecture.
      (he pauses)
The title of this project, which we
recommend, is "The First Total Synthesis
of a Human being."

Mario pauses. There is no immediate response, but rather a
surprising, deep silence. Mario looks around the stone faced
assembly and decides he better continue fast.

                    MARIO
          The project describes the first full
          creation of a human being by chemical
          synthesis of the fundamental building
          blocks that define an individual. Mr.
          Chairman, that, in itself, obviously
          is a tremendous achievement. But the
          project goes far beyond. It describes the
          evolution of the individual, its thinking,
          its doings, its beliefs, its talents,
          and its capabilities. Yes Mr. Chairman,
          it addresses everything about being a
          human - what is it being a human being?
          And it touches on topics as creativity and
          arts.
                    (he pauses)
          Mr. Chairman, the team has been totally
          breath-taken. The project deals with
          everything about a "human" being a
          "human being", so to say. It comprises
          everything - we simply cannot think of a
          better proposal - so, Mr. Chairman, that
          is our recommendation.

Everybody sits astonished for a moment. Mario folds the paper
together.

                    ALBERT RYESLING
          My dear Mario, that almost sounds like
          "by the way, we synthesized a human being
          and here is what we really want to test
          now." How, Mario, can this tremendous
          advance have been made out of our sight.
          And, if I may ask, where are we in regard
          to the legal matters on this?

                    MARIO
          We had an evaluation of the legal aspects
          of the project done, of course. And we
          can say that due to the details of its
          execution we see no unlawfulness. For

good reasons, by the way, there is not
much law directly related to this matter!

                    ALBERT RYESLING
                  (humorous irony)
Please, Mario, explain me again what
it is all about? This certainly sounds
like science fiction, perhaps even some
conspiracy setup. Imagine all the things
that can happen here!

Mario takes a quick look at the nervous Duilio.

                       MARIO
                 (in a humorous tone)
We agree! Imagine the story in the press:
"Some very smart scientists explore the
relationship between physical matter
and higher spirits, and the question
if creativity, faith, thinking, and
creation of art is purely manifested in
our chemical composition or if there
is something apart from that which
contributes to our identities and doings."
                  (he pauses and continues in
                   an even higher humorous tone
                   and body language)
So, here then is how it will continue
by the sensation seeking reporter Mr.
Chairman. Here is what they will ask
you: "Mr. Ryesling, there are indeed
divergent views on these matter among
various institutions in the world - deeply
divergent to put it mildly! Think of
the deep questions of religious nature.
Many of these are the origin of much
controversy and misery in the world -
wars, and what have you. And now you
tell me, "Mister Ryesling", that these
discussions are just rubbish - it's just
about chemistry - full stop!"
                  (Mario pauses)
This is the kind of discussion that this
project will certainly create - and the
sensations that the press can build are
numerous. We know, of course, Mr. Chairman.

Mario holds for a moment. He looks around at the stunned
assembly.

                    ALBERT RYESLING
          Well, my dear Mario. You know how much I
          respect you and everyone in this room.
          Tell me - what are the downsides here.

                    MARIO
          Only few to think about: First of all,
          this proposal is from one of the board
          members and it is based on his work and
          there is a lack of publications. But we
          understand that all will be made public
          in connection with the lecture.
                    (he pauses)
          But, before we continue, could I please
          ask the other members of the sub-team
          to raise their hands and confirm their
          support for the recommendation.

Mario pauses. All five team members around the table raise
their hands. Mario looks at Duilio.

                    DUILIO
          Thank you, gentlemen.

The chairman turns towards Duilio.

                    ALBERT RYESLING
          I knew it was you. I knew you were
          holding something back. You have had
          this enormous project going - and so few
          publications.

                    DUILIO
          Well, with all respect, I have published
          the synthesis and generation of simple
          forms of life. But this project was to
          check if all that goes with life as a
          human being can also be generated by
          means of chemical synthesis - feelings,
          talents, faith, ability to deliver
          in the sphere of the arts - "divine
          inspiration", what is that? Is it real?

So, I first generated the human being and
then I let the person live and breathe
all the aspects of being human. Early
disclosure would of course ruin the
experiment. But now -
          (he pauses briefly)
- now Mr. Chairman, I am ready: I have
the person, and I have the answers to all
the questions; and I will show it all if
you give me the chance.

Albert Ryesling, looks a bit suspicious at Duilio, yet full of
admiration.

                    ALBERT RYESLING
          It's is hard to believe.

                    DUILIO
          But Mr. Chairman. Every word is true.

                    ALBERT RYESLING
          So, you have the person? You will actually
          bring the person?

                    DUILIO
          Yes, Mr. Chairman, that's the plan.

                    THE CHAIRMAN
          And does this person know that?

                    DUILIO
          I assure you that I will sort that out
          before the lecture. Actually within the
          next days. I have organized, so to say,
          that I will see him. As you can imagine I
          know everything about him - well, and how
          to influence him.

                    ALBERT RYESLING
          But Duilio, if we decide to move forward
          with this lecture we have to publish the
          title for the press now. So you have to be
          absolutely sure.

                    DUILIO

> I understand - and I am - I will get the
> consent. As I said, I know him very, very
> well as you can imagine. The lecture Mr.
> Chairman, if I may say so, may well turn
> the world upside down. The impact we are
> looking for is certainly there.

The Chairman looks at the board members for comments and
speaks formally as he is about to concluded the discussion and
close the meeting.

                    ALBERT RYESLING
> So, the proposal on the table is to move
> forward while accepting some risks?

                    DUILIO
> Yes Mr. Chairman, that's my proposal...

                    MARIO
> ... and my recommendation.

The Chairman pauses. He looks at the team and the other
members of the board.

                    ALBERT RYESLING
> And the team - does the team support this
> recommendation?

They all again raise their hands. The Chairman looks at the
board members and addresses them all.

                    ALBERT RYESLING
> Please raise your hands if you support
> the recommendation of the team. In this
> case we will only move forward by total
> agreement.

Around the table board members all raise their hands.

                    ALBERT RYESLING
> Thank you gentlemen. Please inform the
> press via the usual process for approval
> of press releases. The meeting is over.

They all rise. They shake hands. The Chairman goes to Mario
and embraces him. He then goes to Duilio and embraces him
firmly.

EXT. MONASTERY - ROAD TO - DAY

A large, black car with shaded windows is driving deep in
the mountains on narrow and dangerous small roads circling
up steep mountain sides. As the car gets higher up the
mountainsides, trees become scarce. The pavement changes from
asphalt to gravel. The road becomes extremely narrow with no
place for two cars to pass. The scenery is breathtaking. A
few huge, black, eagle-like birds are circulating up along the
rock face. Their screams break the silence. Further down the
road, an old cloister is seen in the distance, impressively
located on the very tip of a single, huge, steep mountain.
It is totally isolated on the small mountain. The walls of the
cloister merge directly with the steep cliff walls reaching
deep down. Below the cloister sulfur containing, hot springs
send acidic poisonous smokes up along the enormous cliffs.
The cloister is only connected to the rest of the mountains
by a small and fragile bridge. Giovanni watches the scenery
and the cloister in the distance with worries. They continue
the drive towards the cloister. They pass the fragile bridge.
The old stone buildings stretch high towards the sky in front
of them. Black birds circle over the court yard. The depth
at both sides of the fragile bridge is frightening. The car
continues into the small courtyard and stops in front of
the main building. The driver exits and opens the door for
Giovanni. He exits the car and stands a short moment in the
courtyard before he walks up to the building. The driver
follows, carrying a small briefcase and a small suitcase. They
enter the building.

INT. MONASTERY - HALLWAY - DAY

Giovanni enters the large hallway. His steps on the stone
floor echo. A broad staircase leads up to a narrow wooden
platform which connects two doors in the corners of the
hallway. A BUTLER (50) with a pale, thin stone-face and dressed
in a black gown appears from a door back in the hallway and
walks over to Giovanni. The driver hands Giovanni's luggage
to the butler. Giovanni nods briefly to the driver. The driver
exits the building. The butler turns to Giovanni.

                        THE BUTLER

(in Italian)
Welcome back. Your room is ready.

Giovanni and the butler walk up the staircase, the butler
in front. At the top of the staircase they turn right. The
butler opens the door and holds it open for Giovanni. They
enter a flat roof connecting the main building with a smaller
building.

EXT. MONASTERY - ROOF - DAY

Giovanni and the butler walk over the roof to the side
building. The roof is surrounded by high stone walls to three
sides. The view from the roof is breathtaking and frightening.
On the open side there is only a low stone wall behind which
a frightening cliff leads vertically deep down. The ground is
hidden in fog and fumes from sulfur containing water streams
at the base of the cliff. On the corners of the roof there are
man-sized statues of twisted human bodies. High up, behind the
stone walls, enormous cliff sides reach to the sky, with their
peaks hidden by clouds and only partially visible. Huge black
birds circulate in the upward air streams along the cliff
sides. Giovanni and the butler reach a robust wooden door to
the side building. The door is old, damaged and covered with
green fungi, but strong. The handle is large and rusty. It
squeaks as the butler opens it. They enter and walk down a
narrow spiral staircase to the guest room.

INT. MONASTERY - SIDE BUILDING - DAY

There is one large room in the side building with a white
wooden floor, white granite walls, a simple bed and a big
solid wooden table. Light shines into the room from small
windows high up in the walls and from a few narrow, vertical
windows in the wall facing the steep cliff. From the vertical
windows one sees the huge abyss reaching down to the steaming
sulfur containing springs in the endless depth below the
cloister. The butler puts Giovanni's luggage in the middle of
the room and faces Giovanni.

                    THE BUTLER
          Your meeting is in an hour. I will pick
          you up.

INT. MONASTERY - MEETING ROOM BIG - EARLY EVENING

Giovanni takes a few steps into the meeting room. In the wall in front of him are three very tall mosaic windows. The ceiling in the room is shaped like large domes held by slim columns throughout the entire room. Large candles all over the room provide light. The room is huge for the very few people present. A large fire burns in a fireplace in the left side of the room. Four tables are ordered two by two opposite each other with a large space between them. Together the tables form a square. By the table, Marchetto, now an elderly but forceful man, is seated, dressed in his precious red cassock. By the table opposite Marchetto are nine empty chairs. The middle chair is positioned with a slightly larger distance to the four chairs on each side. Behind Marchetto stands a pastor in a yellow cassock. Giovanni steps forward to the empty chair. He stands behind the chair. Marchetto signals Giovanni to sit down. The pastor puts a folder on the table in front of Marchetto and opens it. Marchetto sits with his hands resting on the table on each side of the open folder with the palms towards the table. They sit in silence.

Suddenly, Marchetto looks up and stares directly at Giovanni. Like a volcano erupting, Marchetto lifts his hands and hammers them violently against the table on each side of the folder. With enormous energy, he repeats this again and again while the anger and the color of his face reaches extreme hysteric proportions. Marchetto shouts towards Giovanni.

                    MARCHETTO
               (in Italian)
          You idiot - you extreme idiot - you
          unbelievable traitor.

Marchetto holds a copy of a US newspaper high up in his right hand exhibiting the headline: "The Total Synthesis of a Human Being" and the smaller subtitle "a true revolution in our understanding of mankind."

                    MARCHETTO
          Is it possible to be a bigger idiot and
          traitor than you? Is it possible to do
          more damage to all of us and to humanity
          and its faith?

Marchetto fumes in anger. Again, he hysterically again and again violently pounds the table. Finally he pauses. He looks Giovanni directly in the eyes as he speaks ironically.

                    MARCHETTO
          So, Brother. What do you have to say; if I
          may ask?

Giovanni places both hands at the table with the palms down and stretches his arms forward. He lets his hands slide forward as he leans closer to the table and gets closer to Marchetto. He speaks in a low, soothing and controlled voice.

                    GIOVANNI
               (in Italian)
          We all knew we were taking a risk.
               (he pauses briefly)
          We were here in this very room debating
          over and over again how the new sciences
          in biology would threaten our institution
          and its basis - our messages on creation
          of humans, our faith and the existence
          of God. And we decided - with a full
          majority - to get ahead of the game and
          prove the science wrong. We were all
          in it.
               (he pauses)
          And after all, Brother, in spite of what
          has happened, we may still simply argue
          that the program happened thanks to the
          thinking of a human being - by arguing
          that way we would not rock the boat.

Marchetto looks at and addresses Giovanni in the most sarcastic tone and manner thinkable. He is fuming.

                    MARCHETTO
          I know, dear Brother, that it is close to
          impossible to overestimate the stupidity
          of the general public. But Brother - the
          general public - the men and women on the
          street - they are not philosophers.
          They are totally uninterested in the kind
          of mental gymnastics or even acrobatics
          you just performed and which we endlessly
          do within our sacred institution. They

are simply stupid Brother. Yes - stupid.
But nobody Brother, nobody will be
stupid enough to swallow that argument
of yours. If anybody can shake a human
being together from a few chemicals here
and there and blend the creation at his
discretion, if I understand correctly what
you have been organizing, then nobody - I
say nobody
          (screaming)
- nobody buys any of our fundamentals.
That's the simple fact. How on earth can
you be so foolish dear Brother to even
suggest this argument?
          (he pauses and continues in
          and ironical, yet calmer
          tone)
You let this experiment continue and
continue in spite of the fact that you
must have known about the progress.
And you continued to endlessly pour our
funds into this story - not only in the
technical parts, but also - for reasons I
never really understood - in promotional
activities, concerts, contracts with
orchestras and what have you. And you
talked us into paying huge up-front money
to your agent, if I may use that word, to
make it all happen.

Marchetto again pounds the table as he speaks.

                    MARCHETTO
Again, again, again and again you spend
huge financial resources on this professor
and this "thing" he created. For years and
years and years you continued to convince
us that this project had to be carried
just a little bit further in order to
provide the definitive data we would need.

Marchetto holds the paper up again. He trembles as he puts the
paper down on the table. He rises and stands with his hands
on the table.

                    MARCHETTO

> (almost screaming)
> You - must - have - known. You must have
> had plenty of opportunity to intervene.
> You could have stopped it. But what did
> you do? You put us all, and all that is
> holy to us and to this world, in the worst
> possible situation. You failed. You failed
> miserably! You have become guilty of one
> of the biggest crimes against humanity.

Marchetto pauses for a moment. It is totally quiet in the
room. As he continues he whispers.

> MARCHETTO
> What are the forces inside you that make
> this happen. I feel something evil.

Marchetto pauses and looks scrutinizing at Giovanni.

> MARCHETTO
> What - is - it - Brother?
> (he screams)
> What - is -it?

Giovanni talks around the question, trying to calm Marchetto
down.

> GIOVANNI
> I assure you Brother that I have been
> serving the very best of our interests.
> As always, I have been seeking and
> praising the truth, also in this project,
> dear Brother.

Giovanni pauses. He looks down for a moment. He folds his
hands.

> GIOVANNI
> And I promise you that in a very short
> time everything from this project will
> have been destroyed. I promise.

As Giovanni speaks Marchetto has again risen and stands
behind his seat speaking angrily.

> MARCHETTO

> This lecture will not happen! It - will -
> not - happen. And I expect you to destroy
> everything from this project forever -
> the people that know and the data they
> have generated. EVERYTHING. Is that
> clear - otherwise tell me now!
> > (he pauses)
> You have my blessing - and I will give you
> my forgiveness for everything you have
> done and need to do. No exceptions!

Giovanni nods. Marchetto gives sign the meeting is over. The door behind Giovanni is being opened by the butler. He holds the door open for Giovanni to exit. Marchetto remains sitting by the table, pondering while cooling down.

EXT. NEW YORK - LABORATORY BUILDING - OUTSIDE - EVENING

A cab with Ludwig approaches a laboratory building. It drives slowly while the driver reads the street numbers. The buildings along the street stand as high, dark silhouettes. The street is wet and dark. There are only a few street lamps here and there with darkness between the few lamps. THE DRIVER (50) pulls off to the side of the building - a high, massive construction dominated by large glass surfaces.

INT. NEW YORK - CAB - EVENING

Ludwig takes a bundle of dollar notes from his pocket. His movements are slightly nervous.

> LUDWIG
> How much?

> THE DRIVER
> 15 Sir.
> > LUDWIG
> Here are 50 - can you wait?

> THE DRIVER
> OK, but not more than an hour.

Ludwig exits the cab.

EXT. NEW YORK - LABORATORY BUILDING - OUTSIDE - EVENING

Ludwig steps out of the cab and walks to the entrance of the
large building. He tries to look through the wide glass doors,
placing his head close to the glass and shielding for the
little outside light with his hand. The large reception area
is empty. It is dark inside. Ludwig steps back and looks up
at the large building. He pulls his light coat tighter around
himself. He nervously grasps his cell phone from his pocket.
He dials. The phone is being answered. Ludwig's voice is a bit
nervous, impatient, and slightly irritated.

                    DUILIO
               (voice on the phone)
          Hello...

                    LUDWIG
          I am here now - in front of the building.
          How do I get in?

                    DUILIO
               (voice on the phone)
          Just stay where you are. I will be with
          you in a sec.

Duilio hangs up. Ludwig steps back from the entrance of the
large building. He looks at the surroundings. No people are
around, except a few girls standing by the entrance to a
small park a little further down the street. One of the girls
takes notice of Ludwig and walks over to him. Ludwig moves
away from the girl as she gets closer. The taxi driver has
fallen deeply asleep in the car. His head is leaning back as
he visibly snores loudly.

Duilio appears from a side entrance to the building and
approaches Ludwig from behind without Ludwig noticing.
The girl walks back across the street as she sees Duilio
approaching. Duilio is casually and comfortably dressed. He
gets close to Ludwig before he speaks.

                    DUILIO
          I am here!

Ludwig, frightened for a moment turns abruptly around. He
recognizes Duilio from the funeral. He is extremely surprised,
stunned.

                         LUDWIG
          It's you?

Duilio smiles friendly and charmingly.

                         DUILIO
          Yes, it's me.

Duilio goes close to Ludwig and places his right hand on
Ludwig's shoulder and then the other hand on the other
shoulder. He stands right in front of Ludwig and looks him
straight in the eyes. His smile is warm; his eyes are shining
in joy. Ludwig is highly uncomfortable with the physical
contact.

                         DUILIO
          Yes, my son, it is me.

Duilio takes his arms down from Ludwig's shoulders. He goes to
the side of Ludwig. He puts his arm around Ludwig's shoulders
and holds him firmly for a moment while they start walking to
a side entrance, side by side.

                         DUILIO
          Good you came. I knew you would.
          Come this way.

Duilio and Ludwig start walking.

EXT. NEW YORK - LABORATORY BUILDING - SIDE ENTRANCE - EVENING

Duilio guides Ludwig down the side street along the building.
They reach the side entrance. Duilio takes his security card
and opens the door. They enter the building.

INT. NEW YORK - LABORATORY BUILDING - FOYER - EVENING

The small foyer is well illuminated from several lamps in the
ceiling. Security glass doors lead further into the building.
Duilio leads Ludwig to one of the doors equipped with eye
detectors and fingerprint readers.

                         DUILIO
          Please, put your fingers here.

Duilio holds and leads Ludwig's hand to the small glass plate for fingerprint reads.

                    DUILIO
          Now look here, please.

Duilio points at a small eye detector right in front of Ludwig's face.

                    DUILIO
          Just look straight into it.

The security door opens. Ludwig walks in. Duilio repeats the procedure and follows Ludwig.

INT. NEW YORK - LABORATORY BUILDING - OFFICE - EVENING

Duilio's office is very large. All walls to the outside are of glass only. One sees the river and the distant lights from the town. A huge table is covered with piles of papers, scientific journals, books and scientific reprints. All walls in the office to the inside of the building are covered with bookshelves. Two big computer screens on the writing desk are active. There are two large armchairs in the office corner with a small table in between. The room is quiet and has a bit cold atmosphere. On the writing desk there is a huge bouquets of violet flowers. Ludwig stands lost for a moment in the middle of the office watching the view, the bookshelves, the flowers, and the papers. He is very alert. He notices a photograph on the wall over the two big armchairs. The light around the armchairs is warmer than in the rest of the office thanks to two lamps with a soft light over the small table between the chairs. Ludwig moves close to the photograph and watches it carefully. The picture, black and white, is from the village of his childhood. It shows his house. Ludwig's mother, happily smiling, stands in front of the house. She is nicely dressed, young and very good looking. Duilio notices Ludwig's surprise as he recognizes his mother on the picture. Another photograph depicts himself on the cover photo of the CD with his live recording at the Carnegie Hall. Ludwig is stunned.

                    DUILIO
          Yes my Son, it is indeed your mother.
          And the other picture you remember, of
          course.
              (he pauses)

                    Sit down please - make yourself
                    comfortable.

Duilio points to one of the large and comfortable armchairs.
He goes to a shelf on the wall between the chairs under the
photograph.

                         DUILIO
                    Coffee?

Ludwig nods. Duilio fills two big mugs with coffee. He adds
hot milk to one of the mugs and hands the steaming, hot coffee
to Ludwig. Ludwig takes the mug, holds it under his nose and
enjoys the strong and warm flavor. Duilio takes seat in the
other chair. They sit in silence for a short moment.

                         LUDWIG
                    How did you know how I like my coffee? -
                    you didn't ask.

Duilio smiles.

                         DUILIO
                    Well, you will see - I just know.

Ludwig moves a little up in his chair and sits on the edge. He
holds his coffee with both hands and looks straight at Duilio.
He asks quietly and open minded.

                         LUDWIG
                    So how did you know my mother? She
                    never told me anything about you until
                    she died - well, she just gave me your
                    contact information. And then you ask
                    me to pass by urgently - why all this
                    secrecy and urgency? What's going on?

                         DUILIO
                    Your mother did me a big favor - I will
                    show you.
                         (he pauses)
                    Let's go to the lab for a moment.
                    You can take your coffee with you.
                    I'll show you something.

Duilio and Ludwig rise and exit the office.

INT. NEW YORK - LABORATORY BUILDING - LABORATORY

The laboratory is huge, like a large factory hall sounding
with a smooth buzzing from the many synthesis machines,
chromatographs and computers in what seems endlessly long
rows. Ludwig and Duilio reach a small resting area. There are
cabinets by the wall full of bottles with chemicals. Duilio
takes four bottles out of the cabinet. He places them on a
small table with a few chairs around. He sits down and puts
the four bottles in front of him. Ludwig sits down in the
chair opposite.

                    DUILIO
          So, this is how I made you! What all
          these machines are doing is "simply" to
          take a little from one of these glasses,
          then a little from another or the same
          again, then another, and another. And so
          on for a very, very long time and at a
          very, very, very high speed.

Duilio raises his hand and points out over the immense
laboratory space. For a short moment he looks proud. Ludwig
looks around at the many machines with little enthusiasm.

                    DUILIO
          As you can see, we are doing this on
          a huge scale. All of these machines
          operate on a high and unprecedented
          speed. And then, thanks to that, we get a
          "synthesized powder" which is the essence
          of you. This powder defines you as an
          individual!

Duilio pauses. He looks Ludwig in the eyes. Ludwig looks
puzzled, and a little frightened. Duilio takes the bottles one
by one, lifts them and places them firmly on the table in a
nice row. He picks additional bottles from the cabinets and
adds them to the row, one by one. The two men sit in silence
for a while. Ludwig is looking at the long row of bottles.
Finally he pulls himself together.

          So I am made from powder? Is that what
          you say?

He pauses. Nobody speaks.

> LUDWIG
> I don't believe a word of this. And why
> do you pull my mother into this? - I am
> afraid you are wasting my time?

Duilio smiles to Ludwig.

> DUILIO
> Well, your mother knew that I was your
> father, although in a highly unusual way.

> LUDWIG
> But why?

> DUILIO
> Well, it is very simple, son. We wanted to
> find out if one can make a human being in
> this way.
>> (he pauses)
> It is long ago now - there were discussion
> about generating life.
> Could one make a human being in machines
> like these -
>> (he again points to the
>> machinery)
> - and would it be a true human being?
> That was the question. And well, I
> decided to check it out.
> That's what science is all about - we test
> it. And I tell you - for now I am the
> only person that can actually do that.

Duilio again raises his hands and again points at all the
machinery while he talks.

> DUILIO
> Now we know the answer - thanks to you!
> You have turned the world upside down -
> like in your arts!

Duilio smiles proudly. Ludwig, still leaning over the table,
watches the bottles. Then he looks up at Duilio, then over at
the lab space, then again at the bottles. Finally, he looks
Duilio in the eyes, obviously dismayed and irritated.

I am sorry. I cannot accept this. You are
telling me that I am not myself, so to
say. No thanks - I cannot accept how you
are treating me - no way!

              DUILIO
Let's go back to the office.

They rise and start walking. Duilio puts his arm around
Ludwig's shoulder to comfort him. Ludwig appears highly
uncomfortable with the touch.

INT. NEW YORK - LABORATORY BUILDING - OFFICE - EVENING

Duilio and Ludwig enter the office and take seat by the coffee
table. Ludwig sits at the edge of his chair and looks at
Duilio over his now cold coffee. He notices the violet flowers
on the table. Duilio points to two other photographs on the
wall next to the photo of Ludwig's house.

              DUILIO
That's where I found some of the essence
of you - some of it.

Ludwig rises and goes to the wall. He watches the pictures
carefully. He turns around towards Duilio.

              LUDWIG
But this is some kind of a cemetery.

              DUILIO
It is not any cemetery.

Ludwig looks carefully at the pictures again. Then he turns
around towards Duilio.

              LUDWIG
One of the places has a very nice
tombstone, the other has nothing.

He suddenly remembers and looks delighted.

              LUDWIG
This is Mozart's cemetery?

                    DUILIO
          Right - that where I found some of you -
          well extremely little I should say.

                    LUDWIG
          Found - some of - me?

Ludwig considers to leave, but sits down in the large chair.
He leans back and waits for an answer. Duilio moves quite
close to the table and leans forward over the table.

                    DUILIO
          It certainly wasn't easy - part of remains
          here and parts of remains there, a
          little from children and a little from
          grandchildren, grand-grandchildren and
          what have you. Then a lot of computer
          modeling. Everybody, even scientists, will
          tell you it is impossible but, I tell you
          that at the end of the day I did it - I
          was able to put all these pieces of a
          gigantic puzzle together!

Duilio points to the pictures one after the other as he
speaks.

                    DUILIO
          And then we made you, just the same.

Ludwig laughs, but becomes serious really quickly.

                    LUDWIG
          Look, then I would be composing all
          the time. No way - you are out of your
          mind - how can you do this to me. I
          cannot accept it. What on earth are you
          up to?

                    DUILIO
          Well, one thing is having the same
          biological configuration as we call it.
          The other part of the story of course is
          your surroundings. You are Mozart - but
          in a different time and space. The arts
          of Mozart just happened with the right
          composition of ...

Ludwig stands up. He is upset and interrupts Duilio.

                    LUDWIG
          ... Stop. I am not just powder! I don't
          believe a word!

                    DUILIO
          My Son, I know it must be a surprise. But
          actually, what's wrong by being made of
          powder rather than from sperm? What makes
          you a better person if you are made in
          one way and not the other? And how would
          you even know the difference? You are
          doing what you are doing, seeing what you
          are seeing, hearing what you are hearing,
          loving what you are loving, feeling what
          you are feeling, and believing what you
          are believing. It's the same - same - same!

Ludwig articulates almost like conducting as he responds.

                    LUDWIG
          I just don't want to be part of your
          stupid game - period!

Ludwig pauses. He continues in a slightly lower voice.

                    LUDWIG
          I just want my life. I just want to do my
          music. I just want to enjoy.

                    DUILIO
          Sure my Son. And you will. But, just now,
          I actually need you. I need to show the
          world what I have done, and you are my
          proof of all the implications for humanity
          of what I have done.

Duilio rises.

                    DUILIO
          It means everything to me. You and me
          together: we will turn the world upside
          down! You are turning it upside down
          already thanks to your genius as a

musician. And now - now we make it even
bigger. We show what I have just told
you - and you turn the world upside down
again. It's fantastic.
          (he pauses)
It's all arranged already. We go
together - I talk and you are my proof!

Ludwig walks towards the door.

                    LUDWIG
Enough! You want to expose me as a
product of your machines?! Like in a Zoo.
You must be out of your mind. Have you
thought about me in your plan of fame?
What do you think will happen to my life,
to my work with musicians; well with
everything I do, if you show me just as a
robot? Forget it. This is madness!

Ludwig opens the door. He stands quiet for a moment.

                    DUILIO
Please come with me when I tell the story.
It makes you even greater.

                    LUDWIG
How on earth should that happen?
You do the exact opposite. You destroy me.
I forbid you to tell the story. You must
cancel. Forget about it. Cancel whatever
has been set up, or arranged as you say!

Ludwig closes the door firmly with a big bang, turns around,
runs through the corridor, finds the lift down and runs out
of the building to the side street.

EXT. NEW YORK - LABORATORY BUILDING - OUTSIDE - EVENING

Ludwig exits from to the street. The side street is dark and
empty. He runs to the main street and looks for the cab. The
cab is gone. He searches for his wallet in his inner pocket
and realizes he left it in the car. He looks around for other
cabs. The streets are all empty. He loses his senses, derails
and runs across the main street. He follows the street, runs

past the girls hanging around and continues into a small park that leads down to a river.

EXT. NEW YORK - PARK - NIGHT

Ludwig, confused, runs through the park and finds a bench close to the water. He sits down and hides his face in his hands. The Requiem (full choir) violently sounds in his mind. He looks up. The music continues with greater intensity. He looks across the river. The music continues. He shouts out over the water.

                    LUDWIG
          (in German)
     Stop. I don't want you.
          (he tries to wipe the music
          away)
     It is not me. I am not dying. I am real.
     It is not about me! - don't do this to me.
          (almost crying)
     Please don't do this to me.

Ludwig hides his face in his hands. The music finally fades out. A huge POLICE OFFICER 1 approaches Ludwig from behind.

                    POLICE OFFICER 1
     It is not allowed to be in the park at
     this time.

Ludwig looks up, surprised. His eyes meet the suspicious police officer.

                    LUDWIG
     Oh, I am sorry. I did not know.

Ludwig rises and starts walking. The police officer stands in his way.

                    POLICE OFFICER 1
     Can I see your ID please.

Ludwig again searches for his wallet.

                    LUDWIG
     I am sorry. I haven't got it here.
     It is in my luggage.

                    POLICE OFFICER
And your luggage?

                      LUDWIG
It's on the way to my hotel.

                   POLICE OFFICER 1
Which hotel.

                      LUDWIG
Well, I don't remember. I will remember
when I walk down-town.
          (trying to diffuse the
           situation)
For sure I will know when I get there.

Ludwig starts walking past the police officer. The absolutely
not amused officer again stands in his way.

                   POLICE OFFICER 1
I am sorry Sir, but I will have to ask
you to come to the station. Please turn
around so I can hand-cuff you.

                      LUDWIG
This is ridiculous. I am not doing that.

Ludwig starts running. He runs fast along the river. The
police officer runs after him. He catches Ludwig, pulls Ludwig
down on the pavement and handcuffs him. The police officer
pulls Ludwig up and pushes him from behind towards the police
car. He opens the car and pushes Ludwig to the back seat. He
calls over his phone.

                   POLICE OFFICER 1
I have an arrest - an unidentified
individual in the park trying to escape
arrest. I am coming to the station
immediately.

The police officer starts driving. The car disappears down the
road.

INT. NEW YORK - POLICE STATION - FRONT OFFICE - NIGHT

The small room at the police station is packed with arrests.
Junkies are sitting on the floor, alcoholics lie on the floor
sleeping, and prostitutes are standing insulted along the
walls with their arms crossed. A POLICE OFFICER 2 (49) sits by
a small table next to a door leading to the general officer's
office. Ludwig is pushed into the room by the police officer.
The officer releases the handcuffs. Ludwig looks bewildered and
frightened around. He addresses the police officer by the desk.

> LUDWIG
> This is a misunderstanding. I do not
> belong here. Can I talk to the supervisor
> immediately?

> POLICE OFFICER 2
> (barely looking at Ludwig)
> You can wait until it is your turn!

The door opens. Another police officer enters pushing a
handcuffed PROSTITUTE into the room. She sees Ludwig and
immediately stares unfriendly at him. As her handcuffs are
released, she walks towards Ludwig. She walks slowly, bent
forward, obviously drugged. She stops in front of Ludwig and
stares at him while holding her face low and turning it to
look up at Ludwig, upside down.

> PROSTITUTE
> I know this guy.

The prostitute turns and moves closer to Ludwig. He steps
back. She follows him closely She stares him in the eyes. She
talks slowly and loud.

> PROSTITUTE
> I know this man! There is something wrong
> with him - he is not real! I know he is
> not real.

Ludwig freezes by the remarks of the prostitute. The police
officer has followed the encounter with some amusement.

> POLICE OFFICER 2
> (slightly humorously)
> You know him. So maybe you can tell us
> his name?

The supervising officer, SAMUEL (40, middle height, fit, slim,
energetic and with fast, clear eyes, obviously of enormous
intelligence), enters the room. He sees Ludwig and immediately
realizes the situation. He directs Ludwig to enter the next
room. Ludwig walks swiftly past the prostitute. She follows
him to the door. She faces Samuel. She spreads her arms as to
embrace him. The second police officer in the meantime has
moved over behind her. He grasps her arm and firmly pulls her
away from Samuel and Ludwig. While she is being pulled away
the prostitute shouts.

                    PROSTITUTE
        I know him - there is something wrong
        with him. He is not real!

Samuel closes the door and enters the next room with Ludwig.

INT. NEW YORK - POLICE STATION - OFFICE - NIGHT

The room is in good order and well organized, but simple.
There is a light, fragile table in the middle of the room
with simple chairs around. The light is white and cold from a
single light tube in the ceiling. Samuel points to the chair
in front of the table for Ludwig to sit down. While sitting
opposite to Ludwig he reads the handwritten report of the
police officer. He turns to Ludwig.

                    SAMUEL
        So. You are in the park against the
        regulations in the middle of the night.
        You behave like a madman - shouting and
        gesturing. You even shout at the police
        officer. You attempt to run away. You have
        no ID. You tell a totally unconvincing
        story.

Samuel pauses, smiles and reaches out to Ludwig over the table
to shake hands.

                    SAMUEL
        My name is Samuel. So, who are you?

Ludwig in the meantime has composed himself. He is charming
and convincing as he responds.

LUDWIG
I am a conductor - Ludwig Mann is my
name - I am here for a performance and
a recording. In fact, I have rehearsals
coming up today; so, it is urgent that I
get to my hotel and get some rest.

SAMUEL
But you do not even know your hotel. And
nobody knows you - except perhaps the
lady outside!

Sergeant Samuel smiles as he believes Ludwig and understands
his troubles.

LUDWIG
Please, just call my manager. She knows
everything and can arrange somebody picks
me up. The number is in my cell phone.
Your man out there took it from me. Or
just let me show you. My whole travel plan
is there.

Samuel hands Ludwig the phone. He points to another door in
the room.

SAMUEL
This is your lucky day. I heard your
name before. Actually I know some of your
recordings.

Samuel again smiles. He signs the handwritten report and
pushes it over the table to Ludwig.

SAMUEL
But you have to sign the report here. You
can wait out there then.
The police officer there will help you.

Samuel watches the tired Ludwig and notices the time.

SAMUEL
Maybe we better get you to your hotel.

Samuel rises, opens the door to the next room and gives his
instructions.

SAMUEL
One of you, please drive him to his hotel.

Ludwig, relieved, signs the report. He rises and shakes hand
with Samuel.

LUDWIG
I thank you a lot. I will send you a
ticket for the concert - if I could have
your card, please.

Samuel hands his card to Ludwig. They shake hands as goodbye.

SAMUEL
It's much appreciated. And good luck. And
don't walk in the park at that time again!

Ludwig exits the office.

EXT. VIENNA - SUBURB - TOWN SQUARE

A cab drives up in front of the building next to the church.
Josephine steps out of the cab. She stands a short moment
by the cab and carefully looks around on the small square.
She addresses the TAXI DRIVER through the front window of
the car.

JOSEPHINE
(in German)
How much?

TAXI DRIVER
(in Austrian German)
50, Mrs.

Josephine hands the driver a large Euro-note through the window.

JOSEPHINE
(in German)
Can you please wait here. It won't be
long. I will pay for your time - also
some extra tips?

The driver nods. Josephine walks swiftly to the entrance of
the building and rings the bell. The door is opened slightly.

Pastor Graupner looks out. As he recognizes Josephine he opens the door just enough for Josephine to get in. Josephine enters the building.

INT. VIENNA - HOUSE GRAUPNER - EVENING

Pastor Graupner swiftly closes the door behind Josephine. They walk through the small corridor to the office of Pastor Graupner. He rapidly opens the door to the office, lets Josephine in first and follows swiftly.

INT. VIENNA - OFFICE GRAUPNER - DAY

Pastor Graupner closes the door behind them. The room is almost dark. He switches a small reading lamp by his desk on. He sits down and with his hand asks Josephine to sit on the chair on the other side of the desk. Pastor Graupner reaches down for a small safe next to his desk.

> PASTOR GRAUPNER
> (In Austrian German)
> This was not easy. But I can assure you I
> got everything in perfect order.

Pastor Graupner dials a code and opens the safe. He takes two envelopes out of the safe and puts them on the desk. Josephine opens her handbag and takes two thick envelopes. She puts one of the envelopes on the table close to herself. Pastor Graupner hands one of his envelopes to Josephine.

> PASTOR GRAUPNER
> This one is yours. The name and
> everything is exactly as you asked for. I
> could match the birth date, the parents,
> and the nationality. Both parents, as
> you requested, have died. There are no
> brothers and sisters - all databases you
> can think of have been updated. The funds
> you provided were sufficient - although
> just barely I should say.

Pastor Graupner looks at Josephine for some recognition. Josephine, uninterested in Pastor Graupner's troubles, smiles briefly and swiftly focuses on the envelope from him. She examines the contents while she pushes her envelope on the table over to Pastor Graupner. He briefly counts the huge pile of large bank notes. Josephine looks at Pastor Graupner as to ensure his satisfaction.

                    JOSEPHINE
                (in German)
        It's fifty thousand - in as small notes as
        reasonably practical.

Pastor Graupner rapidly puts the envelope close to himself at the desk. He takes the other envelope and puts it on the desk in front of Josephine. He is slightly smarmy as he speaks.

                  PASTOR GRAUPNER
        This one too is exactly as you instructed.
        It was quite a bit more tricky to make,
        I would like to say. But everything is
        exactly as you asked for.

                    JOSEPHINE
        I expected that and I do recognize your
        extra efforts. I certainly do, Pastor. You
        have always been good to me.

Josephine takes the other envelope. It is significantly thicker than the first. She puts the envelope on the table while she still holds it with both hands. Pastor Graupner puts his hand on his envelope on the table.

                    JOSEPHINE
        It is a hundred thousand. This should
        certainly cover for all your troubles -
        and your discretion.

                  PASTOR GRAUPNER
        It certainly will. I do appreciate your
        confidence.

Josephine pushes her envelope to Pastor Graupner. He takes it with both hands. Josephine takes his envelope. The envelope is unsealed. She reads the papers in the envelope without taking them out. She again reads the documents in the first envelope. Pastor Graupner briefly counts the notes in the envelope without taking them out.

                    JOSEPHINE

Well, that should be it then.

They both rise. Pastor Graupner opens the door for Josephine. They exit the office.

INT. VIENNA - HOUSE GRAUPNER - EVENING

Pastor Graupner closes the door to the office behind them. They walk through the narrow corridor. Pastor Graupner opens the main door for Josephine half way. Josephine briefly stands in front of him. They shake hands.

                    PASTOR GRAUPNER
          God bless you Josephine and good luck.

Josephine exits the building.

EXT. VIENNA - SUBURB - TOWN SQUARE - EVENING

Josephine walks out of the half open door to the square. Pastor Graupner swiftly closes the door as to avoid being seen. Josephine walks to the waiting taxi. She steps in. The taxi immediately drives away.

INT. VIENNA - HOUSE GRAUPNER - EVENING

Pastor Graupner walks back through the narrow corridor. He continues through the corridor past the entrance to his office. At the end of the corridor he carefully opens a dark wooden door to the church chapel. He exits the corridor.

INT. CHURCH - PASTOR GRAUPNER - EVENING

Pastor Graupner enters the church chapel and walks up towards the altar. He kneels down in front of the altar and prays. He looks up at the altar. He makes a cross over his chest. He bows his head and again prays with his eyes closed. The chapel becomes dark while he continues to kneel in front of the altar. The chapel becomes dark in the night. Pastor Graupner still kneels and prays.

EXT. EUROPE - CATHEDRAL - OUTSIDE - NIGHT

Josephine stands in the dark night at a cobblestone covered
square with a huge cathedral behind her. The scattered lamps
around on the square provide an insufficient light in the
humid, foggy darkness. The little light from the scarce
lamps is absorbed by drops of fog and form halos around
the lamps. The square is almost empty. Josephine looks with
disgust at the huge cathedral and its large towers which
reach towards heaven but fade in the low-lying fog. She walks
determined to a narrow alley and walks down the alley on its
steep and slippery stones. Her steps are echoing from the
cobblestones. Josephine is dressed as a light living girl in
black, provocative, close fitting trousers, black high heeled
shoes and a black, tight fitting and low necked blouse. She
wears a small, black handbag over her shoulder and matches
the many girls hanging around and waiting for customers; yet
she clearly surpasses the street girls with her elegance,
determination, sensuality, body shape and beauty. A few poorly
dressed men are scouting around between the girls. Here and
there men are talking to the girls and disappear with the
girls into the houses. Josephine stops in front of a tavern.
She pushes the door up with her shoulder and enters.

INT. EUROPE - TAVERN - EVENING

Most tables in the poorly illuminated room are empty. A single
couple sits by a table drinking beer. At the bar, a huge, fat,
vulgar and disgusting WOMAN BARTENDER (50) is serving a few
customers. Some girls are hanging around in the bar. Most of
the girls smoke cigarettes and blow the smoke over the bar.
The dense smoke limits the visibility in the room. Josephine
goes to the bar. She takes seat on one of the high chairs and
sits with crossed legs pointing away from the bar as she leans
her side to the bar desk. She puts her elbow on the bar desk
and lights a cigarette. The huge woman comes to Josephine.

                    WOMAN BARTENDER
               (in German)
          As usual?

                    JOSEPHINE
               (in German)
          As usual.

The woman pours a large glass of Campari for Josephine. She adds an ice cube a bit carelessly making part of the Campari splash over the edge of the glass and onto the bar table.

                    WOMAN BARTENDER
          15!

Josephine pulls a large bank note out of her tight sitting pocket. She flattens it on the bar desk and pushes it over to the woman.

                    JOSEPHINE
          Keep the change - and tell him I am here.

The woman steps back from Josephine, presses a bottom below the bar and walks away. She disappears through a back door. Josephine continues smoking the cigarette. She blows the smoke up in the air with a vulgar expression while she is carried away in the moment. A man CUSTOMER rises from a table in the back of the room and walks up to Josephine. She blows further smoke up in the air as the customer takes seat right next to her. He whispers. Josephine talks in a rough tone.

                    THE CUSTOMER
               (in German)
          So lady - you have your room around here?

                    JOSEPHINE
               (in German)
          Sure, but not for now - I have business.

The woman comes back behind the bar. She waves Josephine to come. Josephine extinguishes the cigarette on an ash tray and empties her Campari in one long, large sip. She follows the woman to the back door and exits.

INT. EUROPE - TAVERN - OFFICE PETER - EVENING

Josephine enters the back office. PETER (60), a tough looking, elderly gang leader with a wrinkled and tried face, sits behind a rough desk. His thin body reflects years of life as a brutal pimp. His meticulous moves and order on his desk reflects his position as the leading expert in preparing and selling fake documents. He speaks with a high trebled voice, always with a subtle tone. There are two huge bodyguards standing behind Peter, both tattooed all over their muscular arms. A large dog lies on the floor next to Peter. With a gesture with his hand he asks Josephine to take a seat. She sits down in the chair in front of Peter in a vulgar posture. Her legs are crossed. She holds her handbag close to her body. Her face has a rough vulgar appearance thanks to her heavy, exaggerated cosmetics and does not suggest the slightest fear in the violent and frightening environment. She lights a cigarette and blows the smoke up in the air.

> PETER
> > (in German with Eastern
> > dialect)
> So my "Belle de Nuit" - have you got the
> goodies for me?

> JOSEPHINE
> > (in German)
> I certainly have..
> > (she pauses, exposes
> > herself and smiles to raise
> > expectations)
> - and as you see, everything as agreed!

Peter leans back and laughs. With his hand he reaches out to one of the bodyguards without turning around. The bodyguard hands him two envelopes. Josephine opens her handbag and takes a thick envelope out. Peter hands the two envelopes to Josephine while she gives him the thick envelope. Peter hands Josephine's envelope to one of the bodyguards who starts counting the money. Josephine briefly looks into the envelopes. She takes the passports out of the envelopes and studies them carefully. She puts the passports back and in her handbag. The bodyguard nods as Peter looks back at him by leaning his head backwards and not turning his body around. Peter addresses Josephine while watching her with great desire and appetite.

> PETER
> They are the best I ever made. You and
> your friend will not get in trouble
> with these masterpieces. We have better
> technologies than the authorities.
> > (he laughs and pauses)
> For your benefit "Belle" I even checked
> all the systems - you know, all the
> databases; even those of the police.

> Everything is right - whoever created
> these names for you did a very good job.
> It is all so consistent that I almost
> started to believe it.

Peter laughs and appears very satisfied as his bodyguard puts
Josephine's envelope in the safe and hands Peter the key.
Peter looks with great desire at Josephine as he addresses the
bodyguards.

                    PETER
          You can leave now.

The bodyguards leave. Peter and Josephine sit quiet while the
door is being closed and they hear the lock click. Josephine
leans back in her chair and spreads her legs. She leans
back while she continues smoking and inhales heavily. Peter
rises and goes over behind Josephine's chair. He kisses the
back-leaned Josephine deeply. She moves her arms backwards
and touches his body. Suddenly he pulls Josephine up of the
chair and pushes her in front of himself to a back door in
the office. He kick it open while holding Josephine very
firmly and pushes her onto the bed in the dimly red lit
room. Josephine protests and fights back in vain and finally
transitions to screams in satisfaction.

INT. EUROPE - TAVERN - BACK ROOM PETER - EVENING

Josephine is dressing, setting her hair and applying fresh
make-up. Peter is lying on the bed, half asleep. Josephine
touches her body while she dresses. She exhales, still in
satisfaction. She briefly looks at Peter and exits the back room.

EXT. EUROPE - CATHEDRAL - OUTSIDE - EVENING

Josephine walks up the narrow alley. At a dark spot she
stops and stands leaning her back against the brick wall and
breathes heavily. She looks up the alley and sees the young,
teenage Josephine walking towards her.

                                        BACK IN TIME

EXT. EUROPE - CATHEDRAL - OUTSIDE - EVENING - BACK IN TIME

The teenage Josephine walks down the dark, narrow alley under the few scarce street lamps. It is raining lightly. The cobblestones on the narrow alley are dirty, wet and slippery. As the teenage Josephine gets half way down the alley, a man dressed in a large black coat and wearing a black hat with a large brim hiding his face suddenly steps out from a doorway and grasps her arm very firmly. The man pulls the young Josephine into the building and pushes her up through a small staircase.

INT. EUROPE - ALLEY - APARTMENT - EVENING

The young Josephine and the man reach the door to an apartment. The man opens the door while he holds Josephine firmly in front of him. He pushes her into the flat.

INT. EUROPE - ALLEY - APARTMENT - EVENING

The man violently pulls half of Josephine's dress off to expose her vulgar dress and sensual body. He forces her on her back on a table and rapes her with all his clothes on. Josephine first pretends protest, but gradually her face reflects joy. She is extremely vulgar and sensual as she screams in delight. Finally she lies quietly, exhausted and relaxed on the table with closed eyes. She again spreads her legs inviting toward the man and smiles while he brings himself in the order and exits the apartment. Josephine quickly brings her clothes, hair and makeup in order and exits the apartment.

EXT. EUROPE - ALLEY - EVENING

The young Josephine exits the house to the dark alley. She walks slowly up the alley and disappears in the fog.

TRANSITION TO PRESENT

EXT. EUROPE - ALLEY - EVENING - PRESENT TIME

Josephine stands with her back against the house wall and watches the young Josephine disappear in the fog. She lights a cigarette, inhales and stands looking down on the ground.

                    JOSEPHINE
                  (whispering)
          Now I soon have him - totally.

Josephine again inhales and blows the smoke up in the air. The smoke gradually hides the picture.

INT. MANHATTAN HOTEL SUITE - DAY

Ludwig, wearing a bathrobe wakes up in the hotel suite by the sunlight pouring into the room. He looks confused at his watch and the alarm clock on the table next to the bed and tries to make sense of the time difference. He looks around as, for a moment, he has forgotten where he is. He sits up in the bed. He composes himself and calls the reception from the phone on the table next to the bed.

                    RECEPTIONIST
                  (voice on phone)
          Good morning Dr. Mann. Anything I can do
          for you?

                    LUDWIG
          Could you please bring me some breakfast.
          And tell me; any messages - or did
          anything arrive for me?

                    RECEPTIONIST
          Oh yes Dr. There is a small briefcase
          here. We bring everything with the
          breakfast.

                    LUDWIG
          Great - thanks a lot.

Ludwig hangs up and sits on the bedside, gradually recovering and waking up.

EXT. MANHATTAN - MIDTOWN - STREET - DAY

Tiffany walks in the streets of Manhattan. She enjoys the early, not too busy hours in the streets and the light of the early day. A heavy rock love song fills the space. She is upbeat, moves with the heavy rhythms, enjoys life, and is much

focused on the music. She gets a text. "Have you arrived?" She
stops walking and types her answer.

INT. MANHATTAN HOTEL SUITE - DAY

A servant enters Ludwig's suite pushing a trolley with the
breakfast. He serves the breakfast on the table next to a
writing desk.

                    THE SERVANT
          Enjoy Dr. This should be as you like it.

                    LUDWIG
          Great - thanks a lot. I have some tips
          for you later - well, no, wait a minute.

Ludwig opens the briefcase and feels on the envelopes inside.
He finds and opens an envelope with a large bundle of cash.
Ludwig takes a dollar note and gives it to the servant.

                    SERVANT
          Oh, thanks - much appreciated.

                    LUDWIG
          Pleasure.

The servant exits. Ludwig sits down by the desk. He pours a
tiny bit of sugar in the latte and stirs it gently. He opens
a big folder with the program for the rehearsals, recordings
and concerts of the week. As he briefly reads through program,
he becomes worried and unhappy. He drinks more coffee as
to recover. The 4th piano concert fills the room. His phone
signals arrival of a message. He reads the message. "I am
here." The music fades to a low level. Ludwig calls Tiffany's
number.

                    TIFFANY
               (voice on the phone)
          Hello - Ludwig?

                    LUDWIG
          Where are you? I need to talk to you.

                              TRANSITION DURING CALL

EXT. MANHATTAN - MIDTOWN - STREET - DAY

                    TIFFANY
          I am up here somewhere - close to the
          park - the major park I believe. I have
          been worried about you.

                    LUDWIG
               (voice on the phone)
          Where can we meet?

Tiffany looks around. She sees a Starbucks a little down the
street.

                    TIFFANY
          There is a Starbucks. I send you the
          street numbers.

                    LUDWIG
               (voice on the phone)
          I will be with you soon.

Tiffany hangs up. She walks to the closest crossing and reads
the street numbers. She texts on her phone and starts walking
towards the Starbucks.

INT. MANHATTAN - MIDTOWN - STARBUCKS - DAY

Tiffany enters the Starbucks, puts her handbag and a newspaper
on two comfortable chairs in the corner. She buys a big cup of
tea and takes seat comfortably in the chair while she listens
to the music in her mind (4th piano concert). As Ludwig enters,
the music stops. Already holding a "to-go" coffee from the hotel
in his hand, he kisses Tiffany discretely and sits down in the
chair opposite to her. His face is happy and worried at the same
time. Tiffany immediately notices his shaken state of mind.

                    TIFFANY
          Are you OK?

                    LUDWIG
          There is something wrong. I just don't
          think I can do these concerts - and the
          recording!

Tiffany is stunned and shocked. She leans forward and speaks in a low voice.

                    TIFFANY
          What - what's going on? - what's wrong
          with you?

Ludwig looks down at the table. He takes a sip of his coffee. Tiffany's glance is warm and loving over her big cup of tea. Ludwig looks up at her.

                    LUDWIG
          I am not real!

                    TIFFANY
          What? Hey. Look at me.

                    LUDWIG
          I have just been made - synthesized - I
          believe that's what it is called. I am not
          a human being. I have just been made up
          in some laboratory.

                    TIFFANY
          Come on. What bloody nonsense is that.
          What on earth has happened to you?

Tiffany grasps both of Ludwig's hands clearly determined to get in the driver's seat and control the situation. She puts her hands around Ludwig's head and kisses him passionately across the table. A young couple at a nearby table looks surprised and amused. Ludwig speaks staccato and extremely excited.

                    LUDWIG
          I met this person yesterday - a guy who
          was at mother's funeral - I had no idea
          who he was. But he has known mother
          many years ago - that's what he says -
          before I was born. Here he has some kind
          of a gigantic laboratory. I was there
          yesterday. It's like a factory. - He
          explained to me how he has made me: from
          powder or whatever it is.
                    (pauses)
          He called me his son. He knew everything
          about me.

Ludwig takes a couple of small paper bags with sugar, straws
and milk from the adjacent table and insanely shakes it all
together to demonstrate his creation. Tiffany and the people
around look baffled at his performance. He stops shaking,
puts his hands on the table with all the "ingredients" hidden
under the hands and finally lifts his hands like a magician
and points first at the powders, then at himself.

                    LUDWIG
          So! That's what I am: just a funny mixture
          of powders and liquids!

Ludwig leans forward over the table towards Tiffany and talks
in a low voice, almost whispering.

                    LUDWIG
          And now "daddy" wants to show me to the
          public! Because he is a genius! A big
          event! Because he has changed the world -
          he says.
                    (he pauses to let the
               message sink in)
          Soon you can visit me in the ZOO, I guess.

                    TIFFANY
          Ludwig. Calm down. This is a piece of
          crap. For Christ sake, forget about that
          nonsense!

Tiffany pauses. Ludwig sits quiet for a moment focusing on the
table and the ingredients for his creation. He speaks in a
very low voice.

                    LUDWIG
          And then, "by the way"- he claims that
          inside I am identical to Mozart. He
          claims that's what he did.

Ludwig pauses and looks over at Tiffany. He gathers the
ingredients on the table and disposes them in the nearby
trash container. He again takes seat opposite Tiffany, a bit
more composed.

                    LUDWIG
          Weird - you remember how critics have
          talked about my interpretations of Mozart?

That I know Mozart's music better than the
composer and all that stuff, right?
          (he pauses)
And, - when I was in Austria some days
ago, this music came to me in a way the
composer himself can have thought and
which I never thought of.
          (he pauses again and looks
           over at Tiffany)
It is so consistent. I think this guy is
right - it is not "bs".

Tiffany moves to the edge of her chair as she decides to talk
Ludwig back to his sense in a for her unusually firm tone.

                    TIFFANY
Ludwig, stop this. It's a bad joke.

Tiffany rises and stands in front of Ludwig. She bends down
towards him and holds her hands around his head. She speaks
totally convincingly and full of passion. In a very seldom
moment for Tiffany, she looks slightly mean as she realizes
how dirty games may be playing against them.

                    TIFFANY
It is a game somebody plays with you -
somebody that envies you, somebody that
wishes to get rid of you. A competitor
perhaps. That's what it is. Look at me.

Ludwig looks up at the upbeat and excited Tiffany. Her
enthusiasm encourages him and calms him bit down.

                    LUDWIG
I really think he is right. He knew
everything about me - my fingerprints, my
eyes, my taste for coffee - everything.

Ludwig takes Tiffany's hands.

                    LUDWIG
He was very sincere. He was passionate.
And he really knew what he was talking
about.

                         TIFFANY
          Now listen, if you don't want to be part
          of it - well, then don't! You have the
          choice, use the power of it. Make it
          simple. Let's get out of here - let's go
          and make music!

Tiffany and Ludwig rise and exit the Starbucks. The young,
student couple follows them with great interest and finally
look questioning at each other. The YOUNG STUDENT 1 addresses
his YOUNG STUDENT 2 girlfriend.

                         YOUNG STUDENT 1
          Is it what I believe I saw?

                         YOUNG STUDENT 2
          I think so - it was Ludwig Mann, right? I
          don't know who the woman was.

                         YOUNG STUDENT 1
          You remember at the lecture yesterday -
          "go to the concert," he said "the best
          conductor ever." Right?

                         YOUNG STUDENT 2
          I remember - I got tickets already.
          He had a few free tickets to poor music
          students like us.

They laugh, rise, exit the cafe and walk hand in hand down
towards the concert and music school area.

INT. NEW YORK - CONCERT HALL - REHEARSAL CORRIDOR - DAY

Tiffany and Ludwig walk through the broad corridor with rooms
for rehearsal. They hear music from each room as they pass.
From one room they hear a brilliant woman singer deep into
the Mozart Requiem. From another room they hear a violin
quartet practicing.

INT. NEW YORK - CONCERT HALL - REHEARSAL ROOM - DAY

Ludwig and Tiffany enter the practice room. The room is large
and has a high sealing. One wall is built only of windows.
Long golden curtains shade for the sun. In the middle of the

room two grand pianos are standing face to face. The entire
atmosphere is music and makes them forget their troubles.

                    LUDWIG
          Great. So, why don't we do the whole thing
          again? Come on!

They sit down at the piano benches and sit face to face. For a
moment Ludwig sees Tiffany as the small girl at the admission
examination by the Maestro. Tiffany sees the young Ludwig with
the Maestro watching him thoughtfully from behind the piano.
She plays the first bars flawlessly. Ludwig joins in at the
orchestra part. The sound gradually transitions to the full
orchestra.

          THE MUSIC TRANSITIONS TO THE MANHATTAN APARTMENT

INT. NEW YORK - PENTHOUSE DUILIO - DAY

Alessia is nervously gathering her things in the apartment.
She takes her cell phone and, in vain, looks for text messages
from Duilio. She dials Duilio's number. The phone does not
ring, but diverts directly to an answering machine. Alessia
tries another number. Again she is directly diverted to
an answering machine. Alessia looks out over the skyline,
concerned but composed and determined. She leaves a message.

                    ALESSIA
               (in Italian)
          It's me. Where on earth are you? Please
          give me a call on the cell as soon as you
          get this message. Just let me know. Empty
          here without you.

Alessia hangs up and calls the other number. At the tone she
leaves a message.

                    ALESSIA
          It's me, I left a message at the usual
          number. It is important.
          Please give a sign of life!

Alessia gets tears in her eyes as she sits by the tall table
in the kitchen. She takes the phone and calls.

                              ALESSIA
                  Could you please connect me? - I am
                  calling to report a person missing.

Alessia sits waiting while she is being redirected.

EXT. EUROPE - MOUNTAIN ROADS - CAR - DAY

A limousine drives up the narrow roads deep in the mountains
towards the cloister in the last daylight. Duilio sits on the
back seat. Next to him is one of Giovanni's helpers dressed
in black tight trousers and a black turtleneck sweater. The
helper is physically very fit, like a bodyguard. Duilio is
unkempt. His face is tired. He looks worried as they pass
through the deserted landscape.

EXT. MONASTERY - COURTYARD - EVENING

The car stops in the courtyard of cloister. The butler
immediately appears form the main entrance and walks down to
the car. Stone-faced he takes Duilio's briefcase and carries it
into the house.

INT. MONASTERY - SIDE BUILDING - EVENING

The butler lights the candles on the table and on the walls
in the guest room of the side building. The room becomes
dimly illuminated. He puts Duilio's briefcase on the table and
then walks back to the entrance.

                           THE BUTLER
                        (in Italian)
                  The meeting is in 20 inutes. I will pick
                  you up.

                            DUILIO
                        (in Italian)
                  I will be ready.

The Butler bows and exits.

EXT. MONASTERY - ROOF - EVENING

While the butler walks back over the roof area, three huge
black birds fly to the roof and sit on the three statues in

the corners. As the butler notices the birds, he walks faster and rapidly reaches the exit from the roof. He exits and locks the door behind him from within the main building.

INT. MONASTERY - CORRIDOR - EARLY EVENING

Duilio and the butler enter the main building. The Requiem fills the scenery. They walk through a narrow corridor to a small corner room on the top floor. The butler leads the way carrying a large candelabrum. They reach the door, the butler opens and with his hand asks Duilio to enter. The butler closes the door behind Duilio and stays in the corridor.

INT. MONASTERY - MEETING ROOM SMALL - EARLY EVENING

Duilio enters the small office room. A choir of the Requiem fills the gloomy space. The walls, built of stones of rock, are painted white, but the contours of the rough stones are clearly visible through the paint. Giovanni sits by a large, rough and dark wooden table with one candle as the only light in the room. There is a large crucifix on the wall behind Giovanni dressed in his black cassock. His eyes shine like snake eyes, intense as though he is able to look through Duilio. Opposite Giovanni's seat there is a single empty chair by the table. With his hand Giovanni asks Duilio to take seat. Duilio sits down. He moves close to the table. The two men sit for a brief moment in silence.

The sound of the Requiem fades but stays with its deadly tones in the background.

                    GIOVANNI
               (in Italian)
          I assume you are fully aware of what has
          happened recently?

                    DUILIO
               (in Italian)
          Well, what I do know is that I
          have conducted the project totally
          successfully. I have delivered
          everything - all as we agreed!

                         GIOVANNI
          I know what you think - but we will have
          to make changes!

                         DUILIO
          And why?

                         GIOVANNI
          I know you have been in contact with
          Ludwig - that was not part of the plan -
          and to make all your results public and
          exhibit Ludwig Mann; not part of the deal
          either.

Giovanni leans back. His face turns mean, evil and
frightening. Duilio senses the danger.

                         DUILIO
          I disagree. Of course this was part of
          the plan. That was the whole point. He is
          the ultimate proof.

Giovanni stares at Duilio with hostility. Duilio, concerned by
the cold and frightening attitude of Giovanni, continues with
even more vigor. The candlelight flickers as if winds were
blowing through the room. The walls exhibit a frightening play
of shadows.

                         DUILIO
          Look, you, Giovanni, you would always be
          the first to know the results I created
          and therefore you could easily reposition
          your holy organization accordingly - you
          could align it with the advancements of
          the sciences. That was the whole idea.
          Everybody in your institution would
          be ready; you would never be taken by
          surprise. And you could use the results
          of my work to your advantage.
                    (he pauses)
          Of course, that cannot be done without
          showing the results - you know that. The -
          results - would - have - to - become -
          public! How can you question that?

Duilio is upbeat as he talks forcefully and full of
conviction. Giovanni has been listening attentively. He sits
quiet for a moment after Duilio's talk. He looks down at the
table. Then he looks Duilio straight in the eyes as he speaks.

                    GIOVANNI
          Things change Duilio.

Giovanni pauses for a moment as he considers his words
carefully.

                    GIOVANNI
          Yes, I certainly admit that Ludwig is a
          perfect case for a reassessment of all
          the fundamentals of humanity. But as it
          stands, we just don't want that debate
          now. And that's why I tell you to stop -
          totally and immediately.

                    DUILIO
          I cannot do that. The science and the
          truth it delivers is an absolute. We
          cannot put it under the carpet. It has to
          come out; and it will, sooner or later,
          whatever you say and have been asked
          to do.
                    (he pauses)
          I cannot be unfaithful to the sciences!

Giovanni rises. He is frightening as he speaks and regularly
pounds the table while the deadly music continues in the
background.

                    GIOVANNI
          Now - let me be crystal clear. We do not
          want this story to become public!
                    (shouting)
          Nobody - I said nobody - shall ever know
          any of this! You opened the gates to this
          knowledge earlier than we agreed. That
          was a grave mistake. Grave indeed!

Duilio gets very angry by the accusations. He stands up and
continues to speak forcefully and angrily.

                    DUILIO
          This is not a breach - it was a necessary
          step.

Duilio pauses as he briefly considers whether to bring his
next point to the table.

                    DUILIO
          And even the last detail of our agreement
          I have delivered on - the "back-up" -
          I have done even that. The back-up is
          successfully under way, a "back-up Ludwig"
          so to say - I did as you asked - even
          though this certainly was not part of the
          agreement!

Duilio pauses increasingly suspicious by Giovanni's request for
the back-up.

                    DUILIO
          I did it with the woman you wanted.
          Your woman somehow - right?
          How on earth can you then accuse me of
          not delivering and honoring our agreement?

Duilio, in anger, pounds the table with both hands. Giovanni
rises and angrily stands by the table. Duilio rises. They
stand face to face.

                    GIOVANNI
          I tell you, cancel it all, get rid of the
          data - get rid of everything. That's what
          I want. I cannot be more clear and I won't
          say it again. Get it done now!

                    DUILIO
          You know me well enough to know that
          there is no way I leave scientific results
          under the carpet. You know that - I
          wonder why you even ask me!

                    GIOVANNI
          I am sorry to hear your that. But, well,
          we are where we are then and we take it
          from there.

Giovanni rises and shakes hand with Duilio. The butler enters
the room. Giovanni's and the butler's eyes meet briefly in
understanding. Duilio and the butler exit.

EXT. MONASTERY - ROOF - DAY

Duilio and the butler reach the entrance to the roof area.
The butler unlocks the door for Duilio to walk over the roof
to the side building. The butler exits the door to the main
building and locks from the inside. Duilio reaches the door
to the side building. He tries to open the door but finds
it locked. He turns around to ask the butler to unlock. He
realizes he is alone on the roof. The choir of the Requiem
totally fills the space, only broken by the screams of the
terrible birds and the wind hitting the huge sides of the
surrounding cliffs. A huge, black bird at the size of an
oversized eagle flies to the roof area and settles on one of
the statues. Duilio goes fast to the door to the corridor of
the main building. He tries in vain to open the door. The
door is locked. In vain, he tries hard to pull the door open.
Two additional big, black birds - also eagle sized - fly to
the roof area and sit on the statues. Duilio runs to the side
building and tries to push the door in. The door is totally
locked. One of the big birds starts walking over the roof
towards Duilio. He tries to frighten the bird by moving fast
against it. The bird retracts a bit but stays on the roof
floor. Three additional very huge birds fly to the roof and
sit on the high walls. Two of the birds jump down and walk
on the roof area. Duilio runs to the low wall and looks out
over the wall. He sees the tremendous and steep depth below.
Three of the birds walk against him. Duilio panics. He shouts
to frighten the birds. The birds retract a little, but come
closer and closer. Five huge birds gather around Duilio. He
tries to hit them. One of the birds rapidly bites a big chunk
of meat from Duilio's cheek. His blood pours out from the face
in a heavy stream. The birds walk closer to him. He reaches
the low wall. Two more birds start hacking on Duilio. One hits
his finger and bites a piece of the finger off. Blood pours
out from Duilio's cheek and finger. Another bird bites another
finger off. Duilio becomes a fountain of blood. The huge birds
totally surround Duilio. He steps up on the low wall and tries
to kick the birds while blood pours out of his wounds. Two big
birds walk on the low wall against him from each side. Duilio
screams while the birds totally surround and cover him. He
jumps out in the air and fall deep, deep down. At the very,
very bottom of the rock a huge crowd of birds gathers over

Duilio eating everything to the last flesh while any remains dissolve completely in the acidic water.

EXT. MONASTERY - COURTYARD - DAY

In the courtyard of the cloister a limousine stands waiting. Giovanni appears in the door of the main building and walks down the broad staircase to the car. He is elegantly dressed in a black suit. The driver opens the door. Giovanni enters the car and takes seat on the back seat. The car drives out of the cloister and down the narrow roads. He watches a group of huge black birds flying along the rock sides in the direction of the cloister. They continue the drive down the steep mountain roads. The sun sends beautiful rays of light between the huge, steep mountains. Giovanni smiles while watching the stunning scenery from the car. The Requiem fades out.

INT. NEW YORK - CONCERT HALL - CONDUCTOR ROOM - DAY

Ludwig sits by the piano in the conductor's room. The score for the 4th is on the piano note holder. He browses through the pages, then rises and puts the score on top of the piano. He briefly watches the numerous pictures on the walls of conductors previously performing in the concert hall. It knocks on the door. He answers. Dr. Schlesinger opens the door. He is casually and practically dressed in light clothes to follow the rehearsals. Tiffany is standing behind him. She is very lightly and elegantly dressed for the rehearsal.

                    DR. SCHLESINGER
        I believe everything is ready Ludwig.

                    LUDWIG
        OK - let's see if we can make it work.

Ludwig is very tense and nervous. As he exits the conductor's room he briefly takes Tiffany's hand and holds if firmly. Tiffany is visibly nervous and tense. Dr. Schlesinger lets Tiffany walk first through the corridor to the concert hall entrance. Ludwig follows right after. Dr. Schlesinger follows Ludwig.

INT. NEW YORK - CONCERT HALL - DAY

Tiffany, Ludwig and Dr. Schlesinger enter the concert hall. The musicians are getting ready and take their seats. The musicians pad lightly on the note holders as Tiffany, Ludwig, and Dr. Schlesinger walk to the podium. Tiffany and Ludwig shake hands with the key musicians. Tiffany sits down on the piano chair and adjusts it. Ludwig steps onto the conductor's console. Dr. Schlesinger stands next to Tiffany and addresses the orchestra, Tiffany and Ludwig.

> DR SCHLESINGER
> Mrs. Yun and Dr. Mann. Let me welcome you
> cordially for this rehearsal and concert.
> We have all been looking forward to this
> day - and the days to come. We have an
> extremely intense program ahead of us; so
> I won't delay you. So please, again all my
> thanks for you to be here today.

Dr. Schlesinger walks back to the entrance of the concert hall. Tiffany sits totally quiet and looks down at the keyboard. Ludwig takes the baton on the empty music stand in front of him. He lifts his arms. It becomes totally quiet. He looks at Tiffany. She sits quiet and focused on the keyboard. Finally she looks up at Ludwig. He smiles his most engaging and comforting smile. Tiffany finds comfort by Ludwig's strong presence and starts playing the first solo part. She plays flawlessly.

> FADE INTO ACTUAL PERFORMANCE

INT. NEW YORK - CONCERT HALL - EVENING

Tiffany plays virtuously through the cadenza.

> TRANSITION TO LAST BARS IN CONCERT PERFORMANCE

Tiffany and Ludwig make a rich, splendid and virtuous ending to the last movement. The applause starts immensely and immediately. Ludwig turns to the audience. Tiffany in a long golden dress sits for a short moment. Ludwig goes next to her chair. He takes her hand. Tiffany rises. Ludwig lifts her hand as the audience all stand up, shouts and applauds. The concert hall trembles. Tiffany stands enchanted as Ludwig raises her hand and they greet the audience. She smiles and shines. They both laugh, downplaying the atmosphere as though they just have fun. Flowers are thrown to them from all over. Several spectators from the audience walk up to the stage and hand flowers to Tiffany. She again lifts her arms and embraces the

audience. The applause increases. Ludwig leads Tiffany out
of the concert hall between the musicians. As they walk, the
musicians tap the note holders as applause. Tiffany and Ludwig
reach the exit.

INT. NEW YORK - CONCERT HALL - CORRIDOR - EVENING

Dr. Schlesinger greets Tiffany and Ludwig smiling, relieved
and happy. The applause continues undiminished. Ludwig is
relaxed for a moment as he has this part of the performance
behind him. He laughs to Tiffany.

                         LUDWIG
          Go in on your own - just you.
          Please. GO!

Tiffany looks at Dr. Schlesinger. He nods and smiles. Tiffany
walks into the concert hall. Ludwig turns to the wall of the
corridor. He puts his arm between his head and the wall and
leans forward towards the wall.

INT. NEW YORK - CONCERT HALL - EVENING

Tiffany walks into the concert hall. She goes to the front
of the orchestra. She stands with the piano on her left.
The applause rises. Tiffany stands totally quiet for a short
moment. Finally, she again embraces the audience with her
entire beauty, smile and charm. She laughs. She walks back to
the concert corridor and exits the concert hall. Ludwig stands
in the middle of the corridor and smiles as she enters. He
holds Tiffany's hand and they enter the concert hall together.
They greet the audience. Ludwig asks the orchestra to rise.
While they receive the applause a young Asian lady, CHU-JIN
(age and appearance very similar to Tiffany), raises from her
seat at the front row and goes close to the podium. She hands
Ludwig and Tiffany each a large bucket of violet flowers.
Ludwig and Tiffany bow down towards Chu-jin and takes the
buckets. For a short moment Ludwig seems surprised by the
flowers and Chu-yin's appearance. Tiffany brings him back to
the moment as she takes his hand and they both bow for the
audience in the never diminishing applause. Ludwig and Tiffany
walk back to the corridor and exit the concert hall. Ludwig
notices a business card among the violet flowers. He puts the
card in his pocket and hands the flowers to a younger staff
member waiting together with Dr. Schlesinger

INT. NEW YORK - CONCERT HALL - CORRIDOR - EVENING

Ludwig enters the concert corridor having conducted the last symphony on the program. Dr. Schlesinger and Tiffany are waiting. A younger member of the concert hall staff brings Ludwig a chilled beer. Ludwig takes a big sip with great joy. As Ludwig is about to address Dr. Schlesinger, he notices Sergeant Samuel appearing in the corridor together with a woman police officer, MILLE JACKSON (AGE 27), a tall and fit black American. Ludwig is surprised to see the Sergeant, but remains in his high spirit as he shakes hands to greet him.

                    LUDWIG
          Great to see you Sergeant. I hope you
          enjoyed.

                    SAMUEL
          Absolutely, it was great Dr. I believe you
          transcended any expectations - and so did
          Mrs. Yun.

                    LUDWIG
          She certainly did. I am glad you could
          come. Well, people are waiting for me
          already, so if you would excuse me -

Ludwig is about walking to the conductor's room.

                    SAMUEL
          Dr. Mann, would you mind if I ask you a
          few questions. It's important.

                    LUDWIG
               (hesitating)
          Do you think you can ask while I change?

                    SAMUEL
          That's fine.

                    LUDWIG
          OK, then, join me in here.

Ludwig walks to the door of the conductor's room and enters. He holds the door for Sergeant Samuel and Mille who follow. Tiffany watches Sergeant Samuel with some suspicion as she walks with Dr. Schlesinger through the corridor towards the exit.

INT. NEW YORK - CONCERT HALL - CONDUCTOR ROOM - EVENING

Sergeant Samuel, Ludwig and Mille enter the conductor's room. Samuel and Mille take seats in the chairs by a small table. Ludwig, with no signs of being shy, changes his dress during the conversation.

                    SAMUEL
          Dr. Mann, - it's about Duilio Paioni.

                    LUDWIG
          I believe I already told you everything I
          know when you called. As I said, I didn't
          know this man before we met.

                    SAMUEL
          Well Dr. He disappeared. His wife has
          asked us to help finding him. And you are
          the last person we know of who saw him.

                    LUDWIG
          I have no clue.

                    SAMUEL
          What exactly were you talking about at
          the meeting - maybe it could give us a
          hint of where to look for him?

Sergeant Samuel pauses for a moment. Ludwig, in the process of changing his dress, stands still and thoughtful for a short moment. Sergeant Samuel and Mille watch Ludwig attentively.

                    SAMUEL
          Why did you go to him in the first place?

                    LUDWIG
          My mother gave me his number, just before
          she died - so, I assumed, she liked me
          to follow up somehow. So I called. I had
          no clue who I was talking to. Anyway, he
          suggested a meeting right away when he
          heard that I would be around. I agreed and
          we met in his office - the rest you know.

                    SAMUEL
          But why should your mother want you to
          meet him?

                    LUDWIG
        Honestly, I do not know - not even after
        seeing him. My guess is that somehow they
        were very connected in the past. I just
        don't know Sergeant. He didn't say and she
        didn't say. I simply don't know.

                    SAMUEL
        Dr. Mann. The police officer that met
        you in the park after your meeting with
        Duilio tells me that you were extremely
        upset.

                    LUDWIG
        All that happened was that my luggage
        with all my precious scores, credit cards
        and my passport was stolen. I felt so
        stupid. That's all.

                    SAMUEL
        I see. Could you tell us, if you don't
        mind, about your father?

                    LUDWIG
        Well, I never knew him. He died before I
        was born. I believe an accident in the
        mountains.

                    SAMUEL
        So, you didn't know your father at all.

Ludwig in the meantime has changed his dress. He sits briefly
at the piano chair. Then he rises.

                    LUDWIG
        No. My mother just wanted to forget, I
        believe. She really didn't like to talk
        about him at all.
                (impatient)
        Sergeant, I really have to leave - people
        are waiting for me. I have an appointment.

Sergeant Samuel and Mille rise. They all prepare to leave the
room.

SAMUEL

Thanks Dr. Just one more question.
Do you know Alessia Callas?

LUDWIG

Absolutely, she is a distinguished singer.
I have to do a recording with her before
I fly back. We have to disc the Requiem -
by Mozart.

SAMUEL

She is the wife of Duilio Paioni.
Are you aware of that? She is the one who
asked me to look for him.

LUDWIG:

No, I had not the faintest idea - I just
have to do the recording with her. Well,
hopefully she is still able to do that.

SAMUEL

I cannot say, but I do know she was quite
upset when I spoke to her.
Did you have any contact to her recently?

Ludwig gets pretty irritated by being continuously
interrogated after a successful concert. He briefly takes seat
in front of Samuel and Mille as he tries to make himself very
clear.

LUDWIG

No, I didn't. You have to understand
Sergeant that all this logistic stuff is
done by our managers; we give them input
on names and the music of course, but all
the logistic work they do - I mean who we
meet when, where and how. Sergeant, I am
a musician. I make music. That's all I do.
What I do hurts me; I have to go beyond
myself every moment. I feel humble to the
music, I feel inferior to it. This is what
I have to deal with every moment - and I
believe I do it well. At least that's what
some people say; And I tell you Sergeant,
I am at the borderline of what is humanly
possible and it totally drains me. I am

at the edge of music. At the edge all the
time. I am exhausted enough. So, I just
don't know all these things you would like
to know. I have no space for it. I really
don't think I can help you much more.

Ludwig rises. Sergeant Samuel realizes he has gone too far in
his questioning. Samuel and Mille rise.

                    SAMUEL
         I totally understand Dr. Thanks so much.
         I may come back to you. And, please feel
         free to be in touch should anything
         come up.

                    LUDWIG
         You are welcome. But as I said - I doubt
         I can be of any value.

They all exit the room.

INT. NEW YORK - CONCERT HALL - CORRIDOR - EVENING

Ludwig, Sergeant Samuel and Mille shake hands in the corridor
outside the conductor's room. Sergeant Samuel and Mille walk
down the corridor. They pass Tiffany and Dr. Schlesinger
impatiently waiting. Ludwig reaches Dr. Schlesinger and
Tiffany. They exit.

EXT. NEW YORK - CONCERT HALL - SIDE ENTRANCE - EVENING

Dr. Schlesinger shows Tiffany and Ludwig the way to a limousine
outside the concert hall. He is energized and exited.

                    SCHLESINGER
         Thanks so much for the most successful
         concert I ever organized - I can honestly
         say that! So, I will see you again after
         the recordings.
              (he pauses while shaking
              hands)
         By the way, Dr. Mann, I am worried
         about Mrs. deBois. I tried to contact
         her several times regarding the Vienna
         concerts - but no answer.

                         LUDWIG
          She should be in Europe. Sometimes she
          pulls the plug. But even so she organizes
          everything. I would not worry.

                         SCHLESINGER
          I have no doubts about that.
                    (he pauses)
          By the way, Alessia Callas would like to
          talk to you. She suggested tomorrow in
          the rehearsal room.

                         LUDWIG
          Great - thanks. That's OK - I will be
          there.

Dr. Schlesinger leaves. Ludwig and Tiffany enter the limousine
which drives away.

INT. NEW YORK - HOTEL - ELEVATOR - EVENING

Ludwig and Tiffany enter the hotel. They go to the direct
elevator to the panorama restaurant and enter. Ludwig presses
the key. As the elevator starts, Tiffany embraces Ludwig with
passionate short kisses. She leans back, still holding Ludwig.

                         TIFFANY
          Let's do something else. We had enough of
          these restaurants. Let's just go to the
          street and find something.

The elevator reaches the restaurant level. The door opens. A
waiter is standing ready to greet the guests.

                         TIFFANY
                    (addressing the waiter)
          Sorry, we forgot something downstairs.

Tiffany presses the key in the elevator. They exit to the
lobby.

INT. MANHATTAN - HOTEL - LOBBY - EVENING

Tiffany and Ludwig run hand in hand through the lobby to the
exit. Tiffany is still wearing her dress from the concert.

The doorman politely holds the door. Tiffany and Ludwig exit
the hotel.

EXT. MANHATTAN - MIDTOWN - STREET - EVENING

Tiffany and Ludwig walk down a crowded street in Chinatown
packed with exited people, endless small booths selling
everything on earth, and numerous small outdoor food places.
They find way to a totally crowded booth selling noodle soup.
The BOOTH OWNER (50, tight Asian in a pretty messy dress due
to endless servings of noodle soup) is busy selling at full
speed to the crowd around. An Asian woman behind him is
busily preparing the soups. Tiffany, in her comfort zone in
the Asian environment, pulls the not so comfortable Ludwig
through the crowd to the booth. She points at a one of several
greasy photos above the booth displaying the various dishes
served.

                    TIFFANY
          Ludwig, let's have that one!
               (she speaks and agitates
               exited to the booth owner)
          Please, can we have one - please.

                    BOOTH OWNER
               (handing the plate on a
               small tray to Tiffany)
          4 $ please.

Ludwig finds a 5 dollar note in his large bundle of dollar
notes and hands it to the owner. They squeeze in by one
of the crowded tables around the booth. Tiffany eats with
great appetite of their shared soup pulling the noodles with
chopsticks high in the air. Ludwig follows with significant
skepticism and some difficulties with the chopsticks, but
gradually goes with the flow. Tiffany is in a great mood.

                    TIFFANY
               (in German)
          Ludwig, are you happy - with what we
          did? - And that we did it?

                    LUDWIG
               (in German)
          Of course. It could not be better - until,
          maybe next time.

                              TIFFANY
                         (persuasive)
               Let's stop now. Let's get out of this - we
               just do Vienna and then that's it.

Tiffany pounds the fragile table. The dishes with noodle soups
jumps around. Soup spills all over the place. Tiffany holds
her hands over her mouth and looks with excuse around the
table and rapidly moves a bit back from the table to avoid
staining her elegant concert dress. The friendly Asians around
the table smile to Tiffany in spite of the inconvenience.

                              LUDWIG
               I am with you - but what about this story
               about me?

                              TIFFANY
               That's crap. - Let's walk around.

Tiffany gives the empty plate back to the booth owner. He
smiles happily as a five star restaurant owner having noticed
the great attention among his customers to the elegant
Tiffany. She takes Ludwig's hand and pulls him through the
busy street. Down the street they reach a crowded stand. An
ASIAN GAMBLER (29, slim, messy dress, pointed beard, long
hair, unkind look) by the table puts a dice under one of three
dice cups. He rapidly moves the cups around. An elderly Korean
man sitting opposite the gambler has put a 5-dollar note on
the table. He points at one of the cubs. The gambler lifts the
cup. The dice is not there. He lifts another cup. The dice is
there. The gambler takes the 5-dollar note. The elderly man
rises. The gambler shouts loud to the crowd.

                          ASIAN GAMBLER
               Who wants to try? I double your bet and
               all you do is to follow the movements.

A small, shy KOREAN GIRL (7, poorly dressed) walks slowly to
the table. She has four coins which she holds tight in her
hand as were they her last money.

                          ASIAN GAMBLER
                         (tempting the girl)
               Do you want to try?

The girl nods and takes seat opposite the gambler. She puts
one coin on the table. The gambler puts the dice under one of
the cups and starts moving them around quicker and quicker.

                        ASIAN GAMBLER
            Now you just follow - and then you win!

The gambler stops moving the cups. He watches the girl. She
sits for a while before she points to one of the cups. The
gambler lifts the cup - the dice is not there. The gambler
lifts the adjacent cup. The dice is there. The small girl
shivers a bit as the gambler takes her coin on the table.

                        ASIAN GAMBLER
            Try again - just watch carefully - then
            you get all your money back when you win.

The small girl looks down in her hand at her three remaining
coins. Reluctantly she takes one more coin and puts it on the
table. The crowd around the table moves closer and stands
close around the girl. Everybody follows the event with
excitement. Tiffany moves forward and stands right behind the
girl. The gambler places the dice under one cup and starts
moving the cups around. He stops. The small girl looks at the
cups and starts rising her hand in the direction of the right
cup. Tiffany puts her hands on the shoulder of the girl.

                        TIFFANY
                    (in Mandarin)
            Wait!

The girl lowers her hand. Tiffany, totally concentrated, looks
the gambler directly in the eyes. In Tiffany's mind it gets
totally quiet and movements slow down as she looks the gambler
directly in the eyes and reads his mind. She holds firmly on
the girl's shoulder. The sound of the surroundings comes back.
Time moves again. Tiffany leans down with her head just next
to the girl's ear and whispers.

                        TIFFANY
            The left!

The girl points first to the right, but as she moves her
hand closer to the cup she changes direction and lets her
hand land on the left. The gambler lifts the cup. The dice

is there. A sigh of relief sounds from the entire crowd. The
gambler smiles as he gives the girl two coins back.

                        ASIAN GAMBLER
             Now you know how to do it, you can put
             all your coins - and then double up!

The girl looks down at her coins. Tiffany whispers to her.

                        TIFFANY
                    (in Mandarin)
             Put all of them.

The girl turns her head and surprised sees the elegant
Tiffany. She whispers.

                        KOREAN GIRL
                    (in Mandarin)
             All of them?

                        TIFFANY
             Yes - I help you.

The girl, reluctantly, puts all her money on the table. The
gambler repeats the process - this time extremely fast. He
stops. Tiffany again watches the gambler, deeply focused. She
leans forward and whispers to the girl.

                        TIFFANY
             The right one.

The girl points to the right cup. The gambler lifts the
cup. The dice is there. A bit annoyed he pays the girl. He
addresses Tiffany irritated.

                        ASIAN GAMBLER
             Why don't you play yourself with some
             significant money.

Tiffany, as in a trance, reaches out to Ludwig. He takes his
money and shows the notes to Tiffany. She takes a 100 dollar
note and puts it at the table. The gambler looks irritated,
puts the dice and moves the cups. Tiffany watches the gambler
rather than the cups. The gambler stops and looks up at
Tiffany. She reads his mind and instantly puts her hand on
the right cup. The gambler lifts the cup. The dice is there.

The crowd cheers. The girl applauds. The gambler, irritated
gives Tiffany her money. Tiffany, still standing behind the
girl, discretely gives the money to her. The gambler packs his
things and leaves.

> TIFFANY
> Now run home dear and tell how you won -
> but never, ever try again. You will always
> lose. Did you hear me?

The girl nods. She turns around. Tiffany embraces her lightly
taking care of her dress. The girl runs away. The crowd
spreads. Tiffany holds Ludwig tight as they walk back through
the crowded street.

> LUDWIG
> My Goodness. How on earth did you do
> that - it was like you knew!

> TIFFANY
> I can see it. Sometimes it is like that.

Tiffany takes Ludwig's hand and pulls him impatiently forward.

> TIFFANY
> Come, let's go to your place - I need you.
> Maybe you need me too - we will make it
> magic, again!

They laugh. As they start walking back in the direction of
the hotel, they pass a roulette where a big crowd is gambling.
There is a large Teddy bear among the prices exhibited.
Tiffany gets excited as she sees the Teddy.

> TIFFANY
> Let's go and win that one.

Tiffany pulls Ludwig over to the roulette. They disappear in
the crowd.

INT. MANHATTAN - HOTEL - SUITE - NIGHT

Tiffany and Ludwig enter Ludwig's suite. Tiffany holds the
Teddy tight, pretending to be childish. They walk over to the
windows and watch the gorgeous view over the park. Tiffany
holds the Teddy between herself and Ludwig and joyfully looks

at Ludwig first from one side and then from the other side of
the Teddy, as though she is hiding behind it and playing hide
and seek.

                    TIFFANY
          Here I am - free as a bird - but all
          yours - if you can catch me!

She laughs excited as she continues playing and runs around
everywhere in the suite. Ludwig follows her and finally pulls
both Tiffany and the Teddy to the bed. They have perfect love.

                                        AHEAD IN TIME

Tiffany and Ludwig lie together in the bed. The Teddy is
behind Tiffany.

                    LUDWIG
          I still wonder how you did it.

Tiffany, naked but covered by a light silk sheet, rises on her
elbows and turns towards Ludwig. She puts her arm across his
chest and puts her head on his chest right in front of his and
talks softly.

                    TIFFANY
          You remember Gyung-hee. She taught me to
          transcend - into the music and into the
          souls.
               (she pauses)
          She could see everything - something
          magic.

                    LUDWIG
          But how?

                    TIFFANY
          I don't know - I just do it.

Tiffany puts her head on Ludwig's chest. They fall asleep.

INT. NEW YORK - POLICE STATION - OFFICE - DAY

Sergeant Samuel is sitting by his desk in his messy, small
office surrounded by big piles of paper. Mille and Larry are
standing by the walls where they can find space. The room is

illuminated by a single light tube in the ceiling. A noisy
air-conditioner makes the atmosphere quite unbearable. Samuel
is summarizing their conversation.

                    SAMUEL
          So, what have we got? - Well, a conductor
          of unbelievable fame who for reasons we
          do not understand at all visits a high-
          tech company and gets arrested after the
          visit due to strange behavior. A missing
          scientist married to a high profile
          singer who will record with the very same
          conductor these days.

Sergeant Samuel leans back. He tries to smile and talks in a
quite humorous tone, but knows by instinct that the situation
could be grave. He looks puzzled at Mille and Larry.

                    SAMUEL
          So, guys what on earth is going on here?

                    MILLE
          (with a thick NY accent)
          Couldn't we at least try to understand
          what happened in this company when these
          folks met - and what is this company
          doing?

                    SAMUEL
          Makes sense. Larry, why don't you go there
          and find out. What are they doing, where
          does the money come from, are there any
          records of visitors - video surveillance,
          lock-in files, - and folks, should we ask
          for a search warrant for the office of Dr.
          Paioni - just in case?

                    MILLE
          I can do that - makes sense. I can get it
          right away. I know the folks over there.

                    SAMUEL
          (appears relieved)
          Great Mille. And Larry, who else knows
          this Paioni. Look him up everywhere. Ask
          all the usual places, hospitals etc. And

Mille, look up whatever is available about
this conductor. But only in the public
domain.

Sergeant Samuel sits thoughtful for a short moment. Then,
determined to get to the bottom of the case, he decides they
better move forward.

                    SAMUEL
          OK folks. Let's move.

Larry and Mille leave the office. Sergeant Samuel finds the
phone on his table behind a pile of paper and makes a call.

INT. MANHATTAN - HOTEL - SUITE - DAY

The morning sun shines into the suite. Ludwig is sitting by
the breakfast table. Tiffany enters. Her hair is covered by
a towel bound firmly around her hair. She is well rested and
energized as she sits down in the couch next to Ludwig. She
pours a large cup of tea. She pulls her legs up under her. She
sits straight up in the coach while she holds the cup under
her nose and enjoys the vapors and drinks with small sips.
They sit in silence for a while enjoying the moment. Tiffany
takes one of the newspapers on the table. On the front-page
she sees a picture of herself embracing the audience after the
concert with Ludwig standing right behind her and with the
orchestra members all standing.

                    TIFFANY
          Look!

She shows Ludwig the picture and turns to the pages inside the
newspaper. She briefly reads through the review of the concert
for herself.

                    TIFFANY
          I know you don't want to hear - but it is
          good.

Tiffany puts the paper down on her lap. She leans back on
Ludwig and closes her eyes. She reaches out for Ludwig's hands
and holds them.

                    TIFFANY
          Ludwig, what more can we ask for?

They sit for a while in silence. Tiffany again looks at the
picture. She puts the paper on her chest and holds it tight.
Ludwig gets impatient due to his dislike for reviews.

                    LUDWIG
          I have to meet this singer at 10 - you
          know, the wife of this scientist. I hope
          she is still fit for the recording.
                    (he pauses)
          ..... You are right, we do Vienna and then
          we get lost from this world.

                    TIFFANY
          Well, make her fit - you can do that
          however desperate she is. And just text
          me when you are back. I will just hang
          around today.

EXT. MANHATTAN - MIDTOWN - STREET - DAY

Ludwig walks out of the hotel. He is energized and in a good
mood. He takes the business card he found in the bucket of
violet flowers and reads the address. Walking down the street
with several small shops, he watches the small exhibits in
the windows. He reaches the address. It is a jewelry shop. He
briefly watches the exhibit of nice jewelry in the window and
enters the small shop.

INT. NEW YORK - JEWELRY SHOP - DAY

Ludwig enters the small, nicely designed jewelry shop.
Throughout the shop glass counters exhibit precious jewelry.
There are a few comfortable armchairs in the room and small
tables with journals exhibiting jewelry and fashion. At the
table and the counter are flowerpots with violet flowers.
CHU-JIN (Asian, same age and strong resemblance to Tiffany,
long black hair set up extremely tight, strong make-up,
elegant and tight dress) stands by the counter working
through the mail of the day and other paperwork. Ludwig is
immediately attracted to her. Chu-jin addresses Ludwig as he
closes the door behind him.

                    CHU-JIN
          Can I help you, Sir?

                    LUDWIG
I got your beautiful flowers yesterday -
I like to thank you.

                    CHU-JIN
It is such a pleasure Dr. Mann. I
I am so glad you noticed and even more
that you pass by.
          (puts the paperwork to the
          side)
I was enchanted when listening to your
music. I'd love to do something in return.
          (she notices Ludwig's
          interest in the jewelry
          exhibits)
Maybe you could find something of
interest?

                    LUDWIG
Well, let's see.
          (he pauses)
What about something nice for a woman
that looks pretty much like you - say as
a surprise gift.

                    CHU-JIN
Are you perhaps thinking of the pianist
yesterday, if I may ask?

                    LUDWIG
Exactly. So, what would you like to get if
it was you?

                    CHU-JIN
Is there perhaps love involved ...?

Chu-jin watches Ludwig very friendly and carefully. Ludwig is
slightly shaken by her gaze and strong presence.

                    LUDWIG
Well - maybe ...

                    CHU-JIN
I believe I have the right stone for you.
You see, stones tell a story - and I can
see it. Let me show you.

Ludwig appears a bit more composed. Chu-jin starts opening
drawers under the counter and searches. She continues talking
while searching.

                    CHU-JIN
          I read the stones - and people.

Chu-jin searches a drawer with numerous rings far down below
the counter. She finds the ring she is looking for - a simple
designed ring in gold with a large, slightly rose diamond
flanked by numerous small diamonds. She puts the ring on a
small tray with black velvet and presents it to Ludwig.

                    CHU-JIN
          This ring Dr. is right for the her.

Chu-jin looks for a box for the ring. Ludwig watches her
lovingly. As Chu-jin notices they both get a bit embarrassed.

                    LUDWIG
          So how is it that you are here in New
          York?

Chu-jin smiles as to an old friend who already knows the most
of her, and talks as if it would be just a minor matter, with
great understatement, but a hundred percent confidence.

                    CHU-JIN
          Well - I lost my parents early - I
          was given away. I learned to look into
          people's minds and the future - I guess I
          was born that way.

Chu-jin looks down at the counter as she continues, a bit
embarrassed.

                    CHU-JIN
          But you know, with stuff like that you
          easily get into trouble. So a few years
          ago I specialized in stones - using them
          a little bit for fortune telling, but
          mainly selling them, to make a living.

                    LUDWIG
          You can look into the minds? - and the
          future?

Chu-jin puts the ring neatly in the small box and hands it, together with the receipt, to Ludwig. He signs. She smiles the smile of a soul mate.

                    CHU-JIN
          The ring was waiting for you. Thank you
          for being my customer - and good luck!

They start walking towards the exit.

                    CHU-JIN
          Let me know if I can do more for you!

Chu-jin gives her hand to Ludwig and opens the door. As Ludwig is just about to leave a thought occurs to him and he turns to Chu-jin.

                    LUDWIG
          By the way, these flowers of yours.
          Where did you buy them?

                    CHU-JIN
          Oh, I did not buy them. I brought them
          with me.

                    (LUDWIG)
               (pretending being a bit
               stupid)
          So one cannot buy these flowers anywhere?

Chu-jin holds the door open for Ludwig as to avoid further questions about the flowers.

                    CHU-JIN
               (again smiling)
          No, I am afraid you can't.

Ludwig is just about finally exiting the shop. He turns around for the second time.

                    LUDWIG
          Well, since you mentioned - could I come
          back with Tiffany - the pianist - to visit
          the fortune teller part of you?

> CHU-JIN
> I knew you would ask that - and sure,
> yes you can. But, I have to warn you;
> you never know. But, if you really feel
> like it -

> LUDWIG
> I do - need - some answers. The truth,
> if this is the right expression -
> assurance -

> CHU-JIN
> Well, you can come back whenever you
> want to.

> LUDWIG
> Maybe later today?

> CHU-JIN
> Any time. I am here.

Ludwig finally exits the shop and walks down the street
towards the concert hall. He looks at his watch, concerned to
be late. He walks a bit faster.

INT. NEW YORK - CONCERT HALL - REHEARSAL ROOM - DAY

Alessia stands by the window. The scenery is exactly the
same as during the event with Tiffany, except for the light:
soft sunlight of the early day shines into the room through
the golden curtains. As Ludwig enters, Alessia rapidly turns
and almost runs through the room to Ludwig. She talks and
agitates with the Italian temper of a brilliant and powerful
singer.

> ALESSIA
> (in Italian)
> Dr. Mann. Thanks for coming. I am sorry
> to spend your time on this day - not
> least after the concert yesterday - but -
> I really need to talk to you.

Ludwig, aware of what is likely to come, attempts to downplays
the drama from the very beginning to rescue his recording.

LUDWIG
(in Italian)
Sure, sure. No problem. I am glad you
asked to meet. I am looking forward to
this recording with you!

ALESSIA
(lowering her voice)
I know. But I have to tell you something;
Something very personal, but it affects
the recording.

LUDWIG
Yes--?

ALESSIA
My husband has disappeared. The police
have been looking for him for a while now.
(with her body language
she indicates the lack of a
trace)
I know him well enough that if he is not
in touch, something is wrong.
(she pauses)
I have to confess: I cannot focus on the
music to the standards you need. I am
so sorry, so sorry. I had been looking
forward.

LUDWIG
I am sorry to hear - but tell me, what
is your husband doing - are you sure you
really need to worry? Maybe it's just
something with his job that keeps him
away - something simple.

ALESSIA
(speaking fast and nervously)
He is a scientist. Molecular science I
believe it is called. Somehow a secret
project. When we were young he always
told me about his work - not anymore. So,
I stopped asking. And lately he has been
so different. I sensed that something was
coming up or something was happening -
and then, then this.

                    LUDWIG
I can't force you. But maybe it would be
good for you to dive down in the music
if there is little you can do anyway. Why
don't we give it a try?

                    ALESSIA
I am sorry. But I feel the weakness
deep … in my bones. I am afraid I cannot
do it.

                    LUDWIG
Well ...

Ludwig goes to the piano. With his gaze, he makes her come
close to him. He looks her right in the eyes.

                    LUDWIG
Come on - let's check it out.

Ludwig strikes few cords. Alessia forgets in Ludwig's magic
presence and intensity and rapidly falls in. The full
orchestra and Requiem with the soprano solo overwhelmingly
fills the room and the picture fades.

     THE FULL REQUIEM ORCHESTRA AND SOPRANO SOLO CARRIES OVER

INT. NEW YORK - CONCERT HALL - FOYER - DAY

Ludwig and Alessia enter the foyer, smiling and in good mood.
The security guard happily greats them. Ludwig greets Alessia
goodbye and goes to a group of chair in the corner of the
foyer. He dials Tiffany from his cell phone. The music fades.
The call goes through.

                    LUDWIG
I am done. Where are you?

                    TIFFANY
           (happy voice on the phone)
Strolling around. Waiting for you.

                    LUDWIG
You know what, I met a very interesting
person.

                    TIFFANY
         The singer?

                    LUDWIG
         No, well yes, her too - anyway. We will
         meet the other person later today.

                    TIFFANY
         Who is it?

                    LUDWIG
         You saw her already!

                    TIFFANY
         What?

                    LUDWIG
         She gave us flowers - you remember?

                    TIFFANY
         I certainly do. But why on earth?

                    LUDWIG
         I tell you.

                    TIFFANY
         I hope you are not getting a bit crazy ...

Tiffany hangs up. Ludwig looks at his phone to make sure it
is on.

INT. NEW YORK - JEWELRY SHOP - DAY

Tiffany, carrying numerous shopping bags, and Ludwig enter
the jewelry shop. Chu-jin stands behind the counter with both
hands resting at the desk. She is dressed in a colorful,
tight and very well fitting modern gown. Her hair is loose
and covers her shoulders and hides most of her face. She
bows slightly forward as she greets Ludwig and Tiffany. Chu-
jin and Tiffany discretely but carefully watch each other,
not knowing what to do about their resemblance. Tiffany,
pretty suspicious, watches the interior of the shop; a little
lost and uncomfortable, as she tries to make sense of the
situation.

CHU-JIN
Very welcome Dr. Mann - and very welcome
Mrs. Yun. I have been expecting you.
Please come closer.

Chu-jin locks the door to the shop and leads Tiffany and
Ludwig to the door in the back. She opens the door for Tiffany
and Ludwig. The door leads to a small kitchen. Tiffany and
Ludwig exit the shop; Chu-jin follows.

INT. NEW YORK - JEWELRY SHOP - BACK ROOM - DAY

Ludwig, Tiffany and the Chu-jin enter the kitchen. It is a
friendly and cozy place, bathed in light. There are fruits
in a bowl and some cookies next to it. Chu-jin takes a bite,
and behaves casually. She leans on the kitchen furniture and,
with her hand, invites Tiffany and Ludwig to make themselves
comfortable. They sit down by the table with the fruits and
cookies.

CHU-JIN
Very well then; as I told you, once I have
contact I have to tell you what I see.

LUDWIG
Yes, we understand.

Tiffany is confused, but excited as she realizes what is
coming up and doesn't interrupt. Chu-jin looks at Tiffany.

CHU-JIN
And you Mrs. Yun?

TIFFANY
Please, just call me Tiffany for now.

CHU-JIN
Very well then. Please help yourself.

Chu-jin pours glasses of water to Tiffany and Ludwig. She
goes to the windows and pulls the curtains. The room becomes
rather dark. Tiffany and Ludwig watch the water in the glass.
It vibrates a little as Tiffany and Ludwig are expecting
something supernatural. Chu-jin comes to the table and sits
down opposite to Ludwig and Tiffany.

                         CHU-JIN
          Now, please relax.

Chu-jin closes her eyes. They all sit very quiet for a while.
Chu-jin's eyelids vibrate slightly. Tiffany and Ludwig close
their eyes.

After a while Chu-jin opens her eyes. Her face has changed.
She is far away in a different world. She talks a little lower
than before and slowly. She suddenly smiles.

                         CHU-JIN
          Tiffany, I feel you - so clearly.

She closes her eyes. Her gaze becomes sad.

                         CHU-JIN
          We will lose you soon like a little
          sister. You will get away from me. But
          you will live - deeply connected in your
          art. And then - I am not sure what I see.
          Somehow you return to your early life -
          I see you, yes sister, I see you somehow
          reliving a magic moment of your life ....

Ludwig sits with his eyes closed. He is well relaxed, and not
tense in any way.

                         CHU-JIN
               (she whispers)
          .... and until then, I see you happy.

Tiffany opens her eyes and looks stunned at Chu-jin. Then
she looks over at Ludwig. He still has his eyes closed. Chu-
jin focuses strongly as she attempts to contact Ludwig.
Her eyelids vibrate and she holds the edge of the table
tight with her hands. After a while she opens her eyes and
addresses Ludwig. Her voice is still low and slow. Her face is
transcendent.

                         CHU-JIN
          I just could not connect to you at all.
               (she pauses)
          Very strange. I just felt empty.
          Totally. Nothing to see.
               (pulling herself together)

                    That never happened to me before.
                              (shakes her head as to get
                              rid of the effort)
                    I am sorry.

They all sit for a while and gradually recover from the
intense event. Chu-jin walks over to the window and opens the
curtains. Ludwig and Tiffany rise. Chu-jin shows the door with
her hand. They all exit the kitchen.

INT. NEW YORK - JEWELRY SHOP - DAY

Chu-jin, Tiffany and Ludwig enter the shop from the back
door. Chu-jin unlocks the front door. She smiles to Ludwig
and Tiffany as she bows goodbye. After a slight hesitation
Chu-jin's and Tiffany's eyes meet with more sympathy. Chu-jin
briefly and lightly embraces Tiffany. She totally relaxes and
sighs relieved as she holds her arms around Tiffany.

The moment slows down as the two women embrace, holding each
other and slowly, almost unwillingly let the other go. Chu-
jin lets her arms fall along her sides and steps a little
back. She looks down on the floor for a short moment. Then she
looks at Tiffany and smiles the best she can in her sad mood.
Tiffany and Ludwig exit to the street. Chu-jin closes the door
behind them. She stands for a moment and sadly watches Tiffany
and Ludwig walk down the street closely together as were she
longing for both of them.

EXT. MANHATTAN - MIDTOWN - STREET - DAY

Ludwig and Tiffany, close together, walk slowly down the
street from the jewelry shop. Ludwig carries Tiffany's bags.
Tiffany holds Ludwig's arm with both hands as they walk.
They stop by a blooming cherry tree. The leaves from the
flowers are falling quietly around them. They watch the
flowers as they fall softly and slowly to the ground. Some
leaves from the flowers land on Tiffany's shoulders and in
her hair.

                         LUDWIG
                    Why do you think she couldn't connect
                    to me?

                          TIFFANY
          Ludwig, stop bothering. You seriously
          believe in this funny kitchen experience?
          Come on.

                          LUDWIG
          But you heard it yourself - she always
          gets contact. That's what she said. So it
          is very simple. It's simply because there
          is no me. End of the story. I am just made
          for Christ sake - I am not real - just as
          this scientist says!

                          TIFFANY
          Now, don't you start all over again.
          You are what you are to me. You are my
          brother, my lover, my soul mate. How could
          you be so if you had no soul? See? Proven.

Tiffany kisses Ludwig passionately. The music (Requiem, soft
soprano solo) from the recording with Alessia fills the
space. Ludwig kneels down by her side and hands her the ring.
As Tiffany opens the small box the light hits the ring and
radiates against her. The whole scenery light up in brilliant
light under the tulip flowers as Tiffany takes the ring like
in a flickering snowstorm of white tulip leaves. She bows over
Ludwig as when they mixed blood in their youth.

        THE MUSIC CARRIES INTO THE REPLAY IN THE RECORDING STUDIO

INT. NEW YORK - CONCERT HALL - STUDIO - DAY

Ludwig is sitting by the huge panel of recording devices
and volume controls in the recording studio. Alessia and the
singers are standing behind him. All are in very casual, work
dresses for recordings. The last bars of the replay fade. Ludwig
leans back and smiles to everybody around - they all applaud.

                          LUDWIG
          Thanks everyone - we got it.
                    (he spreads his arms in
                     excitement)
          Even without a church! What a relief guys.

Ludwig leans back and watches all the musicians and singers.

LUDWIG
Frankly guys, I had my doubts. But you
made it - thanks everyone.

The musicians and singers in the studio all applaud.

INT. NEW YORK - POLICE STATION - OFFICE - DAY

Samuel, Mille and Larry are gathered in Samuel's office.
Samuel is sitting by his desk among the usual piles of paper.
Mille and Larry are standing by the walls. The miserable air-
conditioner makes an even worse and terrible noise. Larry
goes to the devise and hammers it with his hand. The noise is
reduced a bit. They are in the middle of a conversation.

MILLE
... and apparently Alessia is not the
only one looking for him now. An Albert
Ryesling called and asked; very concerned.

SAMUEL
Who is he?

MILLE
Head or chairman of some pretty well
known scientific society. Dr. Paioni is
also on the board there.

SAMUEL
I better go and talk to this guy then.
Larry - anything from the lab?

LARRY
They did the initial DNA profiles of the
samples from the office.
They are now in the database. I asked
them to look for matches.

SAMUEL
And why would you do that - we do not
know who to match to?

LARRY
Well - if you ask, they can look for
matches to whatever happens to be in
the databases and you may be lucky. And

actually there was a match - a very
strong match.

                    SAMUEL
          What? A strong match - and to whom?
          Do you know?

                    LARRY
          Sort of. The sample was from a case quite
          some years ago - there was suspicion of
          some wrongdoing in an abortion case -
          something like that. It is hard to find
          out. The original file is not there -
          deleted they say - but somehow the file
          with the DNA data and a few comments
          survived. Weird - but that's what I am
          told.

Samuel gets very interested. He walks over and switches the
noisy air-condition off. It gets quiet in the room, but hot.

                    LARRY
          The person referred to is a woman, Giulia
          Cara. She is European and apparently must
          have had a miscarriage or an abortion
          over here.

                    SAMUEL
          And - did you follow up on her?

                    LARRY
          Not yet, I can ask in Europe - that's
          where we believe she lives?

                    SAMUEL
          Well, go ahead, you can always ask for
          her records: who is she, where does she
          live, if she is alive - stuff like that.
          Public domain information you can always
          request. Just don't imply anything.

Sergeant Samuel, clearly excited by finally having some
concrete tracks to follow, turns to Mille. She unfolds a
printed paper she has been holding while Larry talked. She
walks over to Samuel's table.

                              MILLE
          I found this. It was on the web-page of
          this society. There is a big thing coming
          up - pretty soon.

Mille puts the print on the desk. Larry walks over to Samuel.
They both read the printed page.

                             SAMUEL
          Wow; "The Chemical Synthesis of a Human
          Being - its Implications for Humanity"!
          What on earth?

They all realize the potential significance of Mille's
finding. Samuel takes his seat and leans back. He ponders for
a moment, then turns to Mille and Larry full of energy.

                             SAMUEL
          Here is what we do. Mille, you go with
          me over to that institution. And Larry -
          please follow up on this match - who is
          Giulia Cara, when was she here, if she
          ever was, where is she now. Everything
          you can get. And please ask our friends
          abroad to look for Duilio. Get an
          International Search going - all the
          usual stuff. And Larry, ask the lab to
          check these data again. I mean, how can
          it be possible to find a match to an old
          case in an office today. This is getting
          too much - what the Hell is going on?
                    (he pauses)
          Guys, this could be big. I smell it. Take
          care to have all formalities in order:
          accurate records, compliance with all
          guidelines and rules - you know what I am
          saying. So, go, go, go and do it!

Energized, they all exit the office.

EXT. NEW YORK - OUTSIDE THE POLICE STATION - DAY

Samuel and Mille walk out of the police station and over to a
line of police cars parked in front of the station. They enter
a car and rapidly drive out of the station area.

INT. NEW YORK - SOCIETY OF SCIENCES - OFFICE - DAY

Dr. Ryesling, Samuel and Mille are in Ryesling's office. The walls in the office are covered by bookshelves, all packed with books, journals, piles of paper, molecular models, artistic drawings, and various old scientific instruments. The large desk is covered with piles of paper. An admin enters carrying a tray with coffee cups and glasses with ice water. She serves Samuel, Mille and Dr. Ryesling.

                    RYESLING
          Thanks so much for coming. As I mentioned
          on the phone we are very concerned here
          about Dr. Paioni.

                    SAMUEL
          We understand - that's why we came right
          away.
                    (he pauses)
          Here is what we have done: we have
          alerted the channels we usually activate
          when someone is missing, and in this
          case we have even issued an international
          search. So far nothing has shown up. So
          we need something more. And Dr., maybe you
          have information we don't have - something
          more we can follow up on?
                    (he pauses)
          Maybe, for example, could you tell us
          exactly what Dr. Paioni was doing in his
          institute. And, did you notice anything
          about him recently - something different?

                    RYESLING
          Well, what he did originally was
          pioneering the structural elucidation and
          preparation of the molecules of life.
                    (he pauses to see if Samuel
                    follows)
          In simple terms Sergeant: he could find
          out what molecules in living cells look
          like - that's what I mean by detailed
          structure - and then he could make them -
          however big and complicated.
                    (he pauses and gets a bit
                    distant)

He was indeed a distinguished scientist.
The papers he publish in his early years
are highly regarded. And he has been,
and he is a tremendous asset for this
institution.

                    SAMUEL
And lately?

                    RYESLING
In the later years he did not publish
much. What he told me was that he was
gathering a wealth of publication for an
extremely significant disclosure.

Mille takes the print of the announcement of the synthesis of
a human and puts it on the table.

                    MILLE
Could this be what he was up to?
Would he be the one actually delivering
this lecture?

                    RYESLING
Yes, indeed - we discussed and agreed
to this title - and yes, he would be
the one.

Dr. Ryesling pauses and continues embarrassed as he knows the
reputation of the Society and of himself are on the line.

                    RYESLING
If he does not show up soon we have
a huge problem - the time to the
anniversary is very short now.

                    SAMUEL
Did you ever see the manuscript or
anything for his lecture?

                    RYESLING
Actually not - not yet I should say.

                    SAMUEL
What about the money for his institute?

                         RYESLING
          I don't know. He kept it for himself. I
          trusted him hundred percent. I still do.
          I assume he had a very rich sponsor of
          some kind. Clearly he needed a lot - and
          I really mean a lot.

They sit in silence for a short while searching for new ideas
as they realize they are getting nowhere. Samuel looks around
on all the scientific materials in the office. Then he looks
back on Dr. Ryesling.

                         SAMUEL
          You knew him well Dr. - did you notice
          anything unusual in the last time -
          something that we could follow up on?

                         RYESLING
          No. We talked a lot as we always did - a
          lot about science and his many interests
          beyond the sciences.
                    (he pauses)
          Maybe his interests for what is beyond
          increased a bit in the last years -
          he went more and more to the edge of
          science. He was clearly very interested in
          what he sometimes called "the spirits", in
          lack of a better term. Well, I don't see
          how that could help finding him.

                         SAMUEL
                    (trying to diffuse the sad
                    atmosphere)
          Well - they, I mean the "spirits" - are
          probably even harder to find. So, let's
          continue to go for Paioni.

They all rise and shake hands. The atmosphere is friendly.
Samuel and Mille exit the office.

INT. EUROPE - POLICE STATION - DAY

In a large, shared, open space office in a European police
station, many police officers work on computer screens and
talk loud on telephones. A police officer, FRANZ WEINER
(40, fit, energetic and good looking), studies the inquiry

regarding Dr. Paioni and Giulia Cara. Checking the clocks on
the wall where the times across the world are displayed, he
takes the phone and dials Samuel. While he waits for the call
to go through he pours a coffee and finds a clean note pad in
his mess of papers.

                    FRANZ
          Hello - is it Sergeant Samuel?

                    SAMUEL
               (voice on phone)
          Speaking.

                    FRANZ
          I am calling regarding the inquiry on
          Giulia Cara; Franz Weiner is my name.

                    SAMUEL
          Great. Do you have anything on her?

                    FRANZ
          I am afraid she died.

                    SAMUEL
          She died? How? - And when?

                    FRANZ
          As far as I can see a natural death; a
          few days ago.

                    SAMUEL
          A few days ago? Damn. We thought she
          could give us a lead to Duilio Paioni. Do
          you by any chance have anything on him?

                    FRANZ
          I saw your search request. And I checked.
          But no - unfortunately not.

There is a short pause.

                    SAMUEL
          Is there any chance you could go to the
          place of Giulia - I mean where she lived -
          and get us some samples of whatever you
          find. We have a DNA match somehow related

to her. I know it is a little farfetched,
but... this is a very unusual case - and
we have essentially nothing.

                    FRANZ
        I don't mind. It's in the old town - it's
        close. I can go there.

                    SAMUEL
        Excellent. Do you have anything on her -
        parents for example, where she was born,
        any of this?

                    FRANZ
        Actually not. Quiet unusual.
        Wherever we looked: no information beyond
        herself.

                    SAMUEL
        Well - for this case it is perhaps not
        that unusual. This case seems to meet
        just dead ends - literally! But please, by
        all means go and see what you can find -
        and be in touch please.

                    FRANZ
        Certainly, I come back. Have a nice day
        over there.

Franz hangs up, puts his papers together and clears the desk.
He writes the address of Giulia down on the note pad and exits
the office.

EXT. EUROPE - OLD TOWN - DAY

Franz drives into the old town in a police car. He drives
slowly through the narrow streets and stops at a small
square. He parks, exits the car and walks to a narrow path
that leads steeply up the hill. He walks up the narrow path
between the very old houses. At the top of the path he
reaches the square in front of the church. He walks over
to the entrance to Giulia's basement apartment. The door is
open. Franz walks down the small staircase and enters the
small apartment.

INT. EUROPE - APARTMENT GIULIA - DAY

Franz enters Giulia's apartment. As he walks through the low
door opening he has to bend in order not to hit the wall over
the door with his head. In the apartment several contractors
are painting the ceiling in the otherwise totally empty room.
Franz addresses one of the contractors who is busily spraying
a coating on the already fully painted walls.

                    FRANZ
               (Austrian in German)
          Hello - so you are fixing this place?

                    CONTRACTOR
               (Austrian in German)
          Yes Sir, somebody is going to move in
          here in two days.

                    FRANZ
          Did you know the woman who lived here?

                    CONTRACTOR
          Sir, I am just fixing the place.
          None of us here know anybody - but
          perhaps ask in the church over there.

                    FRANZ
          In the church....?

                    CONTRACTOR
          The church owns this place - they ordered
          the repair. And hopefully they pay us -
          with real money!

                    FRANZ
          Do you have any idea where the things of
          the lady are.

                    CONTRACTOR
          Everything has been burnt. They told us
          to burn everything. "Everything", they
          said. Even the old lady has been burned -
          well, not by us.

The contractor laughs. Franz looks serious and determined for
some clues.

                    FRANZ
          How did she die - who found her dead? Do
          you know?

                    CONTRACTOR
          She was old. The church found her dead, I
          believe - it is their place.

                    FRANZ
          OK - thanks. Can I give you my card, just
          in case you hear more about the lady or
          her things?

Franz hands his card to the contractor. He exits the
apartment.

EXT. EUROPE - CATHEDRAL - OUTSIDE - DAY

Franz walks up to the square. He looks over at the gloomy
church. The Requiem fills the space as Franz starts walking
over to the church. He carefully opens the large wooden door,
looks into the almost dark room, and enters.

INT. NEW YORK - POLICE STATION - OFFICE - DAY

Sergeant Samuel, Larry and Mille are together in Samuel's
office. Larry hits the noisy air-conditioner hard. Samuel is
in the middle of his speech.

                    SAMUEL
          ...... So, that's what they say over there:
          "everything gone - literally." And still, my
          friends, we have no trace of Paioni. And -

                    MILLE
          I looked Ludwig Mann up. He married very
          recently in Europe.

                    SAMUEL
                (getting in his sarcastic
                mood)
          Well, most people do at some point - some
          even do it several times.
          So, who did he marry?

MILLE
The manager, Samuel - Josephine deBois.
Apparently she is the one that made
him famous. She made him a huge name -
and also a huge fortune - very huge,
it is believed - you know, they have
been asking for enormous fees for their
performances during the latest years -
that's the rumor.

SAMUEL
I see, but nothing wrong by that - what
else about her?

MILLE
We know a lot from the recent years. But
there is nothing to find about her past -
just nothing!

SAMUEL
        (still in sarcastic mood
        and with a crescendo of
        frustration)
"Nothing" - nothing, nothing, nothing.
"NOTHING" surprises me any more folks -
except perhaps if you had told me you
found all her data, everything about
her past, everything about Giulia Cara,
everything about everything. But what
do we get, nothing about everything and
everything about nothing.
        (he pauses a bit embarrassed
        by being upset and continues
        in a calm, soothing tone)
- and Larry?

LARRY
Sorry - same story Samuel. I tried to
trace the mother of Ludwig Mann - again
nothing.
        (he pauses before continuing
        a bit subdue)
Samuel - I wonder how much more we can
really do here.

                    SAMUEL
          You are right. Maybe we just stop here and
          leave it as is -
                    (unsuccessfully attempting
                     to convince himself)
          - who cares after all?

It is quiet in the room. The three stand and think about the
case. Then Samuel hits the table with his hand.

                    SAMUEL
          What about this girl who said she knew
          Ludwig when we arrested him - the
          prostitute?

                    LARRY
          She probably just saw him when he entered
          the park. I wouldn't go after her. They
          are there all the time - we arrest a few
          now and then - just to keep the area a
          bit cleaner.

                    SAMUEL
          OK - well, what can we do? Mille, perhaps
          try to find this Josephine and talk to
          her - ask Ludwig. He should know where
          his wife is, right?

Mille and Larry leave the room. Samuel sits alone by the desk.
The terrible air-conditioner starts making its unbearable
strong noise. Sergeant Samuel walks over to the devise and
hammers the conditioner. It gets very quiet.

INT. NEW YORK - JEWELRY SHOP - DAY

Ludwig and Chu-jin stand face to face right inside the door of
Chu-jin's shop. Ludwig is carrying the scores for the upcoming
rehearsals. The gentle light from the early sun of the day
shines lightly through the windows, illuminating the room
right by the windows only. The rest of the shop is in dim
light. Ludwig and Chu-jin are both slightly embarrassed. Chu-
jin looks down at the floor for a short moment and then up
at Ludwig. As she looks up, the gentle rays of the early sun
make her face clearly visible with its strong resemblance to
Tiffany's.

                          CHU-JIN
          What brings you here this early, Dr.
          Mann? - Please take a seat.

She directs Ludwig to the small table with the violet flowers.
She quickly goes to the kitchen and returns with two cups of
tea. She places the cups on the table. She elegantly takes a
seat opposite Ludwig and looks questioning at him.

                          LUDWIG
          It is about the fortune telling.
          Could you perhaps try again and see if
          you can get contact?

                          CHU-JIN
          I can try - but I am pretty sure it won't
          work. I tried very hard - and I never
          failed before.

                          LUDWIG
          I really want you to read my mind.
          Would you mind?

Chu-jin rises and puts the sign for "closed" at the front
door. She directs Ludwig to the kitchen. Ludwig exits the
shop. Chu-jin follows.

INT. NEW YORK - JEWELRY SHOP - BACK ROOM - DAY

Ludwig and Chu-jin sit as during the previous event with
Tiffany. Chu-jin concentrates deeply, her eyelids vibrate and
her hands hold tight to the table. It is quiet. Ludwig closes
his eyes. After a while Chu-jin opens her eyes. She looks sad
at Ludwig's questioning eyes.

                          CHU-JIN
          Dr. Mann - I cannot - there is nothing
          to see.
                    (she pauses)
          Dr. Mann - anything you can tell me about
          you that might help. I mean, maybe I have
          to approach you in a different way?

Ludwig, with his elbows on the table, his fingers over his
mouth and his fingertips reaching the tip of his nose, looks
Chu-jin in the eyes.

                    LUDWIG
          I don't think it is your fault.
                    (he pauses)
          I have to get to the studio.

Ludwig and Chu-jin rise and walk to the shop.

INT. NEW YORK - JEWELRY SHOP - DAY

Chu-jin and Ludwig stand close face-to-face by the front door.
Chu-jin stretches her hands forward while leaning slightly
backwards. She smiles charmingly but with some sadness. Ludwig
holds both her hands in his for a moment. Chu-jin unlocks and
opens the door to the shop. Ludwig exits and walks down the
street towards the concert hall. Chu-jin stands by the door
and follows Ludwig with her eyes down the street. She walks
back into the shop.

INT. NEW YORK - CONCERT HALL - FOYER - DAY

Sergeant Mille is standing in the foyer of the concert hall
building waiting for Ludwig. She walks over towards Ludwig
as he exits the lift. They meet in the middle of the foyer.
Ludwig recognizes Mille as she approaches him.

                    MILLE
          Excuse me, Dr. Mann, do you have a short
          moment.

                    LUDWIG
          Sure -

                    MILLE

          Just a single question. Do you think your
          wife would mind if we asked her a few
          questions?

                    LUDWIG
          No, not at all. But why?

                    MILLE
          Still no trace of Paioni.

                        LUDWIG
          I can give you her phone number.

                        MILLE
          Excellent - then I won't bother you
          anymore.

Mille gives Ludwig a business card. He takes his cell phone
and looks Josephine's number up. Mille hands Ludwig a pen. He
writes the number on the back of the card. They shake hands
as goodbye and exit the building.

EXT. MANHATTAN - MIDTOWN - STREET - DAY

Mille walks over to the police car parked in front of the
concert building. She inserts a card in a public phone next to
the car and makes a call. Ludwig walks down the street. Mille
gets contact and can be seen talking on the phone.

INT. MANHATTAN - HOTEL - SUITE - DAY

Tiffany and Ludwig are having breakfast in Ludwig's suite.
Most of their luggage has been packed in suitcases standing
ready for the last items to be packed. Ludwig enjoys his
coffee while Tiffany cuts and eats the fine fruits and reads
a newspaper on her lap. She notices a story on the front page.
She stops eating the fruit. She takes her tea and reads much
focused while she drinks.

                        TIFFANY
          I think there is something about the man
          you mentioned.

                        LUDWIG

          Yes - ?

                        TIFFANY
          Listen!
               (reading loud)
          "Scientist disappears before landmark
          talk at the hundred year anniversary of
          the Society of the Sciences. The scientist
          Duilio Paioni has been out of reach
          for several days and is now searched

worldwide. In an interview yesterday
evening with the President of the Society
of Sciences it was confirmed that the
topic of the landmark lecture is on the
"Total Synthesis of a Human Being and
its Implication for Humanity". According
to the president, another lecture on
future materials to interphase the human
brain and computers will now become the
landmark talk.
> (she pauses before she
> continues concerned)

How do they know all this? Is this the
man you talked about?

                    LUDWIG

It sounds so.
> (he hides his face in his
> hands for a moment - then
> looks up)

I don't know what to think about any
of this anymore. I don't even want to
think about it. As I told them again and
again - just leave me out of this.

                    TIFFANY

Agree.
> (she rises)

Let's get out of here.

Tiffany, strongly determined, makes a call and swiftly packs
her last items. Shortly afterward, a servant appears with a
trolley and exits with all the luggage. A clerk enters with
the paperwork. Tiffany signs absent minded for Ludwig without
reading the papers. The clerk bows and exits. Tiffany and
Ludwig exit.

INT. NEW YORK - POLICE HEADQUARTER - FRONT OFFICE

Samuel, Mille, and Larry enter the spacious front office of
Samuel's supervisor ERNST AUSTIN (AGE 62). The admin of Ernst
Austin, a brusquely, uniformed, middle-aged, slim woman, asks
them to take their seats in a group of uncomfortable, poorly
designed chairs. After a while, the admin's phone rings with a
buzzing sound. The admin points to the door of Ernst's office as
a sign for them to enter. They rise and exit the front office.

INT. NEW YORK - POLICE HEADQUARTER - OFFICE ERNST - DAY

Samuel, Mille and Larry cautiously enter Ernst's office. They stand inside the door and wait for further instructions. Ernst sits behind a huge writing desk. He is extremely overweight and is signing documents one after another from a pile of papers. Without looking up he gives sign to Samuel, Larry and Mille to take seat in front of the desk. Finally, he looks up and talks in a highly unpleasant and inquisitorial tone.

                    ERNST
          Can I ask you what is going on?

                    SAMUEL
          Excuse me Sir - in regard to what?

Ernst, obviously irritated by Samuel's response, takes a tabloid newspaper on the desk and reads loud, irritated, exaggerated and didactic.

                    ERNST
          "Is there an artificial human among us?"
                    (he gazes at Samuel and
                    continues)
          "The President of the Society of the
          Sciences cannot exclude the possibility."

He throws the paper on the desk towards Samuel, Mille and Larry. His high blood pressure shows up in the color of his face. He starts sweating and loosens his too small shirt around the neck.

                    ERNST
          How can this stuff reach the street
          without us being prepared?

                    SAMUEL
          The society must have told somebody about
          Paioni.

                    ERNST
          That's why I called Dr. Ryesling.
          And he did not say anything like
          this, --- Sergeant!

                    SAMUEL
          Maybe the journalists are just guessing -
          not unusual.

Ernst, now explosive by the total lack of clarity, speaks in
an increasingly louder voice.

                    ERNST
          Well Sergeant. In this case the press may
          either do pretty good guesses - or they
          may simply be better than you. No way
          could they pull this out of the blue -
          there must be something going on, right?
          So couldn't you at least do me the favor
          to find out if this whole thing is real
          or not. Who is this artificial human? A
          man? A woman? A funny new gender?
                    (points with increasing
                    agitation to the phone while
                    speaking)
          I want this out of the way. I don't
          want my phone here to ring and ring by
          desperate congressmen and even higher
          level officials about this thing. So,
          Sergeant, you better find Paioni and you
          better tell me whether this whole thing
          is true or not; Get it done and get down
          to facts.
                    (he pauses)
          Did I make myself clear? - and don't
          pretend no knowing "what is going on".

Samuel, Mille and Larry rise. As they are about to leave
Samuel turns to Ernst.

                    SAMUEL
          Maybe you could help me a bit. We found
          a DNA match from a sample in Paioni's
          office, to an old case. Could you let me
          have a warrant to obtain a sample from
          Ludwig Mann - he was there before Paioni
          disappeared - the last person we know of
          who saw Paioni.

                    ERNST
                    (pretending to be calm)
          You want me to authorize that you go to
          a high profile individual that is not
          in any way suspected of any wrongdoings
          and request a blood sample: "Sir I think

a DNA sample from you could help me to
find Duilio Paioni and resolve all the
mysteries circulating about him."
             (he explodes)
Where have you been during your lessons
at the police school, stupid?!?

                    SAMUEL
I just thought this would ...

                    ERNST
             (interrupting)
.... I don't care what you think. I care
about you solving this case as presented
to us. That is: find Paioni. - So
Sergeant; do as I say; and do it fast!

Ernst again focuses his attention to the piles of paper on the
desk. Samuel, Larry and Mille quietly exit the office.

INT. NEW YORK - POLICE HEADQUARTER - FRONT OFFICE ERNST - DAY

The admin in the front office barely looks up as Samuel, Larry
and Mille pass through.

INT. NEW YORK - POLICE HEADQUARTER - FOYER - DAY

Samuel, Mille and Larry enter the foyer of the police
headquarters from the lift. They walk to the middle of the
foyer and stand for a short moment together. The foyer is busy
with numerous people passing.

                    SAMUEL
Mille, did you get contact to the wife?

                    MILLE
No, there was no answer at the number
Dr. Mann gave me. I tried a couple of
times. The last time there was not even
a ringing tone. I think the telephone has
been closed.

                    SAMUEL
Hum - and Larry - any more news?

                         LARRY
         The lab confirmed the match; Otherwise
         nothing.

                         SAMUEL
         OK folks, let's get out of this place!

Samuel, Mille and Larry exit the police headquarter.

EXT. NEW YORK - AIRPORT - PARKING - DAY

The limousine with Tiffany and Ludwig stops in front of the
departure area in a New York airport. The driver opens the
doors for Tiffany and Ludwig. They proceed directly to the
check-in area while the driver gathers their luggage on a
trolley and follows them to the check-in.

INT. NEW YORK - AIRPORT - LOUNGE - DAY

A young, male servant in the lounge brings refreshments to
Ludwig and Tiffany. They sit close to each other and watch the
planes leaving and arriving at the nearby runway. Ludwig takes
his cell phone and dials Josephine's number. The call does not
go through.

                         LUDWIG
              (in German)
         I have not been able to reach her for
         several days now - wonder what's going on.

                         TIFFANY
              (in German, slightly
              jealous)
         Try Dr. Schlesinger.

                         LUDWIG
         I don't know if I have his number.

Ludwig scrolls around on his phone. He finds Dr. Schlesinger's
number and dials. The call goes through.

                         DR. SCHLESINGER
              (in German, voice on phone)
         Hello.

                    LUDWIG
              (in German)
         Dr. Schlesinger - it is Ludwig.

                    DR. SCHLESINGER
         Hello Ludwig - where are you?

                    LUDWIG
         On my way back from New York, as planned.
         Did you by any chance hear from Josephine
         in the last couple of days. I cannot
         reach her.

                    DR. SCHLESINGER
         I am glad you called. I could not reach
         her either.

                    LUDWIG
         Could you please try again - just to make
         sure everything is in place. We go on a
         plane now.

                    DR. SCHLESINGER
         Of course.
              (he pauses)
         I will pick you up at the airport later.
         Everything for rehearsals and concerts is
         in place - I know that - no worry.

                    LUDWIG
         OK, great. See you then.

Ludwig hangs up, switches the telephone off and puts it in his
pocket.

INT. NEW YORK - POLICE HEADQUARTER - OFFICE ERNST - DAY

Ernst is sitting by his desk embedded in piles of paper.
His red phone with a direct line to top-ranking government
officials rings. He picks up immediately.

                    ERNST
              Yes.

                          VOICE
                    (extremely upset)
          Could you please turn your TV on.

The telephone is hanged up. Ernst switches the TV on and
browses until he reaches the news channel. A reporter is
in the middle of delivering a report in front of Duilio's
institute.

                        REPORTER
              (on TV standing in front of
                Duilio's laboratory)
     ...... and no sign of the missing scientist
     that was the key driver of the huge
     institute you see here behind me. He was
     going to deliver a landmark lecture on an
     artificial human at the upcoming meeting
     of the Society of the Sciences. Today we
     have breaking news. I am here with Dr.
     SCOTT (40, nerd scientist) an expert in DNA
     profiling. So Dr. tell me what do we know?

                         SCOTT
                    (on TV screen)
     What has been disclosed to me is the
     finding of a match between an old DNA
     sample and a sample collected recently
     in the office of our missing college Dr.
     Paioni. The old sample .....

Ernst hides his face in his hands, switches the TV off,
and smashes his fist violently in the table which is close
to breaking by the hit. His direct line rings in the same
moment. He swiftly goes to the desk and takes the phone.

                          VOICE
                (in an extremely angry tone)
          I assume you heard enough...?

                         ERNST
          I did.

Ernst listens with dismay and holds the phone further and
further from his ears as the voice on the phone explodes.

                    VOICE
    Now listen to me. Read my lips! You better
    clear this whole mess up, right away. From
    the bottom. And you put a lid on this
    case.
          (shouting)
    I - don't - want - artificial - humans -
    around. Is that understood. Nobody up
    here wants it. You understand? If this
    is real; imagine the consequences - the
    whole world order could turn upside down?
    This is not what we need at this time!
    Our national security may be compromised!
    It must stop! Get rid of this whole thing.
    Extinguish it - whatever it takes. Get
    a lid on this for Christ sake - and -
    don't - let - me - have - any - more -
    surprises. Did you hear what I said:
    I - do - not - want - artificial -
    humans - around!

The phone is hanged up. Ernst sits pondering, extremely
dismayed.

INT. VIENNA - CONCERT HALL - OFFICE SCHLESINGER - DAY

Dr. Schlesinger is sitting by the well-organized desk in
his office. All over the walls in the spacious room are
photographs of conductors and musicians, oil paintings,
portraits, bookshelves with old leather bound books and
numerous music scores. The floor is covered by numerous
antique rugs. The furniture are old, classical and precious
models. Dr. Schlesinger is reading through the program of the
day. It knocks at the door.

                DR. SCHLESINGER
          (loud, in German)
    Come in.

The door opens halfway. The concert master JOHAN DIETRICH (40),
slim and lightly dressed for an upcoming rehearsal looks in.

                    JOHAN
          (in German)
    Do you have a moment?

                    DR. SCHLESINGER
          Of course Johan. Come in please.

Johan enters the office. He carries a tabloid newspaper. Dr.
Schlesinger rises. He walks across the room. They shake hands
and take seat in two chairs by the window.

                         JOHAN
          It won't be long. But, - have you read the
          news today?

                    DR. SCHLESINGER
          Not yet - anything I should read?
                    (he looks at the clearly
                    worried Johan)
          - or anything I should be concerned
          about?

                         JOHAN
          A lot actually.
                    (pauses and continues in a
                    low voice)
          It's about Dr. Mann.

Johan opens the tabloid on his lap.

                         JOHAN
          If one can have any trust in these media,
          Dr. Mann seems to be implicated in a
          case in the US. It is about a scientist
          that has disappeared - for quite a while
          now. And somehow - somehow there is a
          rumor that this scientist generated an
          artificial human being.

Dr. Schlesinger looks puzzled. Johan reads aloud from the
tabloid.

                         JOHAN
          "Apparently Ludwig Mann is the last known
          person to have seen Duilio Paioni alive."
          That's the name of the scientist ...
                    (he pauses while skipping
                    some sentences and continues
                    reading loud)

"..... and if you add to that the match of
the DNA found in the office it could be
that indeed Duilio Paioni's experiment was
successful in a second try ...
        (Johan looks up at Dr.
        Schlesinger while he
        continues)
..... and that the resulting human is
Ludwig Mann. Police and law official are
deeply concerned."

                DR. SCHLESINGER
        (laughs)
Well - come on Johan!

                JOHAN
Well; I know - farfetched indeed. But,
you see, my problem is, that the musicians
are extremely concerned. Convinced even -
some of them. They start believing that
Dr. Mann could be sort of unreal. From
another world.

Johan pauses briefly. Whispering as revealing a secret, he
continues.

                JOHAN
"Can it be dangerous to be close to such
a person?" That's the kind of questions
they start asking.

                DR. SCHLESINGER
Now, wait a minute. Dr. Mann has been
around forever. Everybody loves him,
everybody enjoys what he is doing, and
nothing bad has ever happened. This is
ridiculous.

                JOHAN
I do agree with you - but Dr. I
cannot change the sentiment among the
musicians - and the audience!
        (he pauses)
The musicians gathered this morning and
they decided that they won't rehearse.

                    DR SCHLESINGER
          What....?

Dr. Schlesinger sits stunned for a moment and considers.

                    DR. SCHLESINGER
          Thanks Johan. I better get to the
          airport. Ludwig is landing this morning.
                    (he pauses)
          Keep that for yourself, please.

They sit quiet together while they think through their
options.

                    DR SCHLESINGER
          Well then, if that's what it is - could
          you please contact the administration and
          ask them to cancel. I cannot believe it
          Johan. But I hear that is our only option.

                    JOHAN
          Yes Dr. I am afraid so. Of course that
          will just add more wood to the fire. It
          will look like an acceptance of this
          weird story.

                    DR SCHLESINGER
          Find an excuse then - say Ludwig has
          become ill. That he himself cancelled.
          That happened before.

                    JOHAN
          Good idea - I will do so.
                    (he pauses for a moment)
          You know, when I first thought about
          this, I felt it like somebody just wants
          to take Dr. Mann from us. He is the best
          we ever had - he has taken us to the edge
          of music; to places we never imagined.
          Unreal in a way, you might say, but yet
          it became so real - what we never thought
          of became real ... became a reality in
          our world. He reached for the stars - and
          that's what we need.... He expanded our
          world beyond.

              (he pauses and almost cries
                as he continues)
     Dr., it is like something evil is
     touching us.

                DR. SCHLESINGER
     I agree Johan. What a mess. Let's try to
     diffuse it. Tell he is ill - and then we
     let time pass by.

They both rise and leave the office.

EXT. MANHATTAN - HOTEL - OUTSIDE - DAY

A police car pulls up in front of a low profile Manhattan
hotel. Sergeant Mille, uniformed, steps out of the car and
enters the hotel.

INT. MANHATTAN - HOTEL - LOBBY - DAY

Mille enters the not too busy hotel lobby and walks over to
the reception. A young female RECEPTIONIST (25) addresses
Mille kindly as she approaches.

                RECEPTIONIST
     What can I do for you Mrs.?

                MILLE
     There should be a letter for Charles
     Abaco. I am here to pick it up.

The receptionist browses through a handful of envelopes on
the table behind the reception desk. She finds a large yellow
envelope with a handwritten text; "for Charles Abaco
- to be picked up today".

                RECEPTIONIST
     It must be this one, right?

She shows Mille the envelope.

                MILLE
     Sure that's it. Thanks a lot.

The receptionist hands the letter to Mille. She takes it and walks out of the hotel.

EXT. MANHATTAN - HOTEL - OUTSIDE - DAY

Mille opens the large yellow envelope while standing right next to the police car. Inside she finds a smaller white envelope. She puts the white envelope in her inner pocket, tears the yellow envelope in very small pieces which she disposes in a garbage bin nearby. She enters the car.

INT. MANHATTAN - POLICE CAR - DAY

In the police car Mille opens the white envelope. She finds a very thick bundle of large dollar notes. She browses through the notes, puts them back in the envelope and in her inner pocket; she starts driving down the street. As she drives, she leans back, smiles satisfied and speeds up. She laughs.

                    MILLE
              (talking to herself)
          What a deal. I love that woman.

EXT. MANHATTAN - HOTEL - OUTSIDE - DAY

The police car rapidly disappears down the street

INT. EUROPE - AIRPORT - ARRIVAL AREA - DAY

Dr. Schlesinger is waiting in the arrival area of a European airport. He looks at the screen announcing flight arrivals. Tiffany and Ludwig enter the arrival area. They walk closely together and shine of happiness in each other's company. As Ludwig sees Dr. Schlesinger waiting, he smiles and waves. Ludwig and Tiffany swiftly walk over to Dr. Schlesinger. He embraces Tiffany and then Ludwig. He holds Ludwig emotionally and tight.

                    LUDWIG
              (in German)
          So wonderful to see you Dr. Good being
          back.

                    DR. SCHLESINGER
                       (in German)
          I have been looking so forward to this
          moment - but Ludwig, something has
          happened.

                    LUDWIG
          Yes?

                    DR. SCHLESINGER
          Let's sit in there for a moment.

Dr. Schlesinger points to an arrival lounge. They all enter
the lounge.

INT. EUROPE - AIRPORT - LOUNGE - DAY

Tiffany, Ludwig and Dr. Schlesinger enter a small, executive
arrival lounge. They are alone, except for a servant who
provides refreshments. Ludwig and Tiffany sit side by side on
one side of a small, low table. Dr. Schlesinger shows them the
latest tabloid newspapers. Tiffany and Ludwig read together.
Dr. Schlesinger sits quiet, worried and sad while they read.
Ludwig looks at Dr. Schlesinger.

                    LUDWIG
          Well - it is what it is. This is a piece
          of sensational crap.

                    DR SCHLESINGER
          Agree Ludwig, but let me tell you what
          happened this morning -

                                        FORWARD IN TIME

                    DR. SCHLESINGER
          So, the only reasonable proposal I can
          think of is that you "disappear" for
          some time. We will just say that you have
          become ill. Then this hype settles -
          people forget, like with any sensational
          stories: tomorrow there is another
          sensation. You know how it is.

                    LUDWIG
          But how? We cannot just disappear!

                    DR. SCHLESINGER
          I brought my car. You can use it.
          Go to the mountains - you still have your
          place there, right?

Ludwig looks at Tiffany.

                    TIFFANY
               (Tiffany nods)
          Sounds good. Let's just get out of here!

They all rise and exit the lounge.

INT. VIENNA - CONCERT HALL - OFFICE SCHLESINGER - DAY

Dr. Schlesinger enters his office. He looks worried around. He
walks over to the desk and sits down. It knocks on the door.
Johan opens the door carefully and enters quietly as he sees
Dr. Schlesinger. He talks from just inside the door.

                    JOHAN
          I just want to let you know that
          everything has been organized.

                    DR. SCHLESINGER
          Thanks Johan.

                    JOHAN
          And Dr. Mann. Do you know where he is -
          just in case somebody asks?

                    DR. SCHLESINGER
          I don't know Johan - I just don't know -
          and that's probably the best for all of
          us. God bless him.

Dr. Schlesinger hides his head in his hands on the desk.

EXT. EUROPE - MOUNTAIN ROADS - CAR - EARLY EVENING

The day is fading. In a terrific sunset Ludwig and Tiffany
drive the last part of the narrow roads up to Ludwig's
cottage. The cottage becomes visible high up on the edge of
the steep hills.

EXT. COTTAGE - MORNING

The darkness around the cottage starts to fade. The sky becomes lighter in a soft red sunrise. As the sun rises it sends brilliant rays between the snow covered mountain tops.

INT. COTTAGE - MAIN COTTAGE - EARLY MORNING

In the main cottage the rays of the sun illuminate the room softly. Ludwig wakes up. Tiffany is still sleeping by his side. He remains quiet and looks around as if the events that brought them there are unreal. Tiffany wakes up. She looks at Ludwig and moves a bit closer. She puts her hand on his chest. They lie silently together and watch the cottage for a while.

Ludwig gets up and goes to the fireplace. He adds new firewood. He goes to the kitchen area. He picks a big kettle and exits the cottage. Tiffany closes her eyes while staying in the bed and enjoys the quiet moment.

EXT. COTTAGE - COURTYARD - EARLY MORNING

Ludwig enters the courtyard from the main cottage and walks over to the well and the manual water pump. While he pumps the water, he puts his head under the water stream. Refreshed and energized he looks around the gorgeous scenery in the sunrise. He walks back to the cottage and exits the courtyard.

INT. COTTAGE - MAIN COTTAGE - EARLY MORNING

Ludwig enters the main cottage. He puts the kettle on the fireplace. Tiffany rises from the bed and walks over to Ludwig. They sit together in front of the fireplace. Ludwig looks over at the two pianos in the room.

                    LUDWIG
              (in German)
         Maybe I should tune them.

Ludwig walks over to the pianos and start tuning. Tiffany rises and exits the cottage while she smiles of Ludwig's eager for the old pianos

EXT. COTTAGE - MAIN COTTAGE - EARLY MORNING

Tiffany walks outside. She stands in the small courtyard and
enjoys the crisp mountain air and the scenery. She walks over
to the bench and sits for a while at the edge of the hill. She
hears Ludwig tuning the pianos and then trying to play all four
hands of the 448 sonata. She laughs and runs back to the house.

INT. COTTAGE - MAIN COTTAGE - EARLY MORNING

Ludwig tries to play the four hands of the sonata. Tiffany
goes over to the other piano and sits on the piano bench. She
laughs.

                    TIFFANY
          Maybe you need a little assistance
          after all.

Tiffany rises and goes to the side of the piano and stands
with crossed arms while blowing herself up to the greatest she
can be.

                    TIFFANY
               (in German dialect mimicking
               the German woman at the
               admission test)
          And who is next? So you Tiffany.
          And what is your piece? -- Well, I told
          you, the "repetiteur" is not here today
          and we do not have the scores around.

Tiffany pretends crying. Ludwig raises his hand

                    LUDWIG
          I heard that piece - I can play it!

                    TIFFANY
               (still pretending, she
               continues in an angry and
               irritated tone)
          I told you - the score is not here!

Tiffany pretends looking down the concert hall to the Maestro.
Ludwig rises and walks to the middle of the room. He takes
seat on a chair, puts his elbows on a chair in front and
imitates the Maestro by spreading his hands in a questioning

acceptance. They both laugh, sit down by the pianos, turn to face each other, and starts playing flawlessly. Gradually they go wild and play through the music making jazz-like improvisations of the piece (Mozart double sonata). Finally, the second movement is played genuinely and perfectly.

THE SECOND MOVEMENT FOLLOWS THROUGH

EXT. EUROPE - HOUSE LUDWIG - OUTSIDE - DAY

Ludwig and Tiffany drive down the street in the town of Ludwig's childhood. The music continues. By Ludwig's house they slow down. The small wooden house appears untouched. Plants are growing up around the house. Ludwig drives into a small space on the land and stops the car. He exits, stands for a moment by the side of the car and looks down the street. Tiffany exits the car. They walk to the entrance of the house. Ludwig finds the large, rusty key hidden under a stone in front of the door. He unlocks the door and slowly pushes it open. They look into the dark room. The music fades.

INT. EUROPE - HOUSE LUDWIG - DAY

Ludwig walks through the small corridor and over to the window opposite the entrance in the main room. He pulls the curtain aside and opens the window. Light shines into the room through the small window. Tiffany is touched by the small and primitive house. As Ludwig has opened the window, a fresh breeze blows through the house and lifts the curtain.

                    LUDWIG
          This is where I was before I got to
          know you.

                    TIFFANY
               (smiling)
          I love it.

Tiffany sees the old piano in the corner of the room. Ludwig notices where she looks.

                    LUDWIG
          I had to tune it every day. It has an old
          wooden frame, so it's out of tune in a
          matter of hours.

He walks over to the piano. The tuning fork is on the top of the instrument. He takes it.

                    LUDWIG
          This is the one I first used. I got it
          from the instrument maker down the road.
          He learned me to tune the piano.

Ludwig puts the tuning fork back on the piano. They go to the small room. Ludwig opens a small cabinet. He searches and moves the many items in the cabinet around. He finds a small metal box. He opens it. There are a few photographs in the box. Ludwig and Tiffany sit down on the small bed and go through the pictures. Ludwig finds a copy of the picture from the admission examination. He and Tiffany are sitting as small children side by side.

                    LUDWIG
          You played so well already. Where did it
          come from - so divine?

                    TIFFANY
          Gyung-hee was with me all the time.
          She played the traditional Korean
          instrument - I told you Mr. Powder. She
          knew music so well - almost magical. A
          pity she did not play piano. She reached
          beyond.

                    LUDWIG
          But how, what happened?

                    TIFFANY
          Mr. Powder: she came to the house and
          asked for shelter. It was a snowstorm. She
          collapsed outside of the mansion. Can you
          imagine? She had lost everything. Father
          just wanted to get her out of the place;
          but mother took her in. She became her
          servant.
                    (she pauses and looks down
                    as she continues subdue)
          Somehow I felt more connected to her than
          to mother - I think they both felt it,
          but it did not bother them.

Ludwig walks around in the small house and looks into all the
cabinets. He looks behind the few books on the bookshelves.
Tiffany watches everything and imprints it all in her mind.
It knocks on the door. Tiffany and Ludwig look surprised at
each other. They are quiet for a moment. It knocks again, more
forceful. Ludwig goes to the door. He opens. Giovanni, dressed
in a large black coat, is standing outside.

                    LUDWIG
               (in German)
          What can I do for you?

                    GIOVANNI
               (in german)
          Can I come in for a moment Dr. Mann? My
          name is Landini, Giovanni Landini.

                    LUDWIG
          Look, we are just about to leave - not
          sure what you want here. The house is
          being closed down.

                    GIOVANNI
          I know. But I have something important
          to talk to you about. So - if you could
          spare a few minutes.

Ludwig opens the door. Giovanni walks over to Tiffany and
shakes hands. Tiffany shakes hands only reluctantly.

                    GIOVANNI
          Nice to meet you Mrs. Yun.

Ludwig closes the door to the outside.

                    GIOVANNI
          May I sit down?

                    LUDWIG
          Sure.

They all sit by the rough dining table in the middle of the
room. Ludwig and Tiffany look at Giovanni and wait for him to
speak.

                    GIOVANNI
     Dr. Mann. I know about the troubles you
     are in. And, I know Dr. Paioni told you
     who you are.
            (Giovanni pauses)
     Let me tell you straight away - what
     Paioni told you is true. And Dr. Mann -
     you saw his institute, right? So you will
     know that, of course, he did not act on
     his own. Imagine the money he needed -
     that's where I come in. I wanted his
     project as much as he did. So Dr., I got
     the money and he did the work!

                    LUDWIG
     I am sorry; I had enough of this project.
     I couldn't care less about how you fit in
     and where the money comes from. I told
     Paioni that I don't want to be part of
     it - and now I tell you the same. Just
     leave me alone. Don't follow me and don't
     show up like this.

                    GIOVANNI
     Well Dr. It seems to me you are not aware
     of the significance of yourself. We simply
     must follow you and know exactly what you
     are doing. We follow every step you take,
     we listen to every word you say and we
     trace everything that is happening around
     you. We have done that for years - your
     entire life.

Giovanni moves a little closer to the table. Ludwig and
Tiffany are skeptical.

                    GIOVANNI
     You are in serious trouble. But I have the
     means to help you out.

                    LUDWIG
     Why on earth should I trust you?
     All you say could be pulled out of the
     air. This whole story is a piece of crap.
     I got enough of it!

Giovanni pauses for a moment and ignores Ludwig's comments.

                    GIOVANNI
          Let me tell you my proposal. You come with
          me to the center of the program. It is not
          too far. There we can show you as much
          as you want to convince you that we are
          telling the truth. And we can deal with it
          in a way that takes your troubles away.
                    (he pauses.)
          Cooperation is really your only option.
          If you continue the way it is - hiding
          in the mountains and hoping the whole
          thing will go away - you will just get
          in even more trouble. The rumors; they
          are already out there - you know that,
          right? - they will not go away, and the
          evidence will become public. So you will
          be cursed. Nobody will have anything to
          do with you. Nobody will see you as the
          great musician you like to be viewed as,
          everything will be taken away from you. I
          can guarantee you Dr.

Giovanni looks at Tiffany. He talks first softly but escalates
to a fuming loud language.

                    GIOVANNI
          And you Mrs. Yun, you will lose what is
          most precious to you. In spite of your
          heroic stance that you will love Dr.
          Mann dearly "whatever he is" - in spite
          of that, Mrs. Yun, he will perish and
          disappear for you. And you will perish as
          well. You will be cursed for having been
          with him and for having loved him. You
          will be seen as evil. You will transition
          from a gifted, famous, and beautiful
          artist to a cursed and evil witch!

Giovanni again focuses on Ludwig.

                    GIOVANNI
          Come with me. I'll show you the truth and
          a way forward.

Ludwig looks at Tiffany. He looks back at Giovanni.

THE PICTURE FADES AND TRANSITIONS TO THE MONESTARY

EXT. MONESTARY - COURTYARD - EVENING

A black car with a driver, Ludwig and Giovanni enters the small courtyard inside the monastery. It stops by the stairs leading up to the entrance of the main building. The large, robust wooden door is opened from the inside. The stone-faced butler appears and walks down to the car. The driver exits the car and opens the door for Ludwig and then for Giovanni. The driver opens the trunk and gives two handbags to the butler. Ludwig stands next to the car for a moment and watches the gloomy scenery. With his hand, Giovanni invites Ludwig to follow him up to the building. The butler, stone-faced, walks in front of them.

INT. MONASTERY - CORRIDOR - EVENING

The butler, stone-faced, leads Ludwig up the broad staircase and through the corridor to the door to the roof leading over to the side building.

EXT. MONASTERY - ROOF - EVENING

The butler and Ludwig walk over the roof to the side building. The butler opens the door with the big key he carries in his pocket. They enter the side building.

INT. MONASTERY - SIDE BUILDING - EVENING

The butler leads Ludwig into the room. He puts Ludwig's bag on the table in the middle of the room and pours water in the small washbasin in the corner. He lights the candles on the walls. Ludwig stands in the middle of the room. The butler goes to the exit and bows as he exits.

                    BUTLER
          (in Italian)
     I will pick you up in 15 minutes Dr.

INT. MONASTERY - MEETING ROOM BIG - EVENING

Marchetto is sitting by the large table in the meeting
room. Two assistants stand behind him. Two tables standing
perpendicular to the main table are empty. Giovanni, dressed
in black, is sitting by a fourth table facing Marchetto. The
four tables form a square in the large room. As Ludwig enters,
Giovanni rises and asks Ludwig to take a seat next to him.
Ludwig sits down next to Giovanni. He faces Marchetto. The
door behind Ludwig is being closed by the butler from the
outside with a soft but firm sound. The light in the room
is dim from candles along the walls and a huge fire in the
fireplace. The only sound is from the fireplace. Marchetto
is watching Ludwig very, very intensively, scrutinizing every
detail. He starts talking - softly and kindly.

                    MARCHETTO
               (in Italian)
          I am glad you could come Dr. Mann. I have
          some important things to tell you - and
          then Dr. we have some important choices
          to make.

                    LUDWIG
               (in Italian, irritated)
          I appreciate being here, but I must say,
          as I have done at several occasions now:
          I just don't want to be part of whatever
          it is you have cooking.

                    MARCHETTO
               (more determined tone)
          I certainly appreciate your honesty. But
          listen, you are missing the point. Whether
          you like it or not, whether you want to
          be part of what "we have cooking" as you
          say - well Dr. the fact of the matter is
          that "you are it" - there is not such a
          thing Dr. as choosing not to be part of
          it, as you say, because you - are - "it"!
               (he pauses briefly)
          Let me be crystal clear - we made you
          exactly as you have been told: you are
          made of powder - as you expressed it
          yourself recently. And Dr. we did even
          more. We made you famous, a star, right? -
          and we paid for it. Where do you think

all the money came from? I tell you - it
all came from here.
          (hammering in the table)
Here - right here Dr. I personally signed
off for all the expenses to make you what
you are - and I tell you, you've been
horrifyingly expensive.

Marchetto pauses for a moment. There is total silence in the
room. Only the fire and the candles along the wall are heard.

                    MARCHETTO
               (more suiting tone)
So Dr.; here is what I am going to tell
you: you are a big problem for us and we
need to talk about that.

                    LUDWIG
               (irritated)
Just leave me alone. I hear what you say
about me being "it". But honestly, I don't
care. And I am not interfering with your
matters - why on earth should I?

                    MARCHETTO
I probably did not make myself clear. But
let me step back for a moment then. This
idiot sitting next to you convinced us,
that by making you from powder you would
become the proof that the science is
wrong and that our institution is right
in some crucial matters. You would be the
living proof, so to say, that creation is
sacred as preached by this institution
because you would not be a human being
with all that goes with being human. You
would be defect - that was the idea. And
now - look at yourself. What has he done
this idiot? He did just the opposite. He
proved us wrong. With one stroke which is
you - yes you Dr. - with one stroke he
eliminated the basis for our institution
and our basic belief in creation and
humanity.

                              LUDWIG
          What do you want me to say. I just
          don't want to be part of this game -
          even though you say it is impossible,
          by definition, so to say. But honestly,
          whatever you say, I don't care. I am not
          going to mess with your faith, although it
          seems to me that your experiment may in
          fact have revealed some truth about all
          the matters you just mentioned. Why don't
          you just admit that you've been wrong.
          What's wrong with the truth?

Marchetto rises violently. He stands highly agitated, fuming
and leans forward over the table as he speaks.

                            MARCHETTO
                        (almost shouting)
          "The Truth." Did I hear right, you said
          finding the Truth Dr.? Let me be clear.
          This place Dr. decides about Truth and
          Faith. And it must continue to be like
          that. And Dr., we here in this very place,
          we tell and we decide what the Truth is -
          it is as simple as that. This is the world
          order - is that clear Dr.?

Marchetto tries to control himself in his furious state. He
sits down. He is extremely agitated as he continues.

                            MARCHETTO
          It is not on you to decide what is right
          and wrong. And unfortunately Dr. you have
          no choice of being part of this or not -
          I said it already.
                          (screaming)
          You are it! You - are - it! For Christ sake!
                        (in a soothing tone)
          The easiest way for us would be that you
          simply did not exist anymore - and since
          you are not a human being per definition,
          well then we could just eliminate you.
          Nothing wrong with that in any respect.
          There ...

Ludwig angrily interrupts Marchetto.

                    LUDWIG
        What do you mean - I am not a human
        being?

                  MARCHETTO
        With your origin - no way? You - are -
        not - a human - being.
                (faking compassion)
        But, even so, I am going to give you
        a choice - as though you were a human
        being!

Marchetto speaks softly as he continues. He leans forward and
moves closer to Ludwig while holding both hands with palms
down at the table.

                  MARCHETTO
        Let me make my proposal clear to you. I,
        as a human being, I want to express my
        compassion for you - even "something"
        like you! I am willing to have all the
        evidence about you eliminated. If I ask
        for that to be done - well, then there
        will be no trace left anywhere in the
        world and you can simply go back to your
        life and your love. Time passes by, and
        the world will gradually forget about this
        story - and, Dr., we will even support
        getting the rumors about you silenced.
        It will not be that difficult since the
        whole thing is so unbelievable. We will
        show the scientist as a fraudster; we
        will prove him as person that puts his
        personal ambitions above everything and
        who does not spare any means to reach
        his personal goals, including making
        the unbelievable crime of falsifying
        scientific results and evidence. And, on
        top of that, he has been torturing you
        and destroying one of the most brilliant
        human beings that has ever been in the
        arts - a gift from God to humanity. What
        would the art of music be without you?
        Does he care? No, not the slightest - all
        that matters to him is his fame and what
        goes with it. A sinner, a liar.

Marchetto pauses and assumes a more friendly tone as he
continues. Ludwig appears increasingly disgusted by the
fanatic views and positions of Marchetto. Giovanni listens in
silence with a neutral attitude and most of the time looks
down at the table.

                    MARCHETTO
          I just need one thing from you.
                    (pauses and moves even
                    closer)
          I need you to declare your faith and
          devotion to this institution for the rest
          of your life. You will tell the world that
          your unbelievable and divine capabilities
          as an artist have their roots in your
          faith and that all the good and the
          miracles you deliver to humanity come to
          you as divine gifts from God as you reach
          for the stars. You connect humanity and
          God - as a saint! You do miracles and we
          will prove that this, indeed, is the case.
                    (he pauses)
          In other words Dr. - we will work
          together, we will protect each other.
          You help us and we help you in the most
          divine way.

Marchetto leans back as he waits for his message to be absorbed
and appreciated. He continues in a faked indifferent tone.

                    MARCHETTO
          Alternatively, we can leave everything as
          it is. The evidence will be made public.
          And gradually you will be viewed as
          unnatural, as poison. All the problems you
          have today will get worse and worse and
          eat you up. You will be cursed. And so
          will your love. Mrs. Yun will perish and
          so will you. You will both burn in Hell!

                    LUDWIG
                    (getting pretty upset)
          You ask me to deny what you just told
          me is the truth. You ask me to mislead
          humanity by not telling the truth of what
          I am. You are contradicting yourself!

Ludwig pauses a moment. He considers.

                    LUDWIG
          You want me to lie.

                    MARCHETTO
          I just ask you to be faithful and save
          humanity.

Ludwig sits quiet for a while. He looks down at the table. He
looks up and stares Marchetto directly in the eyes.

                    LUDWIG
          I cannot do that - I do not want to lie
          to your advantage. Let's just continue as
          things are. Yes, I will suffer. And so
          what? Well, everything I burn for may be
          taken from me. Even so, I will make it. I
          I cannot lie.

                    MARCHETTO
          This is not the answer I was hoping for
          and, honestly, expecting.

Marchetto takes an indifferent attitude and appears to
distance himself from the situation.

                    MARCHETTO
          Well then - let's take it from there. If
          you change your mind during the night,
          let me know. Otherwise there will be a
          car for you tomorrow morning to bring you
          back. You can leave now.

Ludwig rises. The door is being opened from the outside.
Ludwig's and Giovanni's eyes meet briefly as Ludwig leaves the
room. Giovanni's face is without expression. Marchetto sits
shaken face to face with Giovanni.

                    MARCHETTO
          You idiot. Why did I trust your judgment?
          Now at least show me your loyalty and
          clean this mess up -
                    (shouting)
          - all of it!

Giovanni rises and leaves the room. Marchetto signals his
helpers to leave. They exit. Marchetto sits alone and watches
the fire.

INT. MONASTERY - SIDE BUILDING - MORNING

The daylight breaks and the last rain of the night stops.
Ludwig wakes up in the chair by the table as it knocks on the
door. The butler enters.

                    THE BUTLER
          I was asked to report if you changed your
          mind Dr.

                    LUDWIG
               (irritated)
          No - I did not. Could you please ask for
          the car to bring me back?

                    THE BUTLER
          Very well Dr.

The butler, stone-faced, exits the side building.

EXT. MONASTERY - ROOF - MORNING

The butler walks over the roof and exits the roof to the main
building. He closes the door and locks. He put the large key
in his pocket.

INT. MONASTERY - FOYER - DAY

The butler walks down the broad stairs in the lobby. Giovanni
is standing in the foyer. He looks at the butler. The butler's
face is without expression as he talks.

                    THE BUTLER
          I will follow you to the car, Brother. You
          do not need to wait.

The butler and Giovanni exit the foyer

EXT. MONASTERY - COURTYARD - DAY

The butler and Giovanni walk to the waiting car. Giovanni
enters the car. It starts driving out of the courtyard.

EXT. MONASTERY - ROOF - DAY

Ludwig leaves the side building and closes the door behind
him. He notices the door locks. He starts walking over the
roof. As he gets to the door to the main building he finds it
locked. He tries to pull the door open, but in vain.

INT. EUROPE - CAR - MOUNTANEOUS ROAD - DAY

The car with Giovanni drives down the narrow roads. He looks
up toward the mountain tops. Up by the brink of the rocks he
sees a large flock of huge black, eagle-like birds flying in
the direction of the cloister. He smiles satisfied and evil.
The car drives down the narrow road.

INT. COTTAGE - MAIN COTTAGE - DAY

Tiffany, tired and worried, is sitting by the table in Ludwig's
house. The sun shines through the small windows. It knocks
on the door. Tiffany walks to the door and opens. Giovanni's
large silhouette appears against the bright sky.

                    GIOVANNI
              (in German)
         May I come in please?

Tiffany does not answer but goes back into the room and
sits irritated by the table. Giovanni takes a seat opposite
Tiffany. They sit face to face.

                    TIFFANY
              (in German)
         Where is Ludwig?

                    GIOVANNI
         He will be away for a while. He decided to
         stay in the monastery.

                              TIFFANY
         I knew we couldn't trust you.
                   (she pauses)
         For how long?

                              GIOVANNI
         I cannot say. He will stay until he has
         thoughts things through.
                   (he pauses)
         Mrs. Yun. I have a proposal for you. And
         Mrs. Yun - you better make an important
         choice today.

PICTURE FADES AND TRANSITIONS TO A BRIGHT SUN IN SOUTH AMERICA

EXT. SOUTH AMERICA - HOTEL - OUTSIDE - DAY

Josephine exits a taxi in front of a luxurious South American
hotel. Her hair is long and black. She wears sunglasses and
overall is not easily recognizable as Josephine deBois. She
carries a small and smart four wheeler carry-on, a small
handbag and a leather briefcase.

INT. SOUTH AMERICA - HOTEL - LOBBY - DAY

Josephine enters the lobby and walks to the check-in counter.
A friendly, female RECEPTIONIST (25, slim, smart, attractive,
black hair) welcomes her.

                              JOSEPHINE
                   (in Spanish)
         Checking in please.

                              RECEPTIONIST
                   (in Spanish)
         Do you have a reservation Mrs.?

                              JOSEPHINE
                   (impatient, slightly rude)
         YES, - the name is Victoria Domingo.

                              RECEPTIONIST
         I have you here Mrs. A royal suite for one
         night?

                              JOSEPHINE
              Correct.

                              RECEPTIONIST
              Can I please take a print of your credit
              card - and your passport?

Josephine hands the receptionist her passport and a credit
card. The receptionist swipes the card, checks the passport
and gives both back to Josephine. She prints the keys and
calls a servant.

                              RECEPTIONIST
              He will show you up to your room.

                              JOSEPHINE
              Great - and could you please have a limo
              ready for me; in say - 15 minutes?

                              RECEPTIONIST
              Of course Mrs.

The servant takes Josephine's luggage and leads her to the
elevator.

INT. SOUTH AMERICAN - HOTEL - SUITE - DAY

The male servant (17) shows Josephine around in the suite.
She hands the servant a generous tip. The servant bows deeply
and exits backwards. Josephine quickly refreshes herself. She
applies a thick and strong colored make-up. She combs and
organizes her thick black hair. She takes the briefcase and
her handbag and swiftly exits the room.

EXT. SOUTH AMERICA - BANK - OUTSIDE - DAY

Josephine's limo stops in front of a major bank. The driver
opens the door for Josephine. She exits.

                              JOSEPHINE
              Just wait here - it won't be long.

The driver bows politely. Josephine enters the bank.

INT. SOUTH AMERICA - BANK - LOBBY - DAY

In the bank lobby Josephine goes swiftly to a small counter. A friendly woman RECEPTIONIST (25) greets her.

> JOSEPHINE
> (in Spanish)
> I have an appointment with Mr. Gonzales.

The receptionist checks a meeting list under the counter. She takes a phone and dials a number.

> RECEPTIONIST
> (in Spanish)
> Mrs. Domingo is here.
> (addressing Josephine while
> hanging up)
> He will be with you shortly.

Josephine waits for a short while. Mr. GONZALES (AGE 50) appears. He is an elegant, slim Spanish gentleman dressed in black and wearing a colorful tie.

> GONZALES
> (in Spanish)
> Welcome Mrs. Domingo. Please come with
> me - this way please.

Josephine and Mr. Gonzales walk to the back of the large open space on the ground floor and enter Mr. Gonzales' spacious and elegant office.

INT. SOUTH AMERICA - BANK - OFFICE GONZALES - DAY

Mr. Gonzales directs Josephine to a seat in front of his large desk. Overly satisfied and smiling he takes seat by his desk.

> GONZALES
> (in Spanish)
> So, welcome Mrs. Domingo. I made
> everything ready as we discussed over
> the phone. I just need to see your
> passport - then I can open your account
> and officially welcome you as one of our
> most distinguished customers -

As Josephine starts looking for her passport in her handbag, he continues talking while watching Josephine carefully.

                    GONZALES
          - and we guarantee ultimate discretion.
          We fully understand your needs.

                    JOSEPHINE
          I so appreciate Mr. Gonzales. Again,
          thanks so much for your flexibility. So,
          here is the passport.

Josephine hands her passport to Mr. Gonzales. He opens the passport, crosschecks with the information on his screen and finally enters a few notes in the computer. He presses "enter" and leans back while he watches the screen. He claps his hand and happily smiles to Josephine.

                    GONZALES
          So Mrs., it is all set. And tell me, what
          deposit can I enter today?

                    JOSEPHINE
          200 million please.
                    (she pauses)
          The other transfer we discussed has been
          done already.

                    GONZALES
          Yes - I can see it now. I do appreciate.

Josephine hands Mr. Gonzales the large leather briefcase. Mr. Gonzales calls upon the CASHIER (AGE 55) who rapidly shows up. Mr. Gonzales hands the briefcase to the cashier.

                    GONZALES
          For Mrs. Domingo's account. Let me have
          the receipt as fast as possible.

The cashier bows and exits with the briefcase. Josephine opens her handbag and takes a thick envelope. She hands the envelope to Mr. Gonzales.

                    JOSEPHINE
          As I mentioned over the phone - I like to
          thank you for your flexibility.

                         GONZALES
          Thank you Mrs. - very appreciated indeed.

Mr. Gonzales, without looking at the contents, rapidly puts
the envelope in his inner pocket. The cashier comes back
carrying a receipt and the empty briefcase. He hands both to
Josephine while Mr. Gonzales watches with satisfaction.

                         CASHIER
                      (in Spanish)
          Your receipt Mrs. Exactly 200 million.

                         JOSEPHINE
          Thank you so much. And - well - see you
          soon again then.

They rise and exit the office. Mr. Gonzales holds the door
open for Josephine with extreme courtesy.

INT. SOUTH AMERICA - BANK - LOBBY - DAY

Mr. Gonzales follows Josephine through the large open space
among the many bank employees working on their computer
screens to the exit of the bank. He wholeheartedly shakes
hands with Josephine as goodbye.

INT. SOUTH AMERICA - HOTEL - SUITE - DAY

A servant enters Josephine's suite with a large, colorful
cocktail. He places the delicious drink next to the sofa in
the middle of the room and exits. Josephine rests in the sofa
while she enjoys the drink and the view to the outside exotic
tropical garden. She leans back. She smiles sensually and she
lets her thoughts flow. She thinks back in time.

                              PICTURE FADES TO THE PAST

EXT. EUROPE - ALLEY - EVENING - BACK IN TIME

It is dark and foggy in the narrow passage by the tavern.
It has rained. The cobblestones are wet and slippery. The
few lamps only illuminate the street just below. The light
forms halos around the lamps in the moist air. Some girls are
standing by the side of the passage. A man passes by, chats to

a girl and walks into the building with the girl. Josephine,
in her very young age, is leaning her upper back against the
wall by a dark entrance to an old house. She is stunningly
beautiful, vulgar and sensual. She exhales as she looks up the
steep walls of the house on the opposite side of the alley.
A man dressed in a long black coat and with a wide-brimmed
hat hiding his face comes up to her. Josephine makes herself
extremely attractive and irresistible. They walk together into
the building and up the narrow stairs. Josephine opens the
door to a small apartment.

INT. EUROPE - TAVERN - APARTMENT - EVENING

Josephine and the man enter the apartment, a single room
with a large bed with a tall metal bed foot. The walls in
the room are decorated with pictures of erotic motives and
richly filled with mirrors. The light in the room is in red
tones from small lamps on the bed table and a table with
mirror for make-up. There is a round, robust table by the bed
end. The young man violently pushes Josephine onto the table
and engages in a violent encounter, still dressed. Josephine
enjoys the act, only partially undressed and extremely
sexually appealing. Josephine screams in delight as they
peak. The man, still dressed, retracts. He briefly organizes
himself. Josephine still lies open on the table. She exhales
and whispers sensually while she still provokes the man with
her erotic and sensual body.

                    JOSEPHINE
          I know who you are! - I know you cannot
          live without me - and you don't need to.
          Just ask me - anything.

The man exits swiftly while Josephine remains on the table.

EXT. EUROPE - ALLEY - EVENING

The man runs down through the narrow corridor and exits
to the street. He hides his face as he walks up the alley.
He passes the girls hanging around, reaches the end of the
alley to a large square, and crosses the square to the huge
cathedral on the opposite side. He walks to the large door of
the cathedral, pushes it open and enters.

INT. EUROPE - CATHEDRAL - NIGHT

The man enters the cathedral. With his bowed head hidden by
his hand and coat and with his large hat in the hand he walks
to a side chapel where long, narrow windows reach towards the
high ceiling. He kneels by the altar in the impressive yet
Spartan and gloomy room. He puts his hat on the floor behind
him. As his coat falls down during intense prayer the face of
Giovanni becomes visible.

>   GIOVANNI
>   (whispering in Italian)
>   Forgive me Lord for my sins. Please
>   forgive me. I know I have asked you again
>   and again. Yet, I still sin. Please help
>   me not to sin. Free me from my desires.
>   Free me from the forces within me. Free
>   me from the darkness in my soul. Please
>   my Lord. Help me and forgive me.

Giovanni remains in deep prayer. Finally he rises from the
altar. He lights a candle and places it among the many candles
in front of the altar. He walks back through the empty
cathedral deeply depressed. He reaches the exit. Suddenly he
turns around and looks up through the immense church room
to the main altar. He hears the Requiem which overwhelmingly
fills the space. He shouts violently with all his force
against the music into the room.

>   GIOVANNI
>   NO - NO, I will prove you wrong -
>   wrong - wrong!

The echo of his words, shouted louder and louder, circulate
and echo through the dark cathedral.

>   GIOVANNI
>   (talking bitterly to
>   himself)
>   - and I will be free. I swear, I will. I
>   shall be free. It cannot be right that I
>   cannot get her. It is wrong.
>   (looking bitterly up through
>   the church to the crucified
>   Christ)
>   You are wrong! My desires are right. I
>   will prove you wrong. I swear.

Giovanni turns around. The music continues as he exits the church.

THE REQUIEM CARRIES OVER

EXT. EUROPE - ALLEY - NIGHT

Giovanni runs over the square. He reaches the narrow alley. He walks fast and determined towards Josephine's place. He sees Josephine talking to a man. He reaches them and violently pushes the man aside. He grasps Josephine and pushes her into the house and up the narrow staircase.

INT. EUROPE - TAVERN - APARTMENT - NIGHT

Josephine and Giovanni enter the apartment. He stands face to face with her. He kisses her violently. The music softens to the quartet of singers.

> GIOVANNI
> (in Italian)
> I need you, I want you - I want only you.
> And you want only me.

Josephine smiles. She takes her arms around Giovanni's neck. She kisses him and leans back sensually while she still holds him.

> JOSEPHINE
> I knew you would come back.

> GIOVANNI
> I will give you everything. I know how we
> can get free. I know how we can do it.

INT. EUROPE - TAVERN - APARTMENT - EVENING

The music fades. Giovanni and Josephine stay in the dimly illuminated room and talk all night making their evil plan.

FORWARD TO MORNING

EXT. EUROPE - ALLEY - EARLY MORNING

The daylight breaks through. Giovanni exits the building and walks up the narrow passage. Shortly afterward Josephine appears and walks down the alley.

                              TIME CHANGES TO PRESENT

INT. SOUTH AMERICA - HOTEL - SUITE - DAY

In the exclusive, South American hotel suite Josephine leans back in the comfortable sofa. She has finished her cocktail. Smiling she talks to herself.

                         JOSEPHINE
                    (in Italian)
          What a story - what a plan - and what an
          execution.
                    (she closes her eyes, leans
                     back and whispers into
                     the air)
          Nobody will ever find out - and even if
          they do they won't believe a word of it!

She laughs with her eyes closed.

INT. NEW YORK - POLICE STATION - OFFICE - DAY

Sergeant Samuel sits by his desk and stirs his coffee. Mille and Larry stand by the walls. They all appear exhausted.

                         SAMUEL
          So folks, once again, - again, again -
          where are we - any news?

                         MILLE
          I called Josephine again, several times.
          I never got her. The first few times the
          telephone actually was ringing. Then it
          stopped responding. The telephone company
          told me fees have not been paid. So
          apparently she cancelled the telephone.
                    (she pauses)
          I tried to search her - unofficially - she
          is nowhere to be found. I need a permit

for a full search if you seriously want me
to find her.

                    SAMUEL
Hum - what about family.

                    MILLE
Nothing.

Samuel hides his face in his hands. While still hiding the
face he asks Larry.

                    SAMUEL
And Larry - anything?

                    LARRY
Well, in a way the opposite Samuel - I
asked the lab again to check the match
and confirm the findings. Now they tell
me that there has been a mix-up. The
data file with the match apparently is
not there anymore. And Samuel, when they
tried to confirm the first sequences of
the samples from the office, there was
now so much contamination that somehow
the findings could not be reproduced.
That's what they say.

                    SAMUEL
Are you telling me that the data are not
there anymore?

                    LARRY
Unfortunately, that's what I am saying.

                    SAMUEL
And how on earth did that happened?

                    LARRY
Any explanation - what they tell me is
that there has been so much hacking
recently and so much extra security set
up - so some data have been lost in that
process. They had to transfer all their
files - things like that. But Samuel, if I
may, these are stupid excuses. Hacking has

nothing to do with contamination - they
are hiding something.

Sergeant Samuel gets extremely upset. He hammers the table
and speaks emotionally.

                    SAMUEL
        What the hell is going on? Anyone we
        investigate - officially or unofficially -
        disappears, we have no family or relatives
        to follow up on, the little, but crucial
        data we had appears to be gone, the
        guy we are trying to find is gone, the
        manager of Ludwig is gone, all evidence
        in the home of the woman associated to
        the crucial match we found is gone and
        the woman herself is dead - do I need to
        continue?

                    LARRY
        I agree with you - something is very
        fishy. Somehow we are being closed out.

An ADMIN (25, uniformed) opens the door to the office. Samuel
looks up at her - a little surprised by her sudden entry.

                    ADMIN
        You are asked to come to the headquarters
        at once.

                    SAMUEL
        Tell them I am on my way.

Samuel rises; he takes his jacket from behind the door and
walks swiftly out of the office.

EXT. EUROPE - HOUSE LUDWIG - OUTSIDE - NIGHT

In the small town Ludwig's childhood home is in flames. A
crowd runs up the street to the burning house. A primitive
fire truck passes the crowd and stops in front of the house. A
few firefighters jump out of the truck and start pumping water
over the house. The small crowd running up the street reaches
the house and horrified watches the fire. Ludwig's house
collapses. The piano stands in flames as the last item in the
middle of the burned-down house. The strings of the piano

break one by one and create a mysterious and sharp sound. The
piano turns over and falls down in the last flames and ashes.
The sound from the breaking strings transform to the soothing
sound of the kayagum. The crowd stands stunned listening to
the transcendent music while frightened watching the last
flames. The soothing music of the kayagum fills the space.
Daylight breaks.

The firefighters pour water on the last flames. The wet smoke
drifts down the street. Leopold stands with tears in his
eyes. He walks out of the crowd and over to the ashes. He
walks through the smokes to the burnt piano. He sees a piece
of metal on the ground between the dark and burned wood. He
carefully picks it up in a piece of cloth not to burn himself.
He watches the metal piece and recognizes the tuning fork.
He cleans it and holds it tightly against his body. He looks
towards the rising sun and cries desperately. The sound of the
of the kayagum fills the space.

                        MUSIC OF THE KAYAGUM CARRIES OVER

EXT. COTTAGE - MAIN COTTAGE - OUTSIDE - DAY

The sun rises over the beautiful landscapes around Ludwig's
cottage. The sunrays break between the tips of the mountains.
The bench by the edge of the cottage area stands empty. Smoke
is blowing with the wind from the cottage, totally burnt down
to ashes. Myriads of light rays shine over the ashes, the
enormous landscape and the terrific peaks of the mountains.

INT. NEW YORK - POLICE HEADQUARTER - FRONT OFFICE ERNST - DAY

As Samuel enters the front-office of Ernst, the stout admin
barely looks up, but with her hand directs Samuel to enter
the office of Ernst immediately. Samuel knocks softly on the
door. A voice is heard from the inside. Samuel opens the door
carefully and looks in. He enters the office.

INT. NEW YORK - POLICE HEADQUARTER - OFFICE ERNST - DAY
Ernst sits by his large desk and reads a report.

                        ERNST
        Come in.

Ernst does not look up as Samuel enters. With fast movements
of his hand he impatiently demands Samuel to sit in one of
the chairs in front of the desk. Samuel sits for a while as
Ernst continues to read. Ernst signs a document. He looks up
at Samuel.

                    ERNST
          Can I have a status, please.

                    SAMUEL
          I have no new findings Sir.

                    ERNST
          I am utterly unimpressed by your
          performance Sergeant. What about this DNA
          story?

                    SAMUEL
          I am sorry. It is like a conspiracy
          against us. The laboratory told us there
          is something wrong with the DNA samples;
          and the data - well, we could not
          retrieved them.

Ernst looks up and leans his overweight body forward. His
chair is at the breaking point of its two legs under his
entire weight.

                    ERNST
               (extremely irritated)
          Sergeant, I am disgusted. Here you have
          a big case, which has made my phone
          ring endlessly and which has totally
          obsessed the press - and even stirs
          public sentiments. And now you come here
          and tell me that it is all smoke. I am
          disgusted, Sergeant. You should have
          taken the opportunity to upgrade your
          reputation. But instead - look what you
          have done - my Goodness - you have made
          us all look like fools. Damned!

Ernst pounds the table with frightening power.

                    SAMUEL
          I am sorry Sir, but ...

                              ERNST
          This is enough. I have just authorized
          that you and your people are transferred
          to ordinary police work with the traffic
          police. I would think, but honestly I am
          not sure, that you can do less damage
          there. This is effective immediately. I
          am sending a press release diffusing this
          whole story a little later today. Your
          utterly incompetence Sergeant has almost
          cost me my position as well. That's all.
          You can leave you licenses by the admin.

Ernst again focuses on the papers on his desk. Samuel rises
and exits Ernst's office.

INT. NEW YORK - POLICE HEADQUARTER - FRONT OFFICE ERNST - DAY

Samuel walks through the front office and leaves his license
by the admin. The stout admin takes the license and puts it
in her drawer without looking up. Samuel exits.

INT. NEW YORK - POLICE HEADQUARTER - OFFICE ERNST - DAY

Ernst unlocks a drawer in his desk and takes a thick envelope
out. He briefly look at the contents of large bank notes,
smiles satisfied and puts the envelope in his inner pocket. He
rises and exits the office.

INT. NEW YORK - POLICE HEADQUARTER - FRONT OFFICE ERNST - DAY

Ernst passes the admin who looks up.

                              ERNST
          I will be back a little later - please
          set the press conference up for this
          afternoon.

Ernst exits.

INT. NEW YORK - POLICE HEADQUARTER - PRESS CONFERENCE ROOM - DAY

Ernst, sitting by a microphone by a table with a uniformed
police officer assistant on each side is finalizing the

briefing of the press. The room is packed with reporters and is flickering from flash lights as endless photographs are taken.

                    ERNST
          ---- and I have now taken the appropriate
          disciplinary actions for this unfortunate
          misconduct of the investigation.
                    (he pauses in the dead
                    silent room)
          I shall be happy to answer a few
          questions. Please use the microphones when
          asking.

A young, formally dressed REPORTER 1 on the first row rises. He is handed a microphone by one of several young, uniformed, female admins spread across the room.

                    REPORTER 1
          It was consistently reported that there is
          a match between samples collected in the
          office of Dr. Paioni and some old case -
          could you please again clarify how this
          match could occur?

                    ERNST
          As I said - there is no such match - the
          idea of a match was reported before the
          analysis was finalized - and when data
          and experiments were reassessed there
          simply was no match - nothing. Again just
          to be clear, there - is - no - match!

A young woman reporter, REPORTER 2, rises.

                    REPORTER 2
          Can you please update us on the situation
          around Dr. Paioni?

                    ERNST
          As I mentioned already, we have not yet
          found Paioni - for now our assumption
          is that there is an accident. We do
          not see any evidence for a connection
          between Dr. Paioni's activities and his
          disappearance - most likely he had an
          accident.

                         REPORTER 2
          And what about the lecture that was
          announced - still no connection?

                          ERNST
          Again - no evidence to suggest any
          connection - and I would like to say,
          but this is outside the scope of our
          investigations - there are significant
          question marks around the scientific
          integrity of the Dr. - as you will know,
          the lecture has been pulled. As I said,
          this part of the story is now with the
          scientific community to deal with.
                  (he pauses)
          I believe you are aware how previous
          cases of scientific fraud in the area of
          biology - stem cell research for example -
          have resulted in scientists committing
          suicide.

Ernst looks around in the room, obviously eager to finish the
conference. An elderly, gray haired reporter, REPORTER 3, rises
at the back row and asks for the microphone. It takes a little
while for the microphone to get there. In the meantime the room
is quiet. The reporter talks with a low, slightly hoarse voice.

                         REPORTER 3
          We know for a fact that the world famous
          conductor Ludwig Mann and Dr. Paioni
          were together the night before Dr. Paioni
          disappeared. Could you please clarify
          three points: what was the connection
          between these two men, where is Ludwig
          Mann now, and what is your position on
          the rumor that Ludwig Mann could be an
          artificial creation?

                          ERNST
          As I said, there are big question marks
          around Dr. Paioni - he has cooked a story
          and glorified it by involving high profile
          individuals - yet, as I said, his lecture
          was pulled and with that, as I understand,
          all the results of his scientific works -
          it speaks for itself, right!

                    (Ernst rises)
          Ladies and Gentlemen - I thank you for
          coming here.

Ernst rises and leaves the press room followed by the two
police officers. The reporters rise and start leaving the
press room.

EXT. MANHATTAN - MIDTOWN - STREET - DAY

Sergeant Samuel stops by a newspaper stand on a Manhattan
street. He inserts coins in the automate, takes the newspaper
and stands reading the headline: "Chairman of the Society
of the Sciences steps down in aftermaths of huge scientific
fraud". Samuel folds the newspaper together and hammers the
automate angrily with the folded paper.

                         SAMUEL
                 (talking to himself)
          What on earth is going on?

Samuel walks down the street.

INT. IN A LARGE EUROPEAN CATHEDRAL - EVENING

The huge and impressive cathedral is packed with people. The
room is decorated and illuminated for the finest of events.
A group of priests with Marchetto in front walks slowly up
the church floor. As they pass the public, all dressed in
their finest clothes, everybody bows deeply in respect and
deference. The Agnus Dei of the Requiem fills the room. The
procession moves slowly towards the main altar in the huge
room. By the altar Marchetto turns and stands facing the
public while the rest of the procession gathers behind him.
Marchetto bows and kisses the altar, rises and spreads his
arms towards the public to bless everyone in the room.

     THE PICTURE MERGES TO THE BUILDING NEXT TO THE CHURCH IN THE
                                              VIENNA SUBURB

INT. VIENNA - HOUSE GRAUPNER - EVENING

Agnus Dei continues to flow as the assistant of Pastor
Graupner walks down the corridor towards the entrance to the
office of Pastor Graupner. She carries a tray with a pot of

tea, a teacup and a small dish with crackers. As she stands by the door, she kneels towards the large crucifix at the end wall of the corridor. She knocks softly at the door and waits for an answer. She knocks again a little stronger. As there is no answer she slowly opens the door

INT. VIENNA - HOUSE GRAUPNER - OFFICE - EVENING

The assistant enters. She takes a few steps inside. She looks for Pastor Graupner. He is not by his desk. She turns around, sees a sharp knife on the floor, and suddenly she sees Pastor Graupner hanging by his neck dead. She screams, pulls herself together and holds her hands over her mouth to suppress her scream. She loses the tray. It falls on the stone floor and crashes. Splinters fly in all directions. The tea flows out over the floor, over the splinters and the knife, and finally mixes with the stream of blood flowing from the neck of Pastor Graupner to the floor.

THE PICTURE AND MUSIC FOLLOWS THE STREAM OF BLOOD AS IT FLOWS
TO THE CHALICE IN FRONT OF MARCHETTO

INT. EUROPE - CATHEDRAL - EVENING

The blood flows to and fills into the chalice while Marchetto holds it in his stretched arms. He faces the altar and looks over the bloody chalice towards heaven depicted on the altar painting. He lowers the chalice and bows his head while his disciples and priests of lower ranks, all in white, add wine to the large decorated chalice. Marchetto again lifts the chalice, filled with blood and wine, with both hands and both arms stretched forward towards the public. At the last tones of Agnus Dei he finally lifts the chalice to his lips and drinks the blood to the last drop. He puts the chalice back on the altar and stretches his arms to heaven while finally turning towards the large church room. He blesses the worshipers in a sacred moment and prays for forgiveness for all sins to all as the music dies out and he smiles evil.

INT. NEW YORK - PENTHOUSE DUILIO - DAY

Alessia is in the kitchen area of the apartment. It is messed up. She is eating some junk food and watching TV. The entire flat is messy. The door telephone rings. Alessia doesn't care.

The door telephone rings again. She carelessly goes to the
door telephone by the elevator.

                    ALESSIA
          Yes?

                    SAMUEL
          It is Sergeant Samuel - I wondered if I
          could disturb you for a moment?

                    ALESSIA
          Sure. Please come in. The small elevator
          goes directly up here.

Alessia swiftly runs over to a mirror by the bedroom. She
corrects her hair and clothes and then swiftly clears a small
area on the high breakfast table by the kitchen. The elevator
arrives at the floor. Alessia goes to the elevator door and
releases the lock. Sergeant Samuel enters the apartment.

                    ALESSIA
          I hope you don't mind the mess.

                    SAMUEL
          Of course not. Just showing up here
          unannounced, how could I complain?

He looks around in the impressive room.

                    SAMUEL
          It does not seem messy at all to me.

                    ALESSIA
          Would you like a coffee?

                    SAMUEL
          Sure.

Alessia walks over to the kitchen and adds water to the
Nespresso machine. She opens the drawer for the coffee cups.
There are just three cups left.

                    ALESSIA
          What kind of coffee would you like?

                    SAMUEL
          Ristretto please.

Alessia looks among the few remaining capsules in the drawer.
There is no ristretto. She just takes a regular espresso.
Samuel takes seat on one of the high kitchen chairs. Alessia
brings the coffee to the table.

                    SAMUEL
          I am not officially on the case anymore.

They don't speak. They are two, lonely, sad souls, sitting next
to each other. They don't need words. Samuel empties his cup.
He overcomes his depressed state and talks with renewed energy.

                    SAMUEL
          I just cannot let it go.

Samuel looks energized at Alessia and tries to cheer her up.

                    SAMUEL
          Tell me. I just wondered - now, after
          some time, has anything come to your mind
          that could help finding your husband?
                    (he pauses)
          They are not looking anymore - right?

                    ALESSIA
          As far as I know there is absolutely
          nothing going on.

They sit quiet - long pause.

                    ALESSIA
          Maybe I should tell you about my first
          time with Duilio? Maybe you will better
          understand what he did then?

                    SAMUEL
          Certainly. Please -

                    ALESSIA
          So, here is what happened. It all started
          in the university.

                              TRANSITION BACK IN TIME

INT. US - UNIVERSITY - CANTEEN - DAY - BACK IN TIME

The scenery of the university canteen emerges as Alessia's talking carries over.

                    ALESSIA
          It was when we studied that I first saw
          him - in the canteen of the college,
          actually.....

The young Duilio as a graduate student is in the busy canteen with 5 of his fellow, obviously brilliant and energized students. They are all extremely excited as, in the middle of sandwich or noodle eating, depending on nationality, they read through reprints from a recent publication on the synthesis of a large nucleotide.

                    PETER
               (exited while holding the
               reprint speaks with a strong
               American accent)
          I told you guys - we would get there
          first - this is just amazing. Think about
          it folks - an enormous molecule, nothing
          like this has ever been done before. I
          smell Nobel Prices - and maybe folks, for
          those who can follow up. A new world is
          opening up.

                    IAN
               (British accent)
          Well, wait a minute. Don't forget that
          "we" - "we" figured all these structures
          out - you guys over here always forget
          the good European thinking. What would
          you have done without what we did? The
          real breakthrough came from us - as usual
          you just mechanized it - "bigger and
          better', right!

The students all laugh as they joke about the respective nationalities and patriotic views on scientific contributions. A group of female students settles by the next table. PIERRE (French) shows a considerable interest in one of the girls who reciprocates his interest.

                    DUILIO
          I agree with Peter - and I tell you guys
          that with the speed that this is evolving
          we will soon be able to synthesize life -
          first, just small virus, then bacteria,
          and, I tell you, at the end of the day
          we will make a human being. That's my
          prediction!

Duilio softly hammers both hands down on the table as he
proudly predicts the future. The other folks barely notice.
Pierre, in particular, continues his intense interest in the
girls by the other table. Duilio, to catch attention, moves
his head to block Pierre's sight of the girls and looks him
straight in the eyes.

                    DUILIO
               (faking a French accent)
          And then "mon ami" - then we will not
          even need to show any interest in the
          opposite, beautiful sex - humanity will
          simply be maintained in our synthesis
          machines and we take whatever human we
          need from the molecules in our freezers.
          Custom synthesis our MBA business
          colleagues will say - and big business.

Duilio points to a table on the other side of the canteen
where a group of students in finance are having lunch in
a slightly more formal fashion than the science and art
students. All finance student, male and female, are very
neatly dressed and with proper well maintained hairstyles in
high contrast to the scientific nerds.

                    PIERRE
               (exaggerating his French
               accent)
          Well "mon ami"! in that case I think we
          should really consider studying philosophy
          and arts instead - which has the other
          big advantage that we will have classes
          with our neighbors over there.

They all look to the table next to them and all the girls look
back. Duilio notices the young ALESSIA (20, Italian descent,
black hair, very nicely dressed to enhance her natural and

beautiful body). She smiles to him. A bit shy the girls swiftly
focus on their meals while quietly laughing between themselves.

                    CHO-YIN
              (Korean accent, addressing
               Duilio)
So Mr. Philosophy, here is the question:
Will you really get a human being out
of your freezer - or will you just get
something that may look like a human
being - but without human emotions; -
just a fleshy robot.

                    PIERRE
              (resuming his attention to
               the girls by the next table)
That's what I think Duilio - and it makes
me feel much better.

He smiles again to the girl by the next table.

                    SEIGO
              (Japanese accent)
I tell you Duilio, you would also break
all principles of any major religion
and their views on creation. A lot of
people will certainly not like it - I can
guarantee you that - but it will certainly
be great fun; imagine the discussions!

                    DUILIO
I bet you, if I did this synthesis you
just can't tell if the human I made is
real or artificial -
              (he continues in a humorous
               tone)
- simply, because he is smarter than you,
or more talented, or even better looking -
depending on the molecules we put in
there -

                    PIERRE
              (interrupting)
Why don't we invite the girls over here.
Duilio, please bless us, in your funny
chapel!

Cho-yin leans over the table towards Duilio.

                    CHO-YIN
               (talking in a low voice)
          I tell you my old friend, there is more to
          it than just chemistry. The world beyond
          what we believe exists! You will not reach
          it in this experiment.
               (lowers his voice even
               further)
          I tell you, we have a lot of that, I mean
          what is beyond our reach, in our Korean
          temples - or rather in the desolated
          temples. There are places, Duilio, in my
          country where all the mysticism exists.
          There are people there - mysterious men
          and women; and ghosts even - they know
          things we will never reach and never
          understand. If you make your human,
          there will be something missing. I
          guarantee you.

Seigo has listened to Cho-yin's comments.

                    SEIGO
               (low voice, Japanese accent)
          Duilio, I agree with Cho-yin, you may get
          ten Nobel Prices - but you will never get
          even close to what is going on out there.

The group sits quiet for a while. Pierre picks coffee up for
the entire group. They all again read the reprints on the table
with great interest. After a while Duilio, uneasy, follows his
thoughts rather than reading over the reprints again.

                    DUILIO
          Why don't we test all these things you
          guys talk about? I tell you something. I
          go to one of these magic or mystic people
          you talk about. I study them. And then,
          maybe, we can test the human being we
          make in the laboratory for these "mystic
          capabilities". We just need to understand
          the principles - so to say - of these
          mystic folks.
               (he pauses)

I am sure we will be able to make a
test: will our human being have a soul or
not - "is the human human?" - that's the
question, right?

                IAN
Wow, Duilio, sounds great - but maybe
you should be a little quiet about this
if you want our professor to still have
you around. Your thesis will still be
in chemistry - not in philosophy or
mysticism, right?

They all laugh.

                DUILIO
Well, I can live with that risk. I can go
there.

He pauses and looks at the Cho-yin.

                DUILIO
I assume it is not dangerous?
        (he pauses)
You tell me where to go!

They sit and enjoy the coffee for a while. Duilio, full of
energy, puts his cup down.

                DUILIO
Folks; let's make a bet! When we have a
human being, I mean artificially made -
then we test it. Is everything there -
or are these things you guys talk about
missing?

                CHO-YIN
I take the bet. No way you will generate
everything artificially!

                SEIGO
Same with me.

The all laugh, highly amused by the conversation beyond the
usual scientific topics. The girls by the next table rise and

send their longing eyes as good-buy, for now. Pierre almost
rises as he looks after the girls and talks.

>   PIERRE
>   (with a longing eye for his
>   favorite girl)
>   Well Duilio, as a matter of principle I
>   have to bet against you in this matter of
>   "looove".

>   PETER
>   I like your idea - but, first of all, you
>   will not achieve the synthesis in our
>   lifetime, and then you cannot test for
>   the presence of these "mystic" properties
>   anyway - you cannot test scientifically
>   what is outside of sciences, right?

>   DUILIO
>   Well folks - I will figure out how we
>   test for the other side of life.

>   IAN
>   OK then, I take the bet too Duilio.

They all laugh. Duilio puts his hand on the table and so do
all the other student.

>   DUILIO
>   All right guys - I bet against all of you
>   geniuses.

They all touch hands. Laugh and rise.

>   DUILIO
>   So folks, back to the lab!
>   (he turns to Cho-yin)
>   And now you tell me where these
>   mystics are!

EXT. UNIVERSITY - LAWN - DAY

The lawn is full of students in the afternoon break. Duilio is
sitting alone and writing intensively on a draft publication.
Alessia is walking over the lawn carrying her books and
looking for a place to sit. She notices Duilio, hesitates a

moment, and then walks over to him. Duilio does not notice
Alessia standing next to him before she speaks.

                         ALESSIA
                    (in Italian)
              Can I sit here, next to you?

Duilio happily recognizes Alessia and moves his things a bit
closer as to make space for her.

                         DUILIO
                    (in Italian)
              Of course - sit down. Here.

Alessia sits down, not too close to Duilio and puts her books
and notes on the grass. She smiles a bit shy but charmingly.
She opens one of her books, puts it on the grass between her
and Duilio and lies down on the grass on her side ready to
read.

                         ALESSIA
              What was it you discussed so much with
              your friends in the canteen - it seemed
              like the world was at stake?

                         DUILIO
              Oh, it was about this paper we were
              reading - it just came out - it's about
              the synthesis of the largest molecule
              ever.

Duilio looks proud and excited.

                         ALESSIA
              What is a molecule?

Duilio realizes Alessia's total ignorance about any scientific
subjects.

                         DUILIO
              OK - molecules is what everything here on
              earth is made of, including you and me.

                         ALESSIA
              Really?

DUILIO
Yes, and I tell you, if I just make
the right molecules and put them nicely
together, then I could make a copy of
you - and it would be exactly as you -
that's what we talked about.

ALESSIA
So would it sing like me then?

DUILIO
That's what I am saying - but the other
folks disagreed - that's what we bet
about. You would not have a soul - so to
say, something would be missing.

ALESSIA
So who would you prefer then; me or the
one you made?

Duilio is captured by the charming Alessia and *vice versa*. He
looks down on the grass for a moment before he answers with a
big loving smile.

DUILIO
Well - I better just stay with you;
I am sure that would feel good.

They pause for a minutes and watch the life on the lawn.

DUILIO
So, what are you doing?

ALESSIA
I am studying music - as a singer.
So I sing!

She looks at Duilio with her deep, capturing eyes.

ALESSIA
These days we are studying Mozart - we
are going to perform the Requiem - and
guess what, I am the lead soprano.

DUILIO
What does that mean?

Alessia realizes Duilio's total ignorance outside the field of science.

                    ALESSIA
          OK, Sir. It means that I will be singing
          all the soprano solo parts.
                    (she continues whispering
                    and acting dramatically
                    while leaning closer to
                    Duilio)
          I tell you, this music is quite something.
          One says that when Mozart wrote it he
          believed it was a mass for his own funeral
          and was ordered by the Death, somehow.
                    (she pauses while her deep
                    eyes almost reflect death)
          And I tell you, with this music we are
          looking straight into death - it is like
          being beyond our existence - with this
          music Mozart makes us look straight into
          the world beyond ours!

                    DUILIO
          My Goodness!

Alessia, now sitting on the lawn, talks with full drama, her eyes rolling and radiating while her hands gesture death and her voice tones like reflected from hell.

                    ALESSIA
          We know now that this whole story is
          not true. Someone just wanted to pretend
          having written it - but it does not
          matter at all. What matters is that
          Mozart did believe it; and he wrote it
          in that belief - that is what matters.
          With his music, he brings us face to face
          with death and beyond because of what he
          believed. That's how I feel it.

Alessia pauses. Duilio for a moment ponders deeply about the remarks of Alessia.

                    ALESSIA
          So, what were these things you mentioned;
          molecules?

                    DUILIO
          Yes, molecules.

                    ALESSIA
          Can one touch molecules?

                    DUILIO
          That's what we are doing all the time in
          this world. Everything you see around
          you is made of molecules. They are just
          like small building blocks for everything
          around. Just like LEGO - you know, the
          toy, right?

                    ALESSIA
          I tell you, there is more to this world
          than what you can touch. Just think about
          the music I told you about - just listen
          to Mozart.

Duilio obviously captured by Alessia moves closer to her and
softly touches her hand. She watches his hand touching her
hand. Duilio moves his hand back, pretending innocence.

                    DUILIO
          Just wanted to be sure I could feel you.

They both laugh.

                    ALESSIA
          Why don't you come and listen to the
          concert - it seems you could benefit from
          being a bit more acquainted with music.
          It's in the church. It is just this one
          piece - so you will survive.

Alessia puts her things together and rises carrying her
things. She speaks with charming and loving engagement.

                    ALESSIA
          So, do I see you?

                    DUILIO
          I will be there.

Alessia smiles a charming good-buy as she walks over the lawn.

INT. BOSTONIAN CHURCH - EVENING

The medium sized church is packed with the audience filling
the room all the way up through the church to the full sized
orchestra, the large choir and the solo singers with the
conductor in front. Tall, grayish columns reach to and hold
the roof and the doom. The light in the room is very dim,
even around the musicians. Duilio is standing in the back of
the room listening to the music that captures him. With the
music his eyes follow the magnificent room, the paintings, the
graves in the chapels and the tall columns to the doom above.
He eyes the name Mozart in the program and glues it in his
mind to his future ambitious endeavor.

                    DUILIO
              (whispering to himself)
        That's what I have to make - Mozart - then
        I will know what's going on!

After the last bars of the requiem fades, Duilio remains in
the room while the audience leaves. The musicians and singers
are packing their things together. Alessia sees Duilio and
walks down to him - charmingly, light and happily smiling.

                    ALESSIA
        So, did you like it?

                    DUILIO
        I certainly did - I heard you very well,
        even down here.

They stand a bit embarrassed for a moment.

                    DUILIO
        So, what's the plan - what about going
        somewhere?

Alessia nods exited. They leave the church together.

INT. BOSTON - SMALL COZY ITALIAN RESTAURANT - EVENING

Duilio and Alessia enter a small Italian restaurant. It is
busy with many post-concert visitors. The RESTAURANT OWNER,
a small round bellied, happy, middle aged Italian approaches
them wholeheartedly smiling with embracing arms. He directs

Alessia and Duilio to a small, nice table with a few bottles
of unopened wine to tempt the visitors. He hands Alessia and
Duilio the menu card. Duilio studies the bottles on the table.

                    DUILIO
          Maybe, just a bottle of wine.

He looks at Alessia. She nods. The happy owner immediately
opens a bottle. He finds two large wine glasses and pours the
rich, Italian red wine and retracts. Duilio and Alessia take
the glasses.

                    DUILIO
          So, cheers. Thanks for getting me to this
          event.

They touch glasses and both take a large, soothing sip of the
obviously very well tasting wine.

                    ALESSIA
          So, you are not much into music?

                    DUILIO
          Well, maybe not really.

                    ALESSIA
          Is that because of these - what were they
          called - molecules - they take all your
          time?

                    DUILIO
          Maybe, yes, we spend all our time in the
          laboratory - even evenings and nights.

                    ALESSIA
          I see, - maybe not all of you. I think
          some of your friends showed quite some
          interest beyond the laboratory and the
          molecules.

They sit for a while and enjoy the apparently very drinkable
wine and rapidly get a bit blurred.

                    DUILIO
          What about a little cheese with the wine?

ALESSIA
Sure! and maybe some sweets!

Duilio calls the happy owner who immediately comes to the table.

DUILIO
Can you please organize a little cheese - and some sweets?

RESTAURANT OWNER
It will all be with you in a sec.

The restaurant owner smiles to Alessia and Ludwig, happy for the happy couple. He walks away.

ALESSIA
So, tell me again, what was this bet you made with your friends?

DUILIO
Well, to make a long story short - as I told you - what I said was that if we make a human being artificially then it will be exactly like the rest of us.

ALESSIA
And what did the other folks say?

DUILIO
Well, they said something will be missing - they imagine the soul, feelings or something like that will be missing. There will be some difference - that's what they say.

They both sit pondering a bit about the bet while making big inroads in the wine. The restaurant owner comes to the table and serves a nice setting of cheese and deserts. Duilio and Alessia eat and drink with great appetite.

ALESSIA
(charming in on Duilio)
So, if you made a copy of me - in your laboratory - then it would be exactly as me. You would not know which is which?

                    DUILIO
          Yes, that was my side of the bet - before
          I met you.

                    ALESSIA
          And my music - everything I feel about
          the music. It would be the same?
                    (she pauses)
          I think you must be a bit crazy.

They laugh. They realize they are the last gusts in the
restaurant. The jolly restaurant owner comes to the table.
Duilio realizes time has run. He pays the owner. They exit
the restaurant in high mood, obviously pretty affected by the
wine, but still almost able to walk straight.

EXT. OUTSIDE THE ITALIAN RESTAURANT - NIGHT

Alessia and Duilio are walking down the dark streets in the
direction of Alessia's home. In their drunk state they find
advantage of leaning to each other. Alessia holds Duilio's arm
with both hands. They stop by a crossing of two small, empty
streets. Alessia tries to find direction. She points in the
direction of one of the streets.

                    ALESSIA
          I think it is that one.

                    DUILIO
          Are you sure?

Alessia laughs. She takes Ludwig's hand as they walk down the
street. She sees the house and points happily.

                    ALESSIA
          It's over there.

They continue down the street and finally stop outside an old
townhouse.

                    ALESSIA
          My room is on the very top!

She hands Duilio her hand with a most charming smile.

                          ALESSIA
              Would you like to join?

Alessia gently pulls Duilio's hand. They enter the house.

INT. ALESSIA'S ROOM

Duilio and Alessia have had wonderful love in Alessia's small,
but very cozy, dimly illuminated room. The naked Alessia is
sitting on top of Duilio. She leans forward. With her elbows
on each side of Duilio's head she kisses and talks.

                          ALESSIA
              So, if you make a copy of me, would it
              really be the same - so exactly the same?
              You could just choose me or the copy?

Duilio put his arms around and pulls her down for a long, very
deep kiss. Alessia continues with a slight tone of jealousy.

                          ALESSIA
              And if one day we were going to marry.
              Who would you choose? - you know, you
              can only have one - and you better don't
              disappoint me!

Duilio smiles the obvious answer and again pulls Alessia down.
She pushes her body up from Duilio and sits naked while they
continue their wonderful and happy encounter.

                              TRANSITIONS TO PRESENT TIME

INT. NEW YORK - PENTHOUSE DUILIO - DAY

                          SAMUEL
              Wow - what a story - and now?
              Anything?
                      (long pause)

                          ALESSIA
              Actually yes.
                      (after a while)
              Do you remember these flowers?
              After the last concert. There was an
              Asian woman coming up to the podium from

the audience. She gave Ludwig a huge
bucket.
>   (after a pause)
>   Duilio always had this kind of flowers
>   here - look!
>   (she points to the flowers
>   by the window)
>   They are not for sale - I mean you don't
>   find them in the flower shops - never.

Alessia walks over to a table close to the window. She takes
one of the flowerpots with the violet flowers and puts it on
the table between her and Samuel.

                    SAMUEL
>   I am not sure I get your point. If they
>   are not for sale, then where do they come
>   from? Where did your husband get them?

                    ALESSIA
>   Look, I think he actually went to Korea to
>   study mysticism. Somehow he met a Korean,
>   mystic woman.
>   (she pauses)
>   I forgot about it over the years.
>   But these flowers - I am almost sure
>   he brought them with him from there -
>   and he paid the greatest attention to
>   them - always.

Alessia pauses. In the meantime it has become dark outside.
Alessia lights a few candles.

                    SAMUEL
>   But who was this woman at the concert -
>   do you know?

                    ALESSIA
>   No idea - but I tell you something else.

                    ALESSIA
>   I made a recording - Requiem - Mozart -
>   after the concert with Ludwig Mann. We
>   talked quite a bit during the breaks and
>   also after we had "disked" the piece. And
>   one thing he mentioned was that he had

been in some kind of a jewelers shop to
buy jewelry for the pianist. I think he
was in love with her, honestly. And, you
know, he mentioned that the owner of that
shop was a fortune teller - he said she
was Asian and looked very much like the
pianist. At one point he said to me he
had been so surprised by the resemblance.
          (she pauses)
A pretty strange coincidence - right. And
you know, in my mind I suddenly got the
idea that maybe it was her - I mean the
fortune teller. Somehow I feel it is her!

They sit in silence for a while.

                    ALESSIA
And then there was this bet I just told
you about.
          (she pauses)
They were so funny and so serious at the
same time. It was always like that. And
they still meet every year. I can show you.

Alessia walks over to the other side of the apartment where
Duilio's working space is. From the wall above his desk she
takes a framed photo over to Samuel.

                    ALESSIA
Duilio is there in the middle. This guy
was the French - he was very fond of
the girls as I told you, always - he
was really funny, and then, the other
folks were from all over the world. It
was really an international team - high
performing Duilio said. He was actually
going to meet them again very soon.

Alessia pauses. They both look at the picture for a while.

                    ALESSIA
Well, Sergeant, you asked - and I answered.
          (she pauses)
But Sergeant, where do you think he is -
and why - why Sergeant are nobody really
looking for him anymore?

> SAMUEL
>> I really don't know. I felt that somehow
>> somebody did not want me to find him and
>> to find out what had happened. I always
>> had the impression that something weird
>> was going on.
>>> (he pauses)
>> I still think so.

They sit in silence for a while, trying to make sense of the
situation.

> SAMUEL
>> Do you know where these folks meet?

> ALESSIA
>> At a conference.

She turns the picture around and opens the frame to see the
back of the photograph.

> SAMUEL
>> And where did he say this jewelry
>> shop was?

> ALESSIA
>> Not exactly - but a few minute walk
>> away from the concert hall. That's the
>> impression I got.

> SAMUEL
>> Well, let me see what I can find out.

They rise and go to the elevator door. They greet goodbye.
Samuel enters the elevator. The elevator door closes. Alessia
walks back to the coffee table. She sits in the dim candle
light and pondering watches the violet flowers.

INT. US - RESTAURANT - SEPARATE ROOM - EVENING

The group of previous students, now about 30 years older, are
gathered in a small, separate room of a restaurant packed
with conference delegates. The mood is high with a lively
discussion of the latest results published at the conference

while the group is waiting for Duilio to take the last empty seat by the table.

INT. US - RESTAURANT - EVENING

Sergeant Samuel enters the busy restaurant. He goes to the welcome counter and looks around in the main room. A lady receptionist comes to the counter.

                    RECEPTIONIST
          We are fully booked tonight Sir - it's the
          conference - we have delegates all evening.

                    SAMUEL
          There may be a reservation for a small
          separate group - under the name Duilio
          Paioni, perhaps. It's a group of about
          six. I am a little late.

The receptionist looks through the messy reservation list for the evening but is unable to make sense of the many reservations on the list.

                    THE RECEPTIONIST
          Please follow me. Let's take a look.

The receptionist and Samuel walk through the restaurant. The receptionist opens the door narrowly to the small, separate room. Samuel looks in and recognizes the students from the photograph by Alessia.

                    SAMUEL
          It's right. Thank you.

Samuel enters the room.

INT. US - RESTAURANT - SEPARATE ROOM - EVENING

As Sergeant Samuel enters the separate room the lively conversation among the previous students stops. They all look at Sergeant Samuel.

                    SAMUEL
          Please excuse me for interrupting. Sergeant
          Samuel. May I sit down for a moment.

                         PETER
                 (surprised)
          Sure.

Peter, friendly, takes a chair from the back of the room to
Samuel. Samuel takes seat by the end of the table.

                         SAMUEL
          I assume you know that Duilio has been
          missing for a while?

                         PETER
          Well, yes and no. As you can see, we
          certainly hope to see him here tonight.

Peter points to the empty chair in the middle of the chairs
by one side of the table.

                         PETER
          Maybe you can tell us more?

                         SAMUEL
          Sure, again excuse me for intruding. But
          let me tell you why I am here.
                 (he pauses and focuses to
                 condense a long story)
          We were asked to look for Duilio by his
          wife; Alessia. We got nowhere. For a long
          time we thought it was some kind of an
          accident; you know, this happens, people
          disappear; but in this case, there were
          too many unusual things happening. People
          that could have given us a lead somehow
          also disappeared - some even died - the
          key data we had disappeared; - well, and
          then suddenly the case was terminated
          abruptly - out of the blue.
                 (he snaps his fingers)

Samuel pauses.

                         SAMUEL
          As far as I know, nobody is looking for him
          anymore. But folks, I cannot let it go. So,
          recently I visited Alessia and we talked
          about everything we knew - just to get

ideas. And she told me about you guys and
that you would be here - that's why I am
here. You knew him forever, sort of, right.
        (Samuel pauses again)
Tell me about your bet with him.

                PETER

Oh, the old bet - please do not
overemphasize that - it was in our young
days. We had that kind of fun all the time.

                SAMUEL

Anyway.

                PETER

Anyway. Well, Duilio argued that if we
synthesized a human being in our labs
then this human being would be a totally
normal human being. What we said was that
there would be a difference, something
would be missing - it might look like
and somehow act like a human being, but
the soul or whatever you would call the
rest - that would be missing.

                CHO-YIN

He had to be wrong. I told him about
the spirits - what is beyond. And, think
about it, where would our free will be? We
would just be robots and so to say just
watch what we are doing. Can you imagine?

                PETER

So that's what the discussion was about -
pretty deep in a way.

                SAMUEL

What about his journey to Asia. Did
anybody go with him?

                CHO-YIN

Well - I told him where he could perhaps
study what we were talking about - out in
our remote temples - but, no, I didn't go
with him. But I believe he went.

                    SAMUEL
          Tell me one thing. This large company he
          built up. What happened to that.

                    PETER
          Oh, it is still there - it is a great
          business now. I became the chairman
          recently.

                    SAMUEL
          And where do you guys think Duilio is?

They sit quiet for a while. Peter offers Samuel a drink from
the bottles at a small buffet behind the table.

                    PETER
          Maybe he just shows up. I don't know.

                    SAMUEL
          Did he have enemies?

                    PETER
          Not that I know of. Maybe he got some
          because of the announcement of the
          lecture; it's a very provocative title.
          God knows.

                    CHO-JIN
          We don't have a clue where he is.
          Personally, I would try to follow up on
          what he did outside of the sciences. This
          Korea story, perhaps.

                    SAMUEL
          Well my friends - let me know if
          something comes to your mind. I think I
          know what to do now. - My card.

Samuel hands each of them his card, greets goodbye and exits.

EXT. KOREA - ROAD TO THE TEMPLE- DAY

Samuel, already exhausted, walks up the narrow path to a
temple. He stops as the path gets paved by cobblestones,
fragmented granite columns and other remains from the old
temple. He watches the wide scenery under the path and, on the

other side of the path, the steep cliff side reaching high, high up. As he has regained his breath, he continues.

EXT. KOREA - PLATEAU IN FRONT THE TEMPLE- DAY

Samuel reaches the plateau in front of the temple. He walks to the middle and watches the scenery of the wide landscape under the plateau. He turns around and watches the old, deserted temple. The wind starts blowing and sweeps leaves and fragmented branches around. He walks to the entrance of the temple.

INT. KOREA - TEMPLE - DAY

Samuel enters the deserted temple. The noise from the winds outside fades. He continues walking deeper into the temple and reaches a large room with a basin under a large, but decayed dome. The silence deep inside the temple is broken only by drops of water hitting the small basin. Samuel stops by the basin and looks for signs of life in the large room illuminated only by streaks of daylight from overgrown window openings, defects in the doom and cracks in the walls here and there.

                    SAMUEL
          Hello - anybody here?
                    (he pauses)
          Hello....

Samuel's voice echoes in the room. He continues deeper into the temple. As he passes a group of columns, SORA (49) suddenly appears in front of him. Samuel instinctively moves a few steps backwards. Sora, dressed in a long white gown soiled by green streaks of soil where it spreads over the floor, raises her arms towards Samuel. Her long black hair almost totally covers her invisible face. She stands as a statue in black and white and speaks with a low, slightly hoarse voice in barely understandable English.

                    SORA
          Do not worry Sergeant. We are here.
          We have been expecting you.

Sergeant Samuel composes himself. Sora points to a doorway further inside the temple and, with her hand, invites Samuel to follow.

                           SORA
          Come!

Sora walks slowly towards the doorway. Samuel follows her.
Their steps echo in the large stony room.

INT. KOREA - TEMPLE - INNER ROOM - DAY

Samuel and Sora enter the inner room. It is small and gloomy
with light only from a round opening high up in one of the
walls. In the middle of the room there is one huge, square
granite block surrounded by smaller granite blocks, all of a
height suitable for sitting. Sora takes seat on the huge block
and invites Samuel to sit next to her. She moves her hair
slightly to the side with one hand and smiles to Samuel. Her
still young face radiates an inner tranquility and intense
presence.

                           SORA
          So Sergeant, what can we do for you?

                          SAMUEL
          I have been looking for Duilio Paioni
          for quite a while. One of his old friends
          told me he might have been here; many
          years ago.
                   (Samuel pauses)
          I am here for help to find him.

                           SORA
          He was here Sergeant. Yes, he was.
          He was here to learn from me; long
          time ago.

                          SAMUEL
          What happened then?

                           SORA
          Well - it's long ago, but let me tell you.
          He came here very much like you ...

          PICTURE FADES TO BACK IN TIME, SORA'S VOICE CARRIES OVER

EXT. KOREA - TEMPLE - ROAD TO - DAY - BACK IN TIME

The mountainous Korean landscape is bathed in the midday sun on a clear, hot summer day. The voice of Sora carries weakly over.

> SORA
> Yes Sergeant - it's long ago. He came her,
> very much like you -

Duilio, as a young scientist, is walking up the steep hills in the remote, Korean mountainous area. The desolated temple is seen in the distance high up the steep hillside. As Duilio gets closer to the temple, the steep path is covered by broad granite stones and other remains from the desolated temple above him. To his right, a vertical granite mountain wall reaches high towards the sky. To his left is a deep slope and an impressive view over the landscape. Duilio follows the narrow path up to the plateau. He stops in the middle of the plateau and watches the gorgeous view of the mountains and the valley deep below. He turns and walks to the entrance of the temple. He exits the plateau.

INT. KOREA - TEMPLE - DAY

Duilio enters the temple. Tall slim columns hold the impressive, but partially broken dome. Water drips from the roof into the fountain basin right under the dome. Duilio goes to the small fountain and watches the impressive but scary scenery of desolation. Suddenly, he sees Sora standing motionless by the distant wall of the temple. She is about 20 years of age, tall and slim with long black hair that totally covers her face. She is dressed in a white, but soiled dress that reaches all the way to the ground. The dress spreads over the floor making her resemble a statue molded into the floor. Duilio walks over to her. They stand for a while face-to-face.

> DUILIO
> I believe you knew I was coming. And how?

Sora raises her hand and moves her long, black hair slightly away from one side of her face. Her eyes radiate with an intense presence as she speaks a barely understandable English.

> SORA
> You are here to see with your own eyes
> how I see into the future, the souls, the

>   fate - everything - how I am in touch
>   with the world beyond.

Sora pauses and walks a bit away from Duilio while she speaks
with a certain distance and slight contempt of Duilio's view
of the world.

>   SORA
>   You call it "magic" - for me it is the
>   world - the reality!

Sora pauses and again turns towards Duilio. The silence is
only broken by the dripping of water from the dome to the
basin of the fountain. She continues in a friendly tone.

>   SORA
>   You are welcome. You can stay - and learn!

Sora signals Duilio to follow her. They exit the temple, side
by side.

>   FADES AND MOVES AHEAD IN TIME

EXT. KOREA - TEMPLE - PLATEAU IN FRONT - DAY

Sora is sitting in the middle of the plateau in front of
the temple. She sits on the ground, motionless with her legs
crossed and with her face towards the distant mountains.
Visitors from all over come to her for advice and help. The
visitors sit on their knees in front of Sora in deep respect.
Duilio is sitting in the background, yet close enough to sense
the quiet Korean conversations. While not understanding the
words he studies Sora carefully.

>   CROSS FADE TO A FOLLOWING DAY

EXT. KOREA - TEMPLE - PLATEAU IN FRONT - DAY

Sora is sitting on the plateau in front of the temple. It
is rainy. The heavy rain and dense fog make the surrounding
landscape and mountains invisible. A young Korean woman,
GYUNG-HEE (25), gradually appears and becomes visible out of
the fog. She carries two newborn children (3 months) wrapped
in a brown, primitive and cheap cloth. She falls on her knees
in front of Sora.

                         GYUNG-HEE
                      (in Korean)
                 Please help them.

Duilio moves a little closer.

                           SORA
                   (whispering to Duilio)
                 She played the kayagum as nobody else -
                 those who listened were enchanted. She
                 was declared evil. Her house was burnt,
                 her life is threatened.

Duilio moves close to Gyung-hee. He watches the two children.
Gyung-hee takes the rough cloth away from their faces. Duilio
sees the two twin healthy baby-girls. Duilio thinks deeply for
a short moment. He turns to Sora.

                          DUILIO
                      (whispering)
                 They may reach beyond - as their mother.
                 You may teach them your skills.

In the totally dense fog he moves close to Sora. Water from
the rain and fog condenses on their soaked faces. Sora
moves her hair to the side with both hands. Gyung-hee sits
motionless with her head bowed. Sora reaches out for Gyung-
hee to embrace the two girls. Gyung-hee moves forward towards
Sora on her knees and places the children in Sora's arms. Sora
holds the children firmly towards her body.

                           SORA
                      (in Korean)
                 Your children can stay.

Gyung-hee moves forward to Sora on her knees and bows with
her head to the ground. She rises and disappears in the fog.

                              CROSS FADE FORWARD TO ANOTHER DAY

EXT. KOREA - TEMPLE - PLATEAU IN FRONT - DAY

Sora is sitting straight up with crossed legs on the plateau
facing the landscape. It is a rainy and windy day. Water is
pouring over her and flows along her long black hair reaching
to and spreading over the ground around her. She holds one

of the children close to her body to protect it from the
rain. Myung-hee (25) walks onto the plateau from the narrow
path connecting the plateau to the valley. She is dressed in
a simple gown. Her wet face shines of expectations and hope.
Right in front of Sora she falls on her knees. She sits with
her head bowed. After a while she looks cautiously up at Sora.
The rain drains over both faces. Sora's totally soaked dress,
hair and face merges with the pouring rain. As she speaks,
the rain and the wind grasps her voice and blurs Myung-hee's
view of her face and body.

                    SORA
               (in Korean)
          I received your gifts.

Sora pauses and takes the child, wrapped in a white cloth, out
from the protection of her dress. As she holds the child in
her arms and looks in its eyes with deep mysterious affection.
The sound from the pouring rain fades in the moment. Myung-
hee, still on her knees in front of Sora, sits fully upright
and watches intensively. Sora looks in Myung-hee's eyes. Their
faces and the child are embedded in the pouring and again
noisy rain. Everything else around them is invisible.

                    SORA
          You will relentlessly ensure she is
          trained to master the spirit of music. The
          music is in her soul - her soul is music.

The sound of the kayagum gradually fills the space. Sora hands
the child to Myung-hee. She takes it with both hands and
places it tight to her body under her dress. She sheds tears
of joy, bows and moves backwards on her knees. She rises and
disappears in the rain. In the pouring rain Sora sits and
watches Myung-hee as she gradually fades away. The picture
focuses on and finally fades into her intense eyes.

                                        FORWARD IN TIME

EXT. KOREA - TEMPLE - GARDEN - DAY

Sora and Duilio are walking in a garden behind the temple.
All over the garden are nicely organized flowers in bright
colors. Small paths separate the various species of flowers.
In a small wooden house in the background are numerous
bundles of plants hanging to dry and seeds from plants in

small ceramic bottles. Glasses with flowers covered with
liquids are standing all over a small table. Sora carries the
other small, wrapped child close to her body. Duilio watches
the many plants with great interest and scientific scrutiny.
They stop by a small area with small, long-leaved, violet
flowers. Sora picks a few flowers and bundles them to a small
bouquet. She walks over to the wooden house and takes a small
box with seeds. She walks back to Duilio busily studying the
many varieties of plants.

                    SORA
          All the plants are for cure.

She hands Duilio the violet flowers and the seeds.

                    SORA
          Take these flowers and the seeds with
          you back to your world. They will remind
          you - and connect us.

Duilio takes the flowers and the seeds. They walk back to the
plateau. Duilio bows goodbye. They stand for a short moment.
Sora moves her long black hair from her face. She stays on
the plateau holding the child tight as she watches Duilio walk
down the narrow path to the valley.

                    CROSS FADE 12 YEARS FORWARD IN TIME

EXT. KOREA - TEMPLE - PLATEAU IN FRONT - DAY

Chu-jin, as a small girl (12), and Sora are sitting on the
plateau in front of the temple face-to-face in a meditation
position, focused and connected. The wind over the plateau
grasps their long, black hair. Then everything turns quiet,
like inside the eye of an hurricane around their faces, their
long black hair that reach the ground, and their motionless
bodies. Around them, the wind is still blowing forcefully and
violently shakes the trees all over the landscape. After a
while, they both open their eyes out of the trance. The wind
again grasps their dresses and long black hair. Sora's and
Chu-jin's eyes meet. Sora smiles happily to the young Chu-jin.
She reaches out for her hands. They both rise. Chu-jin follows
Sora as an obedient pupil as they turn towards the temple and
walk inside.

                    TIME SHIFT TO PRESENT TIME

INT. KOREA - TEMPLE - INNER ROOM - DAY

                    SORA
          (she pauses)
     So Sergeant - that was it.

They sit quiet for a while.

                    SORA
     Before he left he asked me for one more
     thing. He had made a bet - he wanted to
     find the truth. It was about the essence
     of what I am and do.
          (she pauses)
     I helped him.

From a door opening in the back of the room Chu-jin enters,
wearing a long white dress like Sora's. Her long black hair,
also like Sora's, covers her face. She takes seat at a stone
opposite Sora and Samuel. As she moves her hair away from her
face, Samuel recognizes her with the greatest surprise.

                    SAMUEL
     It's you?

Chu-jin bows her head.

                    SORA
     Yes Sergeant. I know what has happened -
     and so do you now.
          (she pauses)
     She has learned and she has proven
     herself. She helped Duilio to find his
     answer - you know the outcome.

                    SAMUEL
          (confused)
     Is she a copy of Mrs. Yun?

                    SORA
     I just told you - they were separated -
     twins - the rest you know Sergeant.

Samuel, totally overwhelmed by all the pieces of his puzzle
falling in place, yet in an unbelievable mosaic, shakes his
head, smiles and laughs as he cannot believe.

SAMUEL
I cannot believe it - all the things that
had to happen for your plan to work out.
There are just too many coincidences -
how could all this be orchestrated and
then just happen - by chance? How could
Duilio and Ludwig meet, how could Duilio be
supported for all he did, how could Chu-jin
be there at the same time as Ludwig - I
could go on and on. Too many coincidences -
too much had to happen by chance!

Sora rises and stands for a short moment face-to-face with
Samuel. She distances herself a bit from the disbeliever and
straightens herself up as she speaks very firmly to Samuel.

SORA
In my world, Sergeant,
nothing happens by chance!

Sora bows slightly as goodbye and walks slowly to the doorway
in the back of the room. Chu-jin rises and stands face to face
with Samuel. She makes a light curtsy.

CHU-JIN
I bid you goodbye Sergeant.

Chu-jin follows Sora. They disappear together. Samuel, standing
alone, hesitates, uncertain what to do. Finally, he decides to
leave. He walks through the temple and exits to the plateau.

EXT. KOREA - TEMPLE - PLATEAU IN FRONT - DAY

The wind hits Samuel hard as he reaches the plateau. He
stands a while and watches the landscape. He turns around and
watches the temple. He smiles and laughs as he walks over the
plateau and down the narrow passage.

SAMUEL
(talking to himself)
My Goodness - what a story. Nobody will
never, ever believe it.

A little down the path Samuel stops and leans towards a tree
at the edge of the path to the deep slope below. He admires
the view as he talks to himself.

SAMUEL

    Who even cares if it is true or not when
    either way it is unbelievable. So why
    bother. Why bother about a truth nobody
    believes?

Samuel continues walking down the path and disappears.

INT. EUROPE - MONASTERY - PRAYER ROOM - DAY

In a remote monastery high in the mountains a group of about
fifty nuns are gathered for prayer in a large room. An elderly
nun is leading the prayer. The walls throughout the room are
of rough granite stones. Light shines into the room through a
windows positioned high on three of the walls. The nuns are
all dressed in identical, dark blue gowns. Blue scarfs cover
their heads. After the prayer the nuns kneel in the direction
of the elderly nun. They continue to kneel in silence and
obedience until the nun rises and signals them all to rise and
follow. All the nuns walk out of the room in a single line.

EXT. EUROPE - MONASTERY - COURTYARD -DAY

Tiffany is in the middle of the line. All the nuns walk with
their heads bowed. Tiffany's eyes are longing and sad. The
nuns spread away from the group. Tiffany stands alone in the
middle of the gravel space. She looks longing toward the
entrance to the cloister. She turns around and walks up a small
wooden walkway to the top of the huge, massive stone wall that
surrounds the entire cloister. She takes her hand under her
dress and takes the ring out in the open. She sees the streaks
of light radiating from the beautiful stone and she sees
Ludwig in the light conducting while the music fills her mind
(Requiem). Dreaming, she sees Ludwig's beautiful strokes in front
of the orchestra, his total dedicated conduction and his immense
energy. She turns around and walks back to the prayer room.

INT. EUROPE - MONASTERY - PRAYER ROOM - DAY

Tiffany enters the prayer room. She quietly watches the neat
and Spartan room. She notices a door in the back of the room.
She walks to the door and opens. Outside she sees a narrow,
half-roof covered terrace leading to additional rooms in a
separate section of the monastery. Tiffany exits the prayer
room and walks slowly and quietly onto the terrace walkway.

EXT. EUROPE - MONASTERY - TERRACE - DAY

Tiffany walks through the narrow terrace. Behind the terrace is a vertical, huge cliff, but to the open side of the terrace walkway there is an immense view over the mountains and the valley below. Tiffany enjoys the impressive view. By the end of the terrace she sees the entrance to the administration office of the abbess of the monastery. Opposite the door to the administration office a half open door leads into an additional room. Tiffany looks into the room through the half open door. She gasps as she sees two grand pianos in the otherwise empty room. She silently exits the terrace to the piano room.

INT. EUROPE - MONASTERY - PIANO ROOM - DAY

Tiffany, tiptoed, enters the piano room and silently closes the door behind her. She goes to one of the old, but well-kept grand pianos. She softly touches the keyboard. The piano is out of tune. She sits down by the piano with her back to the door and strikes a few cords. Her mind is carried away as she starts playing the beginning of the 4th softly. As she gets to the orchestra part she imitates the orchestra on the piano. She smiles, forgets her sadness and is carried away. Suddenly, the door behind her is closed with a loud sound. Tiffany holds her breath and turns around. She sees the ABBESS (50, tall, proud, determined, yet kind looking) standing inside the door. The abbess walks over to the piano and stands with her left hand on the piano opposite Tiffany and looks at her as she is waiting for an explanation. Tiffany, terribly embarrassed, rises.

                    TIFFANY
          I just saw the pianos from outside and
          thought I would check if they are in tune.

Tiffany, embarrassed, looks down on the floor. She holds her arms straight down in front of her and folds her hands.

                    ABBESS
          Why are you so embarrassed dear Sister.
          I heard your play. Why should that
          embarrass you?

                    TIFFANY
          I am sorry. I did not ask for your
          permission to touch the instrument.
          I am so sorry.

                        ABBESS
          Well, you have it now - and maybe you
          could do something about the tuning of the
          instruments. The tuning rod is over there.

The abbess points to a small cabinet in the corner of the
room. She walks over to Tiffany by the keyboard. They stand
close face to face. The abbess lifts her hand and softly
touches Tiffany's chin.

                        ABBESS
          Take your time Sister. You can use this
          place as much as you like. At some point,
          please invite your sisters to listen.

The abbess goes to the door. She exits and closes the door
softly behind her. Tiffany sits down exhausted on the piano
chair with her hands on her lap. She looks around in the room.
She lets her hand softly touch over the entire keyboard. She
walks over to the small cabinet, opens it, takes the tuner
rod and walks back to the pianos. She removes the cover over
the piano strings and starts tuning. White light flickers in
the room while Tiffany hits the first keys and aligns the A
with the tuning fork.

                              TIME SHIFT FORWARD 7 YEARS

        THE GLARING WHITE LIGHT FROM THE SKY CONTINUES AS THE
     SINGLE TONES SOUND. THE PICTURE TRANSITIONS FROM THE GLARING
     WHITE TO A BEAUTIFUL OCEAN REACHING THE HORIZON AND FINALLY
       SETTLES IN A GRAND LOBBY OF A HUGE SOUTH AMERICAN MANSION
       INT. SOUTH AMERICA - MANSION - LOBBY DOWNSTAIRS - EVENING

The large lobby in a South American mansion is richly
decorated with precious oil paintings, sculptures, and
goblins. It is quiet in the late evening. The lobby is dimly
illuminated by a few small lamps on small tables. Suddenly
a woman's screams of delight sounds weakly from the distance
into the room. A staircase leads up through the lobby to
a series of rooms upstairs. A door to one of the rooms is
slightly open. There is a weak red light in the room.

INT. SOUTH AMERICA - MANSION - LOBBY UPSTAIRS - EVENING

Upstairs the sound increases. Josephine is visible inside
the room through the slightly open door. She is sitting

on the edge of the bed extremely provocatively dressed in black. She is wearing a strong, sensual make-up and sits with her legs provocatively spread as she engaged a man in the room. An extreme sexual encounter follows with the man raping the enjoying Josephine screaming in delight. The man finally retracts while Josephine continues exhaling on the bedside while she pushes herself backwards up on the bed. She stretches her hand out to Giovanni. He pulls her up. They stand face to face and engage in a sensual and long lasting kiss. Giovanni, realizing that the door to the room is not fully closed, pushes it to close with his foot. The lobby is again silent in the late evening. SUNO (25, African descent, slim, gracious, tall) stands totally quiet, slightly scared and almost invisible in the lobby. As the door upstairs is pushed to a close, Suno silently exits the lobby while the first feeble light from the morning sun shines into the room.

EXT. SOUTH AMERICA - MANSION - TERRACE - DAY

Josephine is sitting comfortably on the very large terrace in front of the mansion. The sea, visible from the terrace, stretches to the horizon. On the terrace there are colorful flowers and plants, all extremely carefully and well kept. Josephine - comfortably and elegantly dressed - sits with a colorful fruit drink while she enjoys the magnificent view. Behind her on the terrace, Suno, nicely, correctly and stylishly dressed in black is preparing a table for the lunch. From behind Josephine, two hands appear to softly and sensually touch her shoulders. Josephine enjoys the hands touching her body, touches them softly and kisses them. The hands touch her breast. She leans her head fully backwards and closes her eyes while she is being softly kissed. She exhales and enjoys. She holds the two hands firmly as she rises from her chair to stand face to face with Giovanni, dressed elegantly, yet casually.

The table is ready. Giovanni and Josephine go hand in hand to the table and sit opposite each other. Suno moves a big parasol to shade the table, carefully made with attention to every detail. Josephine looks around and addresses Suno a bit irritated, almost rude.

                    JOSEPHINE
               (in Spanish)
          Where is Ludwig - could you please
          find him.

                              SUNO
                    (in Spanish, slightly fearful)
              He is playing inside - I will call him.

Suno offers Josephine bread from a basket and a bowl with
salad. Josephine serves herself and puts some salad on the
plate next to her. She hands the salad to Giovanni. He serves
himself. Suno pours small glasses of white wine to Giovanni
and Josephine and pours sparkling water in the glasses by
all three plates. The bubbles from the water flicker in the
sunrays. Josephine looks impatiently for Ludwig and calls loud.

                            JOSEPHINE
                         (in Italian)
              Ludwig - come out here. Mom and Dad are
              waiting. Ludwig!

The five year old Ludwig comes running to the table. He is
identical to the five year old Ludwig Mann, just dressed
nicely and cleanly. He runs fast to the chair and jumps
backwards up on the too high chair. Josephine kisses him on
the cheek, a bit mechanical, unemotional and distant. Ludwig
starts to eat the salad and finishes it fast.

                            LUDWIG
                         (in Italian)
              Mom, can I go back in?

                            JOSEPHINE
              Yes, but you have to come back for more
              food in a moment.

Ludwig runs back to the house. Josephine and Giovanni continue
the meal.

                              THE PICTURE FADES TO EVENING

INT SOUTH AMERICA - MANSION - LOBBY - EARLY EVENING

Suno is in the lobby cleaning and ordering the many small
tables, sculptures, paintings, lamps and furniture. It is quiet
in the house. Suddenly she hears a door close. Surprised she
walks to a window in the back of the lobby with a view on the
back-garden. Down by a back-gate in the tall wall surrounding
the mansion she sees Josephine exit the garden. She is dressed

in a tight, black dress. Just as she exits the garden she takes
a coat on that covers her dress. Suno goes back to the lobby.
She looks around and notices the half open door to the bedroom
upstairs. She walks up the staircase and looks into the room.
The room is dark as the light is off and tight curtains are
pulled over the windows. Suno takes her hand into the room
to the electric switch and turns the light on. She sees
Josephine's table for make-up in some disorder and the drawers
not closed properly. Suno exits the lobby to the bedroom.

INT. SOUTH AMERICA - MANSION - BEDROOM - EVENING

Suno enters the bedroom and walks over to the make-up table.
On the table there are many pieces of tissue. Suno moves the
tissues slightly and notices the leftover of lipstick, mascara
and perfume - all in extreme excess. She opens the half
open drawer. The drawer contains multiple pieces of black,
provocative lingerie. Suno takes a piece to her nose and
notices the extremely strong perfume flavor. She closes the
drawer and silently exits the room.

                                        FORWARD TO EVENING

INT. SOUTH AMERICA - MANSION - LOBBY - EVENING

Giovanni arrives at the house and enters the lobby. He looks
around for a sign of life.

                        GIOVANNI
            Hello - where are you?

Giovanni waits for an answer. He walks upstairs and looks into
the rooms, but finds nobody. He goes back to the lobby. Suno
enters the lobby from outside holding Ludwig in her hand.

                        GIOVANNI
            Where is Josephine?

                        SUNO
            Not sure. She left in the afternoon.
            I have been with Ludwig to an arrangement
            by one of his friends.
                    (she pauses and listens to a
                    sound outside)
            I think a car coming.

Josephine enters the lobby wearing a couple of shopping bags and a coat covering her dress. She is surprised when seeing Giovanni.

                    JOSEPHINE
          Oh, you are back already - I thought you
          would be out all night.

                    GIOVANNI
          We finished early - so where have you
          been?

                    JOSEPHINE
          Oh, just shopping, as you can see.

Josephine lifts the shopping bags towards Giovanni. Then she quickly walks over to a small mirror in the lobby. She puts the shopping bags on a small table and takes a tissue from her bags. In front of the mirror she discretely removes an excess lipstick from her lips and briefly orders her hair. Giovanni watches with discrete suspicion. She looks over at Ludwig.

                    JOSEPHINE
          Come and give Mother a kiss - and Papa.

Ludwig obeys and runs, not too happily, over to Josephine for a kiss. He runs to Giovanni who lifts the not too happy Ludwig up for a kiss. Finally Ludwig runs happily over to Suno. Ludwig moves close to Suno as she holds her arm lovingly around him and finally takes him by the hand. Suno and Ludwig exit the lobby.

                    GIOVANNI
          Are the shops really open that late?

                    JOSEPHINE
          Sure my dear - and even if they were
          not - I always have access dear; you know
          dear.

Josephine starts walking swiftly upstairs. She sends Giovanni a sensual smile and blows a kiss through the air. She exits the lobby upstairs to the bedroom. Giovanni, alone in the lobby, stands pondering in suspicion.

EXT. SOUTH AMERICA - ALLEY - EVENING

Josephine, extremely provocatively dressed up in black is
standing leaning her back against a house wall. Numerous
other girls are in the alley or standing by the walls.
Josephine lights a cigarette and blows the smoke up in the
air. A CUSTOMER (50, large and overweight South American man)
approaches her.

                    CUSTOMER
               (in Spanish)
          How much?

                    JOSEPHINE
          You tell me afterward.

The customer and Josephine enter the house.

INT. SOUTH AMERICA - MANSION - LOBBY - EVENING

Giovanni arrives to the house and enters the lobby.

                    GIOVANNI
          Hello - I am back!

There is no answer. Giovanni looks at his watch. He runs up
the stairs and opens the doors to all the rooms. They are all
dark and empty. He enters the bedroom.

INT. SOUTH AMERICA - MANSION - BEDROOM - EVENING

Giovanni enters the bedroom. He switches the light on and looks
searching around. He goes to the table for make-up. He notices
a piece of tissue with excess deep red lipstick. He takes it
to his nose and inhales the strong fragrance of heavy perfume
while he watches the perfume bottle on the table. He quickly
opens the drawers in the make-up table. One drawer is empty.
Giovanni closes it violently and instantly leaves the room.

EXT. SOUTH AMERICA - ALLEY - EVENING

The door to the house in the alley opens. The customer exits
from the house and walks swiftly and shy down the alley. As
he passes the girls hanging around they vulgarly approach
him. Josephine enters the alley from the house. She wears

fresh lipstick and cosmetics but in disarray with her hair and clothes not perfectly set. She lights a cigarette and exhales while she again leans on the house wall. A CUSTOMER 2 (35, fit muscular, poorly dressed man of South American descent) appears in the alley. He walks over to one of the girls and whispers to her. The girl points discretely at Josephine. The customer hands the girl a large money note and approaches Josephine.

                    CUSTOMER 2
          Are you ready Mrs. - again?

                    JOSEPHINE
          More than you will believe - ready for
          people like you. I know what you asked
          over there.

The customer laughs. He pushes Josephine into the house. Giovanni appears in the alley. He immediately addresses one the girls. He has a large money note in his hand. The girl whispers in his ear and points to the house. Giovanni immediately gives her the money, walks over to the house and enters.

INT. SOUTH AMERICA - ALLEY - HOUSE - EVENING

Josephine is with the customer. She stands in front of him spreading her legs and exposing her body.

                    JOSEPHINE
          Now feel that I am as you want - right?

Josephine pushes her abdomen closer to the customer. He feels with his hand and smiles satisfied. Josephine sits on the edge of a table and pushes herself further backwards onto the table. She leans back while exposing her body completely. The customer starts raping her violently.

The door to the room is suddenly and violently opened. Giovanni rushes into the room. He sees Josephine and the customer. He immediately takes and instantly opens a switchblade from his pocket. It makes a strong sound as it opens. Giovanni beats desperately with the knife and hits Josephine deep in the neck. The customer, frightened to death, immediately retracts, grasps his clothes and runs naked out of the room. Josephine lies on the table. She exhales in spite of her heavily bleeding wound. She opens her mouth sensually towards Giovanni and lifts her abdomen towards him.

Giovanni with a hysteric, desperate scream rushes between
Josephine's legs and violently continues the rape of the
enjoying Josephine while he hysterically screams in delight
and desperation. With blood flowing from Josephine's neck they
peak in endless delight. In their heavenly pleasure the knife
in Josephine's neck is displaced. Josephine screams to heaven
in delight until her scream is abruptly silenced by blood
flowing abundantly out of her mouth. She peaks and dies at
the same moment. Giovanni retracts. He steps back and watches
Josephine. Her body is totally collapsed on the completely
blood covered table. Giovanni touches Josephine's arm and
seeks her pulse. As he feels no pulse he touches the neck
seeking a pulse. With his hands soaked in blood he finds no
pulse and realizes Josephine is dead.

Giovanni swiftly brings his clothes in order. He cleans the
blood from his hands on Josephine's blood soaked body. He
looks around in the small room, finds Josephine's bag, takes
it, switches the light in the room off and exits. From the
outside he locks the door with the key from Josephine's bag
and swiftly walks down the stairs.

                              FORWARD IN TIME TO MANSION

EXT. SOUTH AMERICA - MANSION - TERRACE - DAY

Suno and Ludwig are sitting by the table on the terrace in
front of the large mansion. Suno is quiet and worried. Ludwig
eats of the bread from a basket on the table. He sits close to
Suno who comforts him.

                    LUDWIG
          Where is Papa and Mother? - they have
          been away now for four days.

                    SUNO
          I believe they went for vacation
          together - sometimes parents need to be
          alone Ludwig.

                    LUDWIG
          They should take me with them - and you!
          I want you to always be with me.

Ludwig, lovingly moves closer to Suno as though he seeks
shelter. Suno holds her arm caring and lovingly around him.

                              SUNO
        Right Ludwig - but sometimes parent do
        something on their own.

Ludwig and Suno continue to eat. Suddenly Suno sees a car from
the distance driving up the large hill and approaching the
mansion. The car stops by the gate to the land of the mansion.
Four disguised men exit the car and goes to the gate. They
try to enter the code to open the gate, but in vain. They look
around to find a way to get across the high wall around the
mansion. Suno gets frightened. She rapidly runs into the house
and swiftly reappears with a big bundle of money notes. She
hides the money under her dress.

                              SUNO
        Come Ludwig - we better get away. Come.

Suno takes Ludwig by the hand. They run to the backside of
the house and exit through the garden back-door.

INT. SOUTH AMERICA - MONASTERY - DAY

Suno and Ludwig are in the office of the ABBESS (50) of a
South American monastery. Ludwig sits very close to Suno. The
room is very simple and furnished with only a table and a few
chairs. Behind the abbess hangs a large crucifix on the wall.
They are in the middle of a conversation.

                              SUNO
                    (in Spanish)
        ... So, please - please let us be here.
        Please let me join you.

                             ABBESS
                    (in Spanish)
        But how can you be so sure?

                              SUNO
        Please, believe me. I have been in that
        house for years now. I know what is going
        on - and now they are gone. I assure
        you - they have left him. He needs a safe
        place. I know that - I guarantee you. I
        love him, and I can help..
                    (she pauses)
        ... and I can pay.

Suno takes a bundle of money notes. The abbess looks at the
money, Ludwig and Suno for a while. She smiles friendly and
compassionately as she has made her decision.

                    ABBESS
          OK then.
               (she looks at Ludwig)
          You can be here and grow up. Suno will be
          with you and we will all take good care
          of you. And you must do as we say!

Ludwig nods. Suno rises. She embraces Ludwig and holds him
tight with tears in her eyes. The abbess makes a call. Shortly
afterwards a NUN (25) enters. The abbess points at Ludwig and
Suno.

                    ABBESS
          This is Ludwig and Suno - they will stay
          with us. And you will be responsible for
          them.

The nun goes to Ludwig. She sits on her knees in front of him.

                    NUN
               (in Spanish)
          You will be fine here. We will take good
          care of you.

The nun holds her hand towards Ludwig. He holds her hand. The
nun rises and turns to Suno.

                    NUN
          Come - let me show you around.

Ludwig and Suno, hand in hand, follow the nun. They exit the
office.

INT. MONASTERY - MEETING ROOM - EVENING

Marchetto and Giovanni are alone in the large meeting room of
the monastery. Giovanni is in his black cassock. Marchetto is
in his red cassock. A few candles on the table and from the
fireplace is the only light in the room. They are at the end
of a long conversation. Giovanni sits with his head humbly
bowed and close to the table. He looks up at Marchetto over
his folded hands.

GIOVANNI

.... so please let me have your
forgiveness. I know I have sinned, I
know I have betrayed, I know I have
been unfaithful to you and our sacred
institution - but Brother, I know now,
through the most horrible of learnings,
that I will serve to the end of my days
with no compromise.

Giovanni pauses, bows his head in obedience while he waits
for the response. Marchetto leans forward to get closer to
Giovanni. As he speaks Giovanni lifts his face. The two men
are very close, face to face.

MARCHETTO

Brother, the ways of our Savior are magic.
We are forced through sufferings to reach
purity. And so have you been Brother. Your
sufferings have been immense, but the
higher is the purity you have reached.
(he pauses)
And you have hold your promise of
cleaning it all up?

GIOVANNI

Everything.

MARCHETTO

The pianist and the boy?

GIOVANNI

They were taken care of over there,
before I left. They are gone.

MARCHETTO

Excellent - so it's only the two of us
now. I am grateful Brother.

Marchetto rises and walks to the fireplace. He stands for a
while in silence and watches the flames. He starts speaking
softly while still looking into the fire.

MARCHETTO

Brother, I am an old man now - I have
been thinking about the future. I have

been thinking about how to ensure the
future of our sacred institution.
      (he turns around)
Brother, I have decided to offer you
to continue my tasks and to take my
position. After all that has happened,
I am convinced of your total commitment
and purity, and I am convinced that you
can provide the leadership needed moving
forward.
      (he pauses)
I feel a need to deeply focus on the
essence of being during my last days
before I meet our Savior.

Marchetto walks over to Giovanni and stands next to him.
Giovanni rises. They stand face to face. Giovanni, immensely
moved, has tears in his eyes. Marchetto puts his hands on
Giovanni's shoulders as he speaks.

               MARCHETTO
Will you do it, dear Brother?

               GIOVANNI
I will.

The two men embrace each other, holding each other tight.

               MARCHETTO
Brother - we will do the transition
tomorrow. Your current humble dress will
be replaced and you will received our
blessing.

The two men embrace again. Giovanni exits. Marchetto walks over
to the fireplace. He stands in deep thought watching the fire.

               FORWARD TO NEXT MORNING

INT. MONASTERY - SIDE BUILDING - DAY

Giovanni is standing by the windows in the guest room
watching the scenery. It knocks on the door. Four boys (12)
from the church and an older PARISH (25) enter carrying the
prestigious clothes for Giovanni's transition. The parish helps
Giovanni to dress while the young boys hand him the many

pieces of the sacred dress, one by one. At the end, Giovanni stands in a gorgeous dress in the middle of the room. He walks over to the mirror and watches himself with great satisfaction. He nods to the parish that he is ready. The boys open the door and they all exit the room.

EXT. MONASTERY - ROOF - DAY

Giovanni, the boys and the parish walk onto the roof. As they reach the middle, the day suddenly darkens. They look up and see a huge black cloud formed by hundreds of black birds covering the sky. The parish and the church boys look frightened at the cloud of birds and start walking as fast as appropriate towards the exit. Giovanni turns and looks up. From above, we see his spreading arms and his snake eyes fueled with anger radiating towards the birds. The cloud disperses. Light again shines on the roof. Giovanni walks towards the exit held open by the church boys. He exits the roof followed by the parish.

INT. MONASTERY - CHURCH - DAY

Giovanni, followed by the church boys and the parish, enter the church room in the monastery. By the altar Marchetto and five high ranging church officials are waiting, all dressed in the finest official dresses. Giovanni walks up to the altar and kneels in front of Marchetto who puts his hand on Giovanni's bowed head and delivers his blessing. Marchetto turns and walks to the altar. He takes the chalice, lifts it in both hands and walks towards Giovanni while holding the chalice high in his stretched arms. In front of Giovanni Marchetto lovers the chalice. Giovanni stretches his arms and takes the chalice. He drinks the holy wine while the Agnus Dei fills the space. Marchetto watches intensively until the last drop has been drunk. Giovanni hands the chalice back to Marchetto. He takes it, turns around and hands it to one of the church boys. The boy carries the chalice back to the altar and fills it with fresh wine. The boy brings the chalice to Marchetto. He drinks and makes the sign of the cross with his hands. The boy carries the chalice to each of the church officials. They all drink and make the sign of the cross with their hands.

Giovanni rises. Standing face to face with Giovanni Marchetto takes his embroidered mitra and places it ceremonially on Giovanni's head. He kneels down. Giovanni holds his hand towards Marchetto who kisses it humbly. Behind Marchetto the

other church officials are lining up and one by one kneels
in front of Giovanni and humbly kiss his hand. Giovanni looks
satisfied up towards the altar and the pictures of sufferings.
He turns towards the large church room, rises his hands and
while, the Agnus Dei fills the space, gives his blessing to
Marchetto and the officials.

Giovanni, followed by the church boys and the parish, leaves
the church. Behind him the church officials follow. Marchetto
stays in the church and prays by the altar,

INT. MONASTERY - CHURCH - EARLY EVENING

The last light of the day shines into the church in the
cloister. Marchetto is kneeling by the altar. He rests his
bowed head in his hands. He looks up at the altar.

                    MARCHETTO
               (whispering)
          My Lord - forgive me, your humble servant.

Marchetto again puts his face in his hands and sits unmoved.
With the last daylight Marchetto fades into the darkness of
the night. Finally Marchetto rises and exits the dark church.

INT. MONASTERY - ROOM GIOVANNI - EVENING

Giovanni is on his bed still fully officially dressed and not
covered, like a dead on his coffin in the spacious room for
the leading church official. It knocks softly on the door. The
door is gently opened and a CHURCH BOY looks humbly into the
room. The church boy looks over at Giovanni.

                    CHURCH BOY
          Anything else Your Highness.

As there is no answer the boy moves closer to Giovanni on
the bed.

                    CHURCH BOY
          Anything else Sir.

The boy bows his face as he is uncomfortable having moved so
close to Giovanni. Marchetto enters the room behind the boy.
The boy gasps frightened as he turns and sees Marchetto.

                    MARCHETTO
            Don't be scared my boy.

Marchetto walks over to Giovanni's bed. He watches the
unmoved, pale, death mask-like face. He touches Giovanni's
neck. After a short while he turns to the boy.

                    MARCHETTO
            Please call the officials, immediately.

The church boy immediately runs out of the room. Alone with
Giovanni, Marchetto remains by the bedside. He bends down and
whispers in Giovanni's ear.

                    MARCHETTO
            Did you really think I was that stupid.
            You never understood my disgust for your
            evil desires and my total devotion to our
            sacred institution. You were a fool and
            you are damned, you idiot.

The door opens. Marchetto turns and faces the five officials
entering the room, still officially dressed. Marchetto bows
his head and then faces the officials with tears running
down his face. The officials walk to the bed and realize the
situation. The ELDERLY OFFICIAL (70) turns to Marchetto and
talks with a trembling voice.

                    ELDERLY OFFICIAL
            This is a sign Brother. Your total
            dedication to our holy spirit must
            continue.

The elderly official turns to Giovanni and removes the
embroidered mitra. He lifts it with both arms stretched
towards Marchetto who kneels down. The official places the
mitra on Marchetto's head and blesses him. Marchetto rises.
The officials all kneel down in front of him. Marchetto
goes from one to the other and they all kiss his hand in
obedience. Agnus Dei again fills the room as Marchetto spreads
his arms over the officials and delivers his blessing.

INT. EUROPE - MONASTERY - PIANO ROOM - DAY

In the music room Tiffany is playing the last part of the
Beethoven's 111 as it knocks softly on the door. Tiffany

immediately stops playing. The abbess enters. Tiffany rises
and stands with her hands folded. The abbess points to two
chairs by the window and, with a gesture, asks Tiffany to sit.
The abbess takes seat in one of the chairs. Tiffany takes seat
in the other. She sits at the edge of the chair with her hands
on her lap. She looks nervously, shy and a bit embarrassed at
the abbess.

                    ABBESS
          Don't be embarrassed Sister - you have
          every reason not to be. You have enriched
          this place and you have diligently
          followed all our prayers and work.

                    TIFFANY
               (smiling, shy and humble)
          I am so glad to hear.

                    ABBESS
          I have been contacted from one of our
          sister cloisters abroad - far abroad. The
          abbess there told me something I like to
          discuss with you.

                    TIFFANY
          Yes ...

                    ABBESS
          She told me sister, that not so long
          ago they received an orphan child. The
          parents cannot be found, there are no
          relatives.

                    TIFFANY
          So sad - but good the child came to us.

                    ABBESS
          Indeed sister - but what she also told
          me is that the child apparently has
          extraordinary talents for music. And
          sister, since they thought it would be
          good to develop this side of the child,
          she asked for my advice.

The abbess pauses and looks straight at Tiffany.

                    ABBESS
     I thought, dear Sister, that I could
     propose the child comes here and that you
     help it with the music. Our sisters will
     help with the other educations the child
     needs, and a sister who knows the child
     will also come here to help.

                    TIFFANY
     Of course - I shall be glad to do my
     best.

                    ABBESS
     I will tell her, dear sister.

They both rise. They stand for a moment face to face. Tiffany
first looks directly at the abbess, then she looks down. The
abbess raises her hand and briefly touches Tiffany's hand.

                    ABBESS
     Thank you, dear sister.

The abbess walks to the door. She exits and closes the door
softly behind her. Tiffany remains standing and looks at the
two pianos.

                                        FORWARD IN TIME

INT. EUROPE - MONASTERY - PIANO ROOM - DAY

Tiffany is playing a Mozart sonata. It knocks on the door.
Tiffany rises and stands by the piano facing the door. The
abbess enters.

                    ABBESS
     They have arrived, dear Sister. They will
     come over here now.
          (she points at the door)
     Please.

Tiffany walks over to the abbess by the door. The abbess
signals Tiffany to exit. Tiffany exits the room. The abbess
follows.

EXT. EUROPE - MONASTERY - TERRACE - DAY

Tiffany and the abbess stand waiting outside the piano room
and look down the narrow terrace walkway to the door in the
opposite end of the walkway. After a while, the door opens
and is held open by Suno, visible through the open door.
While holding the door open with one hand, Suno holds the
child by the other hand and gently pulls the child in front
of her in order for the child to enter the terrace first. The
small child appears, but stands still and slightly resists
walking through the door. Suno, behind the child, gently
pushes it forward. The child walks through the door and enters
the terrace walkway. Tiffany holds her breath and suddenly
takes her hands to her mouth to hold a gentle outcry as she
recognizes the small Ludwig, exactly as she saw him at the
admission test for the Maestro classes.

Tiffany instantly bends down in her knees, sitting squats to get
to the level of Ludwig. She stretches her arms towards him and
smiles with tears in her eyes. Ludwig, seeing Tiffany, instantly
becomes less shy and starts walking towards her through the
narrow terrace walkway. Suno follows Ludwig a few steps behind.
The abbess moves to stand behind Tiffany and watches the
stunning encounter. Ludwig stops right in front of Tiffany and
looks bravely at her. Tiffany stretches her hands towards him.
Ludwig lifts his hand and puts it in Tiffany's hands.

                    TIFFANY
               (in Spanish)
          Welcome.

                    LUDWIG
               (in Spanish)
          Thank you.

Ludwig looks Tiffany straight in the eyes. Tiffany rises while
still holding Ludwig in her hand. Ludwig turns and stands
next to Tiffany facing Suno. Tiffany and Ludwig turn around.
Still hand in hand, Tiffany and Ludwig stand face to face with
the abbess.

                    TIFFANY
          Say hello.

Ludwig, still holding Tiffany's hand, looks bravely at the
abbess.

                         LUDWIG
              Hello.

                         ABBESS
              You are welcome.

                         TIFFANY
              Let me show you where we can play - there
              are two pianos.

Tiffany smiles to the abbess and Suno. She takes Ludwig by the
hand and walks over to the door of the piano room. She opens
the door to let Ludwig look in. As he sees the two pianos he
looks up at Tiffany, eager to get into the room. Tiffany lets
Ludwig enter the room first and then follows.

INT. EUROPE - MONASTERY - PIANO ROOM - DAY

Tiffany and Ludwig enter the piano room. Tiffany leaves the
door half open, but it is softly closed fully from the outside
by the abbess. Tiffany takes Ludwig by the hand over to the
second piano. She points at the score on the note holder. She
lifts him up to stand on the piano chair with his head right
at level with the score.

                         TIFFANY
              Can you read the notes?

Ludwig turns around, looks at Tiffany and nods happily. He
looks at the scores on the piano and recognizes the Mozart
double sonata, even though only a single bar is visible. He
points to the score.

                         LUDWIG
              I heard that one once!

Tiffany holds her breath and takes her hands to her mouth as
she remembers the exact first words and the voice she heard
of Ludwig when they were at the admission test by the Maestro.
She stands breathless. Ludwig turns around and looks at her.
Tiffany composes herself. She lifts Ludwig and puts him down
on the piano chair. She adjusts the chair for Ludwig to reach
the keyboard.

                              TIFFANY
             Shall we try? Maybe the second movement?

Ludwig nods energetically. Tiffany goes to the other piano
and takes seat at the piano chair. She looks at Ludwig across
the pianos. Ludwig smiles, fully comfortable. His face asks
Tiffany to start. They both put their hands at the keyboards.
They looks at each other over the pianos. Then they look down
and start playing.

The double sonata flows flawlessly as rehearsed a thousand
times. Ludwig and Tiffany play without body language, but with
focus and tranquility in the music which instantly totally
connects them.

                 THE PICTURE FREEZES BUT THE MUSIC CONTINUES WHILE
                 ACKNOWLEDGEMENTS FLOW OVER THE SCREEN

                       -- THE END --

Printed in the United States
By Bookmasters